The Complete Gentleman,

The Truth of Our Times,

AND

The Art of Living in London

BY

HENRY PEACHAM

EDITED BY

Virgil B. Heltzel

PUBLISHED FOR

The Folger Shakespeare Library

BY

CORNELL UNIVERSITY PRESS

Ithaca, New York

Preface

I SHOULD like to express my thanks to the staff of the Folger Shakespeare Library for their unfailing courtesy and helpfulness in expediting the preparation of this edition of Peacham's writings, and particularly to the reference librarian, Miss Dorothy Mason, who was always ready with help on difficult problems, to Miss Margarita Metaxatos for checking passages of Greek, and to Miss Virginia LaMar, who read the manuscript with great care and offered valuable suggestions. I am indebted also to the British Museum for permission to reprint the apparently unique copy of *The Art of Living in London.* I am deeply grateful to the trustees of the Library for a grant-in-aid, without which this work could hardly have been done. To the director of the Library, Dr. Louis B. Wright, this edition owes much for his interest in the subject and for his helpful advice whenever need arose.

V. B. H.

Contents[*]

[*] The original table of *The Complete Gentleman* has been omitted. Chapters XIV and XIX of the original text have here been omitted for reasons given in the Introduction.

Contents

Introduction

HENRY PEACHAM is known as the author of *The Complete Gentleman* (1622) to many persons who have never read the work, but he deserves to be more widely appreciated for having given us that thoroughly English and altogether noble book of advice to young gentlemen. His equally important social criticism, too, deserves more attention than it has received. It is the purpose of this collection to present in modern dress the greater part of Peacham's most important writings dealing with the ideals to be pursued and the evils to be shunned by young gentlemen of his day. Few men of his time were better educated than he, even fewer reveal a closer observation of life in Stuart England, and none at all, I feel sure, more fully represents the Renaissance ideal of the pursuit of good learning and versatility in achievement, or exhibits to better advantage an unusual variety of interests and talents to be found in one individual—for he was painter, musician, mathematician, writer of English and Latin verses, traveler, social critic, and scholar ("by profession I am a scholar")[1]—and neither harsh schoolmasters nor poverty nor unsympathetic kinsmen prevented his cultivation of them. The essential facts of his career, even though not necessarily the important ones, are fairly well known.

[1] *Graphice* (1612), sig. A2ᵛ.

Introduction

He was born about 1576 at North Mimms, Hertfordshire, "near to St. Albans,"[2] the son of Henry Peacham, the scholarly author of *The Garden of Eloquence* (1577) and rector successively of North Mimms and Leverton in Lincolnshire. Young Henry attended the local school, was admitted to Trinity College, Cambridge, in May of 1593, and was graduated B.A. in 1595 and M.A. in 1598. "Left young to the wide world to seek [his] fortune,"[3] he became master of the private school at Wymondham, Norfolk, but for reasons quite apparent to the readers of his essays he soon gave up the profession. "Ever naturally from a child," he says, he had been "addicted to the practice" of painting and had been beaten for it by "ill and ignorant schoolmasters, . . . yet could they never beat it out of [him]."[4] In 1606 he published the first English book of practical instruction in drawing and painting, *The Art of Drawing with the Pen and Limning in Water Colors*. It was dedicated to Sir Robert Cotton, unto whom, as Peacham was later to declare, "not only Britain, but Europe herself is obliged for his industry, cost, and care in collection of so many rare manuscripts and other monuments of venerable antiquity, being of the same most free and communicative to all men of learning and quality."[5] The work was expanded and, with a dedicatory epistle to Sir Edmund Ashfield, was published in 1612 as *Graphice* or with the variant title it was to retain thereafter, *The Gentleman's Exercise*. It had a new edition in 1634 and was reprinted in 1661 with *The Complete Gentleman*.

In 1610, like many other struggling authors seeking the patronage of Prince Henry, Peacham presented to him a manuscript containing some of the "divine instructions" excerpted from King James's *Basilicon Doron* (1599), done into Latin

[2] *Thalia's Banquet* (1620), sig. C4ᵛ.
[3] *Truth of Our Times* (1638), below, p. 184.
[4] See below, p. 129.
[5] *The Complete Gentleman* (1634), sig. Cc2.

x

verse "with their pictures drawn and limned by mine own hand in their lively colors." [6] The Prince's acceptance of the work no doubt made Peacham known to the many literati who gathered about that popular young patron, so that in the next year he was among those many wits of London who contributed mock poems to the "Panegyric Verses" prefixed to Tom Coryate's *Crudities*, which was also dedicated to Prince Henry. In 1612 Peacham dedicated to the Prince his most ambitious work, a book of emblems titled *Minerva Britanna*. In his address to the reader he declares, with characteristic pride, that the English, though belatedly, would in time equal the best of the French and Italians in this kind, and he would have his reader know also that, except for Geoffrey Whitney's collection and a few translations, his own is the first book of emblems published by an Englishman. On November 6 Prince Henry died and, like many another poet, Peacham lamented his passing in an elegy, *The Period of Mourning, Disposed into Six Visions, together with Nuptial Hymns* (1613). Two years later he celebrated the birth of Prince Henry's nephew, son of Prince Henry Frederick, County Palatine, in a poem titled *Prince Henry Revived* (1615).

Probably as a result of the recognition these events gave him, he was commissioned in 1613, it is said,[7] to travel abroad as private tutor to Hannibal Baskerville and the sons of Thomas, Earl of Arundel and Surrey. Whether he tutored these youths or not, he did travel abroad for two years, visiting France and Italy (where he studied music under Horatio Vecchi of Modena), western Germany, and Holland. He was entertained by many prominent people and had sufficient time and interest to make the impressive observations so often revealed in his later writings. After his return to England he published in 1615 a pamphlet on "the affairs of Cleves and Gulick." His book of

[6] *Minerva Britanna* (1612), sig. A2.
[7] See *The Worth of a Penny* (1669), "An Advertisement to the Reader."

epigrams, *Thalia's Banquet,* dedicated to Drue Drury and published in 1620, reveals a wide circle of acquaintances and friends he had acquired, particularly among the country gentlemen of England, whose welfare was to be the chief theme of his writings; and although his next book, *The Complete Gentleman* (1622), was actually addressed to the son of an earl, the group of readers he really had in mind were the country gentry of England. In 1624 he wrote *An April Shower,* an elegy to his late friend and patron, Richard Sackville, Earl of Dorset, and after a ten-year period of inactivity he wrote another funeral elegy, *Thestylis atrata* (1634), to Frances, Countess of Warwick. He resumed publication in 1636 with *Coach and Sedan,* a dialogue of light social satire, dedicated to Sir Elias Hicks.

In the few remaining years of Peacham's life he was, he tells us, without employment, and he probably experienced the pinch of poverty. Nevertheless, he wrote a number of brief pieces, many of which were published posthumously. To his apparently sympathetic patron, Henry Carey, Earl of Dover, he addressed in 1638 his *Valley of Variety,* notes gathered from Pancirolla and other authors, and in the same year he presented to his "much respected friend," Henry Barnwell of Turrington, "in Marshland near to King's Lynn in the County of Norfolk," his collection of essays, *The Truth of Our Times.* Four years later he published his brief but significant essay, *The Art of Living in London.* His half-dozen or more political and other pamphlets written in his last years need no mention here save that they show him a staunch royalist, a champion of Anglicanism, and a trueborn Englishman. The work most often in demand through the remainder of the century, *The Worth of a Penny* (1641), deals in delightful manner, by way of choice anecdote and sharp observation of economic conditions, with Peacham's favored topics of frugality and thrift. The date of his death is as uncertain as that of his birth, but it is thought to have been in 1643.

Introduction

The Complete Gentleman was written for young William Howard, son of Thomas, Earl of Arundel and Surrey. It was entered in the Stationers' Register on July 3, 1622, and thus may have been intended as a gift to the young nobleman on his tenth birthday (November 30).[8] Peacham's object was "to recover" young William and, as it turned out, other young English gentlemen, "from the tyranny of these ignorant times and from the common education, which is to wear the best clothes, eat, sleep, drink much, and to know nothing."[9] He believed that next to the fear of God good learning is "the fountain of all counsel and instruction," and that by it "our affections are persuaded and our ill manners mollified."[10] Having observed in his travels the "great forwardness and proficiency of children in other countries [and] the backwardness and rawness of ours," due in large part, he thinks, to "the remissness of parents and the negligence of masters," he composed this book "by fits" during attacks of a quartan fever. The result is a singular work of its kind, because it not only offers the usual good counsel of the genteel tradition but includes as well, in textbook vein, a more than usual amount of instruction of a somewhat technical nature in drawing and painting, heraldry, antiquities, and military drill as matters which the gentleman should have some knowledge of, however elementary. To the first edition of 1622 were added in the second printing of 1627 the chapters on military drill and fishing, and in the edition of 1634, upon which the present text is based, were included the chapters "Of Antiquities" and "Of Sundry Blazons, Both Ancient and Modern."

In his address to the reader Peacham names many of his great predecessors who were teachers of good counsel, and it

[8] George E. Cokayne, *The Complete Peerage* (2nd ed., London, 1953), XII, pt. I, 188.
[9] See below, p. 5.
[10] See below, p. 4.

is quite evident that he had read them all. The tradition of courtesy from which he drew was a long one extending back through the more recent humanist writers, both native and foreign, to Quintilian, Plutarch, Cicero, and Aristotle. To the best of this tradition Peacham was faithful without servility, and the popularity of his book during the next two centuries undoubtedly had much to do in forming the ideals set forth by later writers on the subject. Indeed, it is probable that until the publication of Chesterfield's letters no writer on courtesy was better known than Henry Peacham. As sincerely as Sir Thomas Elyot, who influenced his thinking, he believes that differences of rank among men are ordained by Providence, but he carefully distinguishes between Christian and civil nobility. For true nobility is not conferred by a title but is achieved by some virtuous action which the title merely recognizes. For him, as for all true men of the Renaissance, learning is "an essential part of nobility," [11] and for imparting good learning to young gentlemen schoolmasters have primary responsibility. Many of Peacham's strictures upon schoolmasters had been anticipated, but few authors before or after him have equaled his caustic but sincere indictment of them and their employers. Neither does he spare the negligent or indulgent or overproud parents about whose remissness he is rather more concerned. Even fifteen years later, in *The Truth of Our Times*, he devoted a spirited essay to each group.

The ideas Peacham puts forth in his discussion of the young gentleman's choice of company were to become the stock in trade of courtesy writers for the next two centuries. His chapter on style and the reading of history, both as a mosaic of pronouncements from the best authors and as a compendium of his own good sense, reminds one of Ben Jonson's *Timber*. His enthusiasm in recommending English authors as models of style is noteworthy: More, Sidney, Hooker, Sir John Hayward,

[11] See below, p. 28.

Bacon, and Daniel. Long before others, Peacham saw the usefulness of geography to the student of history, and he appreciated the contribution that travel, coins, statues, and ancient inscriptions could make to the study of history. He looked upon antiquities not as dead things, but as things full of meaning, and he was aware at the same time of the aesthetic appeal of many of them. He may have been prompted to introduce this subject—the first to do so in English courtesy literature—and to deal with it at such length by his acquaintance with the antiquities then to be found in Arundel House. His patron, Thomas Howard, Earl of Arundel and Surrey, was the first great virtuoso in England, and after 1615 he spent many years on the Continent forming his famous collection of marbles, paintings, and coins. Peacham's "survey of the earth" expresses something of the wonderment we come upon several years later in Burton's "Air Rectified," and that he had been touched by some of the new enthusiasm for mathematics that we later detect in Francis Osborne and others is apparent in his chapter on geometry. His advice as to the necessity of healthful exercise and recreation is briefer than but not inferior to that of Elyot or Ascham.

Peacham writes with conviction and feeling about poetry and music. Poetry is a sweetener of severer studies, has moved men to great actions, and is believed to have cured bodily diseases. He omits mention of Greek poets, but gives the standard list of Roman, beginning with Virgil; and he has more to say of the Latin poets of England—Joseph of Exeter, George Buchanan ("the chief"), More, Lily, Chaloner—than of the more numerous vernacular poets. His list of the latter from Chaucer to Daniel contains no dramatist—if Sackville be excepted—for the reason, perhaps, that the greatest drama of the age had not yet won favor and respectability as poetry in his sight. Music, the sister of poetry, is defended as a means of praising the Creator and of solacing oneself in the midst of sorrow and care, and the exercise of music is a "great lengthener of life." "Those stung with the tarantula are cured only by music." With William Byrd, to whom he later gives a glowing citation, he believes that singing is a healthful exercise and that by it children may be cured of stammering. Urged by the promptings of patriotism, Peacham included in his list of musicians a goodly number of English composers, who, he declares, are "inferior to none in the world (how much soever the Italian attributes to himself) for depth of skill and richness of conceit." He does not, however, make a similar claim for England's painters, few of whom had risen above amateurism. He thinks drawing and painting are "most commendable and so many ways useful to a gentleman," and to prove his contention he shows how it was practiced in ancient days by both prince and patrician. These considerations induce him to include some practical instruction and, perhaps for inspiration of his pupils, a series of brief notices of Italian painters; and since a "noble or gentleman who beareth arms and is well descended" should be able to blazon his own coat, derive his pedigree, and know his kin by blood or marriage, Peacham deals with heraldry at even greater length.

In his discussion of the gentleman's "carriage in general" Peacham insists upon temperance and moderation as essential to the achievement of reputation, "without which our most graceful gifts are dead and dull," and he advocates thrift and frugality in preserving one's estate, in apparel, and in eating and drinking. Choose religious and learned companions, he advises, from whose discourse and counsel you may benefit; be affable in company; and "have a care ever to speak the truth." All these practices are to be observed abroad as well as at home, but the young gentleman must be sure he knows his own country before he ventures to travel abroad. Peacham's chapter on travel with which he ended the first edition of his book—perhaps because he regarded travel as a supplement to formal training—gives advice on what to see in France and

Spain, but no such discussion of travel in Italy or Germany is given because "they have been so exactly described by Master Sandys and others." With this chapter should be read the essay on the subject in *The Truth of Our Times.*

A few words about *The Truth of Our Times.* As has been suggested, a number of the essays match chapters of *The Complete Gentleman*—those on schools and schoolmasters, parents and children, and travel—and others expand topics treated in the earlier work. Although these essays appeared some fifteen years later, Peacham is still the wise counselor to the inexperienced and the unwary. But whereas *The Complete Gentleman,* despite the fact that it had been written to a ten-year-old boy, was laden with recondite learning and classical lore, the essays are relatively free of such things, marginal annotations are seldom used, and the writing has assumed a more familiar, anecdotal, and humorous cast. His style is more incisive and epigrammatic, and his examples and illustrations and figures are often more apt. An obvious fault—if indeed it be a fault in works separated by more than a few years—is his fond repetition of certain favorite allusions, anecdotes, and jokes, and of quotations from David and Solomon and the classical languages. The familiarity and freedom of the essay enabled him to give more frequent expression to the satirical outlook of his generation as well as to indulge in reminiscence and the airing of prejudice. He can be caustic, but he is never violent in his strictures, and their harsh edges are often turned by his ever-present humor. The influence of the popular "character" is to be detected here and there, especially in his "absolute clown" and "A Religious Honest Man." [12] His essay "Of Common Ignorance" anticipates, to a minor degree, of course, Sir Thomas Browne's *Vulgar Errors.* Like James Howell and other later writers Peacham begins to record detailed observations and to illustrate his ideas with personal experiences and

[12] See below, pp. 216, 222–223.

striking remarks he has heard. He knows the city and has savored of its fascination, but he loves the country and country folk. He preaches the great virtues of his class and time that were to endure in English life, and his concern is rather with the young country gentlemen, who, he believed, were to be, as they later proved themselves, the salvation of England.

What image emerges from his writings? We see in him, I believe, a true patriot who was modestly proud of his country and yet not blind to the achievements of other nations, who adhered to the established church and honored his king. He preached the sober virtues of thrift, frugality, and moderation in living, but nearly always with touches of humor, and he displayed breadth and tolerance in an intolerant age. He rightly regarded himself as a scholar by profession, but on a minor scale he was much more—poet, painter, musician, mathematician, and philosopher. He possessed in abundance the common sense, discretion, and sound judgment which he so earnestly wished the young gentlemen of England to practice.

NOTE ON TEXTS

The omissions from the text of the following modernized version of *The Complete Gentleman* have been prompted by several considerations. The greater portions of the chapters on heraldry (armory, blazonry—for Peacham uses all three terms), the brief chapter on military drill, and a portion of the chapter on drawing and painting are somewhat technical and are obviously indicative rather of Peacham's special interests than of those of the traditional writer of books of good counsel. They are closer to the textbook than to the material in which they are imbedded. Moreover, Peacham himself recognized and often recommended fuller and more expert books on such subjects. His own *Gentleman's Exercise* (1612), for example, gives a much fuller account of the art of drawing and painting and contains a dialogue on blazonry as well. The omissions indicated provide space for the essays, which have been too long neglected, but which are so closely related to the subject matter of *The Complete Gentleman* as to form a supplement to that work. Finally, the omitted portions of the book can be found in most libraries in G. S. Gordon's reprint published in 1906 at the Clarendon Press.

The Truth of Our Times, which was carelessly proofread, or not proofread at all, especially in the latter half or third, had no second edition, though in 1942 it was reproduced in facsimile by Robert R. Cawley. *The Art of Living in London,* first printed in 1642, was reprinted by Thomas Park in the *Harleian Miscellany,* IX (1812), 84–89.

The text of *The Complete Gentleman* is based upon the Folger Shakespeare Library copy of the 1634 edition, and Folger copies of the 1622, 1627, and 1661 printings have been consulted for correction of doubtful readings. The text of *The Truth of Our Times* is based upon the Folger copy checked against the facsimile of the Huntington copy mentioned above, and *The Art of Living in London* is reproduced from a photostat of the apparently unique copy in the British Museum.

The modernization of an early-seventeenth-century text is beset with some troublesome difficulties, particularly in applying the principles of modern punctuation to passages whose syntax is now obsolete. Peacham was characteristically addicted to the long sentence, made so by excessive co-ordination and strings of qualifying subordinate clauses. I have broken up many of these prolix passages, but in only a few instances have I permitted sentence fragments to stand alone. Peacham's sometimes fanciful spellings of proper names have been given present-day spellings to aid the reader in searching for them in works of reference, and some few words have been altered in form—for example, *fift* to *fifth, thorough* to *through, burthen*

to *burden, ware* to *wore,* and *then* to *than*—but the verbal
ending *-eth* has been retained throughout. These changes do
no violence to the language, since original spellings nowadays
seldom represent to us the words as the Jacobean ear heard
them. Abbreviations have been expanded and all obvious misprints silently corrected. All foreign passages not translated or
paraphrased by the author have been translated in the notes.
Direct quotations are placed in quotation marks or printed in
reduced type. Marginal annotations, except for mere key or
index words, which have been omitted, have been placed in
the footnotes, with only the English parts modernized. All
such notes are marked by an asterisk (*). Peacham shows little
consistency as to form in his Latin references to other works.
Many are fragmentary or incomplete, and a few are obscure
or unidentifiable. There has been no attempt to normalize them
here, but sometimes clarification has been attempted, misprints
have been corrected, abbreviations have been silently expanded,
and in a few instances the punctuation has been made con-
sistent with Peacham's usual practice. Biblical references have
been given modern style. All other changes or additions are
enclosed in square brackets. The commentary has been kept
to a minimum upon the assumption that the reader will have
access to standard works of reference, although some attempt
has been made to explain some of the more germane or remote
allusions. Glossing, in all except a few instances, has been con-
fined to words which do not appear in *Webster's New Collegiate
Dictionary,* latest edition.

THE COMPLETE GENTLEMAN

(1634)

By Henry Peacham

Ad optimae spei, generosissimaeque indolis adolescentem,
Dom. Gulielmum Howard, *illustriss. ac vere honoratiss.*
Thomae *Comitis* Arundeliae, *summi totius Angliae*
Mareschalli, &c. filium secundo-genitum.[1]

> *Ingenio, genio, dum vis Generosus haberi,*
> *Ingenua haec discas, ingeniose puer.*
> *Stemma nihil, cultis animum nisi moribus ornes,*
> *Et studeas studiis nobilitare genus.*[2]

---

[1] "To the truly noble youth of greatest hope, Lord William Howard, second son of Thomas, Earl of Arundel, High Marshal of all England, etc."

[2] "So long as you wish to be esteemed as of noble mind and character, clever boy, you will learn these noble things: A family tree is nothing unless you furnish the mind with good manners and take pains by your studies to make yourself worthy of your high birth."

To the truly noble and most hopeful knight of the honorable Order of the Bath, William Howard, second son to the Right Honorable Thomas, Earl of Arundel and Surrey, Earl Marshal of England, etc.

WHAT motive, noble sir, may induce others in their dedications, I know not. Sure I am, none other hath incited me than the regard of your own worth and that native ingenuity and goodness of spirit I have ever perceived in you since it was my good hap to enjoy your acquaintance and to spend some hours with you at your book in Norwich, where you had your education under the reverend, religious, and my honorable good lord, the then Lord Bishop of Norwich.[3] And indeed to whom of right should rather appertain these my instructions in regard of their subject, which is the fashioning of nobility after the best precedents, than to yourself, every way so nobly descended. Besides, it is affirmed that there are certain sparks and secret seeds of virtue innate in princes and the children of noble personages, which, if cherished and carefully attended in the blossom, will yield the fruit of industry and glorious action, and that not only above the strength of the vulgar, but even in the scion and before the time which nature hath appointed. So Achilles,[4] while he was yet very young, undertook to shoot the fiercest lions and boars and was so nimble on foot that he was able to take a wild beast without either toil or dog. Alex-

[3] Samuel Harsnet, who was Bishop of Norwich from 1619 to 1628.
[4] *Pindar in Nemeis,* Ode 3.

3

ander [5] also, when an Egyption priest saluted him, being very young, by the names of son and child, replied, "But you shall find me a man before the walls of Athens." But to omit heathenish examples, Solomon,[6] we read, when he was but even a child, begged wisdom of God and grace to govern well, and Ignatius,[7] that holy martyr, writeth how that Solomon was scarce twelve years of age when he decided that hard controversy between the two harlots. Nor was Josiah above eight years old when he walked religiously before God. And methinks, sir, as in that Cornelian stem whereof Scipio was said to be the top (*in quo, ut plura genera in unam arborem, videtur insita multorum illuminata sapientia* [8]), already you grow apace, reflecting, as from a fair glass, that princely moderation and honesty of heart of the good Duke, your great-grandfather, the honorably disposed mind of my lord, your noble father, together with his love and admiration of whatsoever is honest or excellent, so that verily you need no other pattern to the absolute shaping of yourself than the images of your forefathers. But as Aristotle [9] saith of the vine, by how much it is laden with clusters, by so much it hath need of props; so say I of greatness and nobility. Ever fruitful and apt to abundance, it hath hourly need of support and help by all timely advice and instruction to guide and uphold it from lying along.

Wherefore, since the fountain of all counsel and instruction, next to the fear of God, is the knowledge of good learning, whereby our affections are persuaded and our ill manners mollified, I here present you with the first and plainest directions (though but as so many keys to lead you into far fairer rooms)

[5] *°Ioannes Monach[us] in vita Alexandri.*

[6] *°Regum I. cap. 3. ver. 9* [I Kings 3:9].

[7] *°[St.] Ignatius lib. Epist. cap. 3.*

[8] *°Cicero.* ["In whom, as upon a single tree, one may see fruits of many grafts, so upon that family was ingrafted and set off the wisdom of many ancestors."]

[9] *°Arist[otle] in Ethicis.*

4

and the readiest method I know for your studies in general and to the attaining of the most commendable qualities that are requisite in every noble or gentleman. Nothing doubting but that after you have herein seen the worth and excellence of learning, how much it addeth to nobility, what errors are hourly committed through ignorance, how sweet a thing it is to converse with the wisest of all ages by history, to have insight into the most pleasant and admirable sciences of the mathematics, poetry, picture, heraldry, etc. (whereof I here entreat together with the most commendable exercise of the body, with other general directions for carriage, travel, etc.), you will entertain this discourse as Ulysses did Minerva at his elbow, as your guide to knowledge, the ground not only of the sweetest but the happiest life. And though I am assured there are numbers who, notwithstanding all the books and rules in the world, had rather than behold the face of heaven bury themselves in earthly sloth and basest idleness, yet, Sir William Howard, at the least let us recover you from the tyranny of these ignorant times, and from the common education, which is to wear the best clothes, eat, sleep, drink much, and to know nothing. I take leave from my house at Hogsdon by London, May 30.

Who is and shall be ever yours,
HENRY PEACHAM.

To My Reader

I am not ignorant, judicious reader, how many pieces of the most curious masters have been uttered to the world of this subject, as Plutarch, Erasmus, Vives, Sadoleto, Sturmius, Osorius, Sir Thomas Elyot, Master Ascham, with sundry others, so that my small taper among so many torches were as good out, as seeming to give no light at all. I confess it true. But as rare and curious stamps upon coins for their variety and strangeness are daily inquired after and bought up, though the silver be all one and common with ours, so fares it with books which as medals bear the pictures and devices of our various invention. Though the matter be the same, yet for variety sake they shall be read, yea, and, as the same dishes dressed after a new fashion, perhaps please the tastes of many better. But this regard neither moved me. When I was beyond the seas and in a part of France adjoining upon Artois, I was invited oftentimes to the house of a noble personage who was both a great soldier and an excellent scholar. And one day above the rest, as we sat in an open and goodly gallery at dinner, a young English gentleman, who, desirous to travel, had been in Italy and many other places, fortuned to come to his house, and, not so well furnished for his return home as was fitting, desired entertainment into his service. My lord, who could speak as little English as my countryman French, bade him welcome and demanded by me of him what he could do. "For I keep none," quoth he, "but such as are commended for some good quality or other, and I give them good allowance—some an hundred, some sixty, some fifty crowns by the year." And calling some about him, very gentlemanlike, as well in their behavior as apparel, "This," saith he, "rideth and breaketh my great horses; this is an excellent lutenist; this, a good painter and surveyor of land; this, a passing linguist and scholar who instructeth my sons," etc. "Sir," quoth this young man, "I am a gentleman born and can only attend you in your chamber or wait upon your lordship abroad." "See," quoth Monsieur de Ligny, for so was his name, "how your gentry of England are bred, that when they are distressed or want means in a strange country, they are brought up neither to any quality to prefer them, nor have they so much as the Latin tongue to help themselves withal." I knew it generally to be true, but for that time and upon occasion excused it as I could. Yet he was received and after returned to his friends in good fashion. Hereby I only give to know that there is nothing more deplorable than the breeding in general of our gentlemen, none any more miserable than one of them if he fall into misery in a strange country. Which I can impute to no other thing than the remissness of parents and negligence of masters in their youth. Wherefore, at my coming over, considering the great forwardness and proficience of children in other countries, the backwardness and rawness of ours; the industry of masters there, the ignorance and idleness of most of ours; the exceeding care of parents in their children's education, the negligence of ours; being taken through change of air with a quartan fever, that leisure I had ἀπὸ παροξυσμοῦ,[1] as I may truly say, by fits I employed upon this discourse for the private use of a noble young gentleman, my friend, not intending it should ever see light, as you may perceive by the plain and shallow current of the discourse, fitted to a young and tender capacity. Howsoever, I have done it, and if thou shalt find herein any thing that may content, at the least not distaste, thee, I shall be glad and encouraged to a more

[1] "From irritation."

8

serious piece; if neither, but out of a malignant humor disdain what I have done, I care not. I have pleased myself, and long since learned Envy, together with her sister Ignorance, to harbor only in the basest and most degenerate breast.

Chapter I

Of Nobility in General: that It Is a Plant from Heaven; the Root, Branches, Fruit

If we consider arightly the frame of the whole universe and method of the all-excellent Wisdom in her work, as creating the forms of things infinitely diverse, so according to dignity of essence or virtue in effect we must acknowledge the same to hold a sovereignty and transcendent predominance, as well of rule as place, each over either. Among the heavenly bodies we see the nobler orbs, and of greatest influence, to be raised aloft, the less effectual, depressed; of elements the fire, the most pure and operative, to hold the highest place. In compounded bodies of things, as well sensible as insensible, there runneth a vein of excellence proceeding from the form, ennobling, in the same kind, some other above the rest.

The lion, we say, is king of beasts; the eagle, chief of birds; the whale and whirlpool[1] among fishes; Jupiter's oak, the forest's king.[2] Among flowers we most admire and esteem the rose; among fruit, the pomeroy and queen-apple. Among stones we value above all the diamond; metals, gold and silver. And since we knew these to transfer their inward excellence and virtues to their species successively, shall we not acknowledge

[1] A sort of whale or monster.   [2] *Spenser in his *Faerie Queene*.

a nobility in man of greater perfection, of nobler form, and prince of these?

Can we be curious in discerning a counterfeit from the true pearl, to choose our scions of the best fruit, buy our flowers at twenty pounds the root or slip, and not regard or make difference of lineage, nor be careful into what stock we match ourselves, or of what parents we choose a servant?

Surely, to believe that nature (rather the God of nature) produceth not the same among ourselves is to question[3] the rarest workmistress of ignorance or partiality, and to abase[4] ourselves beneath the beast. Nobility, then, taken in the general sense, is nothing else than a certain eminency or notice taken of some one above the rest for some notable act performed, be it good or ill. And in that sense are *nobilis* and *ignobilis* usually among the Latin poets taken. More particularly, and in the genuine sense, nobility is the honor of blood in a race or lineage, conferred formerly upon some one or more of that family, either by the prince, the laws, customs of that land or place, whereby either out of knowledge, culture of the mind, or by some glorious action performed they have been useful and beneficial to the commonwealths and places where they live.

For since all virtue consisteth in action, and no man is born for himself, we add "beneficial and useful to his country"; for they hardly are to be admitted for noble who, though of never so excellent parts, consume their light as in a dark lanthorn in contemplation and a Stoical retiredness.

And since honor is the reward of virtue and glorious actions only, vice and baseness must not expect her favors, as the people of Rome created C. Flavius from a tribune senator and aedile for stealing of a book of records; Euthicrates, Euphorbus, and Phylagrus were ennobled for treason; and Cottier by Louis the Eleventh, the French king, unworthily advanced

---

[3] Accuse.   [4] From 1622; 1634 abuse.

from a mender of stockings to be lord chancellor of France.

Neither must we honor or esteem those ennobled or made gentle in blood who by mechanic and base means have raked up a mass of wealth, or because they follow some great man, wear the cloth of a noble personage, or have purchased an ill coat at a good rate, no more than a player upon the stage for wearing a lord's cast suit, since nobility hangeth not upon the airy esteem of vulgar opinion, but is indeed of itself essential and absolute.

Besides, nobility, being inherent and natural, can have, as the diamond, the luster but only from itself. Honors and titles externally conferred are but attendant upon desert and are but as apparel and the drapery to a beautiful body.[5]

Memorable, as making to our purpose, is that speech [6] of Sigismund the Emperor to a doctor of the civil law, who, when he had received knighthood at the Emperor's hands, left forthwith the society of his fellow doctors and kept company altogether with the knights; which the Emperor well observing, smiling before the open assembly, said unto him: "Fool, who preferrest knighthood before learning and thy degree, I can make a thousand knights in one day but cannot make a doctor in a thousand years." Now for as much as the weal public of every estate is preserved *armis et consilio*,[7] this fair tree by two main branches dispreadeth herself into the military and civil discipline. Under the first I place valor and greatness of spirit; under the other, justice, knowledge of the laws, which is *consilii fons*,[8] magnificence, and eloquence.

For true fortitude and greatness of spirit were ennobled, we read, Iphicrates, that brave Athenian who overthrew in a set battle the Lacedaemonians, stopped the fury of Epaminondas,

[5] *Aeneas Silvius lib. 4, de gestis Alphonsi. Georg. Fiscellus.*

[6] *This happened at the Council of Constance, where the doctors and knights were about some serious business divided into two several assemblies.

[7] "By arms and counsel." [8] "The fountain of counsel."

and became lieutenant general to Artaxerxes, King of Persia, yet but the son of a poor cobbler.

Eumenes, one of the best captains for valor and advice Alexander had, was the son of an ordinary carter.

Diocletian was the son of a scrivener or bookbinder; Valentinian, of a ropemaker; Maximinus, of a smith; Pertinax,[9] of a woodmonger; Servius Tullius, son of a bondwoman (thence his name *Servius*); Tarquinius Priscus, of a poor merchant, or rather peddler, in Corinth; Hugh Capet, the first of that name, King of France, the son of a butcher in Paris, who, when Louis the Sixth, son of Lothaire, was poisoned by Blanche, his wife, for adultery, being a stout fellow and of a resolute spirit, having gathered a company like himself, and taking his advantage of the time and distempered humor of the state, carried himself and his business so that he got the crown from the true heir, Charles, the uncle of Louis.

Lamusius, the third King of the Lombards, was the son of a common strumpet, found laid and covered with leaves in a ditch by King Agelmond, who, by chance riding that way and espying a thing stir in the ditch, touched it with the point of his lance to see what it was; which the infant with the hand taking fast hold of, the King, amazed and imagining it as a presage of some good fortune toward the child, caused it to be taken out of the ditch and to be brought up, which after, nursed in the lap of Fortune by many degrees of honor, got the crown of Lombardy.[10]

Neither are the truly valorous or any way virtuous ashamed of their so mean parentage, but rather glory in themselves that

---

[9] *Pertinax or Stubborn, so surnamed because he came from his father, who would have made him a scholar, he choosing rather to be a woodmonger. [*Julius*] *Capitolinus*, I. See the *Treasure of Times* [perhaps, Thomas Milles, *The Treasury of Ancient and Modern Times*, 2 vols., 1613–1619].

[10] *Ex Historia Longobard.* ["from *The History of the Lombards*," by Paulus Diaconus].

their merit hath advanced them above so many thousands far better descended. And hence you shall many times hear them freely discourse of their beginning and plainly relate their bringing up and what their parents were. I remember when I was in the Low Countries and lived with Sir John Ogle at Utrecht, the reply of that valiant gentleman, Colonel Edmunds, to a countryman of his newly come out of Scotland, went current; who, desiring entertainment of him, told him my lord, his father, and such knights and gentlemen, his cousins and kinsmen, were in good health. Quoth Colonel Edmunds, "Gentlemen," to his friends by, "believe not one word he says. My father is but a poor baker of Edinburgh and works hard for his living, whom this knave would make a lord to curry favor with me and make you believe I am a great man born," etc.

So that the valiant soldier, you see, measureth out of whole cloth his honor with his sword, and hence in ancient times came Rome, Athens, Carthage, and of late the Ottoman Empire to their greatness. Honor being then highly prized, every one aimed at nobility and none refused the most desperate attempts for the good of his country. Thus the Decii, Cato, Marcellus, with infinite others, became ennobled and had their altars, statues, columns, etc., and were well-nigh adored with as great respect as their gods themselves.

From no less meanness of birth and beginning we find many great and famous bishops, civilians, orators, poets, etc., to have attained to the greatest dignities, both of church and commonwealth, and to have checked with their fortunes even Glory herself. Pope John the Two and Twentieth was a poor shoemaker's son; Nicholas the Fifth was son of a poulter; Sixtus the Fifth, of a hogherd; Alphenus but a tailor's apprentice, who, running from his master, went to Rome and there studied the civil law and so profited that for his learning and wisdom he was created consul; Ulpian but meanly born, yet tutor to Alexander the emperor. Cicero was born and brought up at Arpinum, a poor and obscure village; Virgil, the son of a potter; Horace, of a trumpeter; Theophrastus, of a botcher; with infinite others I might allege as well of ancient as modern times.[11]

For doing justice the Romans of a private man and a stranger chose Numa for their king, and on the contrary, as Plutarch writeth, comparing them together, Lycurgus of a king for justice sake made himself a private man. For, "A goodly thing," saith Plutarch, "it is, by doing justly to obtain a kingdom, and as glorious to prefer justice before a kingdom; for the virtue of the one (Numa) made him so esteemed and honored that he was of all thought worthy of it; of the other, so great that he scorned it." [12]

In like manner, for their good laws and doing justice were advanced to their thrones and goodly tribunals Minos, Rhadamanthus (though subjects of poets' fables), Aratus, Solon, etc. And how fairly beyond their laurels the name of Just became Aristides, Trajan, Agesilaus, with many others, I leave to history to report.

For magnificence and obliging the places wherein they lived by great benefits were ennobled Tarquinius Priscus, a stranger and a banished man; and of later times Cosmo de Medici in Florence, upon whose virtues, as upon a fair prospect or some princely palace, give me leave a little, as a traveler, to breathe myself, and show you afar off the fair turrets of his more than royal magnificence, being but a private man, as I find it recorded in his history by Machiavelli.[13] "This Cosmo," saith he,

was the most esteemed and most famous citizen (being no man of war) that ever had been in the memory of man, either in Florence or any other city, because he did not only excel all others of his time

---

[11] A favorite topic with P. Cf. *The Worth of a Penny*, 1669 ed., pp. 17 ff., and below, pp. 182 ff.

[12] *Plutarch. in Lycurgi et Numae Comp.* ["Comparison of Lycurgus and Numa."]

[13] *Machiavell[i], Hist. Florentin. lib.* 7. [The following quoted passage is from Thomas Bedingfield's translation (London, 1595), pp. 172–173.]

in authority and riches, but also in liberality and wisdom. For among other qualities which advanced him to be chief of his country he was more than other men liberal and magnificent, which liberality appeared much more after his death than before. For his son Piero found by his father's records that there was not any citizen of estimation to whom Cosmo had not lent great sums of money, and many times also he did lend to those gentlemen whom he knew to have need. His magnificence appeared by divers his buildings, for within the city of Florence he builded the abbeys and temples of S. Marco, S. Lorenzo, and the monastery of S. Verdiana, and in the mountains of Fiesole, S. Girolamo, with the abbey thereto belonging. Also in Mugello he did not only repair the church for the friars, but took it down and built it anew. Besides these magnificent buildings in S. Croce, in S. Agnoli, and S. Miniato, he made altars and sumptuous chapels. All which temples and chapels, besides the buildings of them, were by him paved and furnished thoroughly with all things necessary. With these public buildings we may number his private houses, whereof one within the city, meet for so great a personage, and four other without, at Careggi, at Fiesole, at Casaggivolo, and at Trebio, all palaces fitter for princes than private persons. And because his magnificent houses in Italy did not in his opinion make him famous enough, he builded in Jerusalem an hospital to receive poor and diseased pilgrims. In which work he consumed great sums of money. And albeit these buildings and every other his actions were princely, and that in Florence he lived like a prince, yet so governed by wisdom as he never exceeded the bounds of civil modesty. For in his conversation, in riding, in marrying his children and kinsfolks he was like unto all other modest and discreet citizens, because he well knew that extraordinary things, which are of all men with admiration beheld, do procure more envy than those which without ostentation be honestly covered.

I omit, as followeth shortly after, his great and excessive charge in entertaining of learned men of all professions to instruct the youth of Florence: his bounty to Argyropulo, a Grecian, and Marsilio Ficino (whom he maintained for the exercise of his own studies in his house and gave him goodly lands near his house of Careggi), men in that time of singular learning, because virtue rears him rather to wonder than imitation.

To proceed, no less respect and honor is to be attributed to eloquence, whereby so many have raised their esteem and fortunes, as able to draw civility out of barbarism and sway whole kingdoms by leading with Celtic Hercules [14] the rude multitude by the ears. Mark Antony, contending against Augustus for the Roman Empire, assured himself he could never obtain his purpose while Cicero lived; therefore he procured his death. The like did Antipater, a successor to Alexander, by Demosthenes, aspiring to the monarchy of Greece. And not long since a poor Mohammedan priest by his smooth tongue got the crown of Morocco from the right heir, being the house of Giuseph or Joseph. And much hurt it may do if, like a man's sword, it be used by a turbulent and mutinous orator; otherwise we must hold it a principal means of correcting ill manners, reforming laws, humbling aspiring minds, and upholding all virtue. "For as serpents are charmed with words, so the most savage and cruel natures by eloquence"—which some interpret to be the meaning of Mercury's golden rod with those serpents wreathed about it. Much, therefore, it concerneth princes not only to countenance honest and eloquent orators, but to maintain such near about them as no mean props, if occasion serve, to uphold a state, and the only keys to bring in tune a discordant commonwealth.

But it shall not be amiss, ere I proceed further, to remove certain doubts which as rubs clog the clear passage of our discourse, and the first concerning bastardy: whether bastards may be said to be nobly born or not. I answer with Justinian, *Sordes*

[14] *Described by Lucian to be aged, bald, and wrinkled, brown-colored, clad with a lion's-skin, holding in his right hand a club, in his left a bow, with a quiver at his back, and long small chains of gold and amber fastened through little holes to the tip of his tongue, drawing a multitude of people willing to follow after him, only shadowing unto us the pomp of eloquence. *Plato in Timaeo. Pier. Valerius, lib. 6.*

inter praecipuos nominari non merentur.[15] Yet it is the custom
with us and in France to allow them for noble by giving them
sometimes their father's proper coat with a bend sinister, as
Reginald, Earl of Cornwall, base son to the Conqueror, bore
his father's two leopards passant gardant or in a field gules
with a bend sinister azure; the like Hamel, base son to Geoffrey
Plantagenet, Earl of Surrey; some, their father's whole coat or
part of the same in bend dexter, as John Beaufort, a bastard of
Somerset, bore party per pale argent and azure, a bend of England with a label of France; Sir Roger de Clarendon, base son
to the Black Prince, his father's three feathers on a bend sable,
the field or. I willingly produce these examples to confirm our
custom of ennobling them, and though the law leaneth not on
their side, yet stand they in the head of the troops with the most
deserving, yea, and many times, according to Euripides,[16] prove
better than the legitimate. Who are more famous than Romulus
and Remus, who laid the first stone of Rome? more courageous
and truly valiant than Hercules, Alexander, our King Arthur
of Britain, and William the First? more critically learned than
Christopher Longolius, Jacobus Faber? more modest and of
better life than Caelius Calgaguinus, the delight of his Ferrara,
with infinite others, and where decretals and schoolmen may
bear the bell, those two grandees, Gratian and Lombard?

A second question ariseth, whether he that is noble descended
may by his vice and baseness lose his nobility or no. It is answered that if he that is ignoble and inglorious may acquire
nobility by virtue the other may very well lose it by his vice.
But such are the miserable corruptions of our times that vices
go for prime virtues, and to be drunk, swear, wench, follow the
fashion, and to do just nothing are the attributes and marks
nowadays of a great part of our gentry. Hence the Agrigentines
expelled their Phalaris, the Romans extinguished the memory

---

[15] "Base persons do not deserve mention among persons of distinction."
[16] *Gnesion amictos in Andromeda. [Andromache 638]*.

of the whole race of the Tarquins, with those monsters of nature, Nero, Heliogabalus, etc., the Sicilians, Dionysius the Latter, with others.

Thirdly, whether poverty impeacheth or staineth nobility, I answer: riches are an ornament, not the cause of nobility, and many times we see there lieth more worth under a threadbare cloak and within a thatched cottage than the richest robe or stateliest palace. Witness the noble Curii and Fabritii, taken from a poor dinner of turnips and watercresses in an earthen dish to lead the Roman army and conquer the most potent kings of the world.

Fourthly, concerning advocates and physicians, whether we may rank them with the ennobled or no. Advocates or counselors, being interpreters of the law, their place is commendable and themselves most necessary instruments in a commonwealth; wherefore, saith the civil law,[17] their calling is honorable; they ought to be freed of mulcts, public charges, and all impositions, and to be written or sent unto as unto persons of especial worth and dignity.

Touching physicians, though the profession by some hath been thought servile, and in times past was practiced by servants, as Domitian, saith Seneca, *imperavit medico servo, ut venenum sibi daret,*[18] and that slovenly epithet of *Scataphagos* be by Aristophanes [19] bestowed upon Aesculapius; yet it is an art nothing servile and base, but noble and free, since we know not only emperors and kings but saints, yea, our blessed Saviour, to have cured the sick; as Constantine, Adrian, Edward the Confessor,[20] King of England; Mithridates, King of Pontus, whose

---

[17] *Extat Lex Constantini* [i.e., as it appears in the Law of Constantine], *lib.* 10. *Codicis.*

[18] "Commanded his medical servant that he should give him a potion."

[19] *Aristophanes in Pluto.*

[20] *To whom was first given, being a devout and most religious king, the gift of curing the King's Evil; whence it hath been derived to our Kings of England, his successors.

antidote yet beareth his name; Artemisia, Queen of Caria, who first found the virtue of mugwort, bearing her name in Latin; Gentius, King of Illyricum, now Slavonia, who immortally liveth in the herb Gentiana, as also Lysimachus in his Lysimachia, Achilles in Achillea, or the yarrow; Apollo, Podalirius, Moses, Isaiah, Solomon, Ezekiel. "Honor the physician," saith Ecclesiasticus; then again, "All physic or medicine is from God, and he shall receive a reward from the king, the skill of the physician shall exalt his head," etc. And as Ptolemy sometime objected against Zoilus concerning Homer, so may I unto our lordly *misiatrous* or physic-haters. Which of them all, treble their revenues, can maintain so many as one poor Galen or Hippocrates, who, though dead many hundreds of years since, feed many thousands of families even at this present? I here intend no common chirurgeons, mountebanks, unlettered empirics, and women doctors (of whom for the most part there is more danger than of the worst disease itself), whose practice is infamous, mechanic, and base.

Fifthly, concerning merchants. The exercise of merchandise hath been, I confess, accounted base and much derogating from nobility, except it be exercised and undertaken by a general estate or the deputies thereof. Aristotle therefore saith [21] that the Thebans and Lacedaemonians had a law that none should be esteemed and held capable of honor in their commonwealth except they had ten years before given over trading and merchandise. And Valerius Maximus reporteth that among things the Romans had, to disparage Tarquinius Priscus withal and make him odious to the people, was that he was a merchant's son. St. Chrysostom,[22] upon that place of Matthew, "He cast out the buyers and sellers out of the temple," gathereth that mer-

[21] *Hippolytus à Collibus. Axiom. de Nobilitate* [*The Principles of Nobility*].
[22] *Chrysost. super Mathaeum* ["Chrysostom on Matthew"], *Francis. Patricius de Repub. lib.* I. *cap.* 8.

chants hardly and seldom please God. And certain it is that the ancient Romans never preferred any that exercised merchandise to any eminent place or office in their commonwealth, perhaps agreeing in one with Aristotle, who, speaking of merchants and mechanics, saith: *Vilis est huiusmodi vita, et virtuti adversa*— This kind of life is base and contrary to virtue.[23]

But some may object unto me the great estates of Venice, Genoa, Florence, Lucca, etc., where their nobility is nothing disparaged by the exercise of merchandise. I answer: as their coins at home they may raise themselves higher or lower at their pleasure, but abroad (like city mayors[24]) in other countries, they fall under value and a great deal short of their reckoning.

But if the owner of the earth and all that therein is hath so bestowed and disposed of His blessings that no one country affordeth all things, but must be beholden not only to her neighbors but even the most remote regions, and commonwealths cannot stand without trade and commerce, buying and selling, I cannot, by the leave of so reverend judgments, but account the honest merchant among the number of benefactors to his country while he exposeth as well his life as goods to the hazard of infinite dangers, sometimes for medicinal drugs and preservatives[25] of our lives in extremity of sickness; another for our food or clothing in times of scarcity and wants, haply for useful necessaries for our vocations and callings; or lastly for those *sensus et animi oblectamenta*,[26] which the Almighty Providence hath purposely for our solace and recreation and for no other end created, as apes, parrots, peacocks, canary, and all singing birds;[27] rarest flowers for color and smell; precious stones of

---

[23] *Arist[otle] *politic.* 7. *cap.* 4.   [24] 1634 Majors; 1622 Maiors.

[25] *Of *Salomon's* merchants. See Chronicles 2. chap. 1. verse 16 [i.e., II Chron. 1:16].

[26] "Amusements of the senses and the spirit."

[27] *Chron. 2.9. verse 21 [i.e., II Chron. 9:21].

all sorts, pearl, amber, coral, crystal; all manner of sweet odors; fruits infinitely differing in form and taste; colors of all sorts for painting, dyeing, etc.—but I proceed.

Sixth and last, touching mechanical arts and artists. Whosoever labor for their livelihood and gain have no share at all in nobility or gentry, as painters, stageplayers, tumblers, ordinary fiddlers, innkeepers, fencers, jugglers, dancers, mountebanks, bearwards, and the like, except the custom of the place determine the contrary, as Herodotus and Xenophon[28] witness to have been observed both among the Egyptians, Scythians, and Corinthians. The reason[29] is because their bodies are spent with labor and travail, and men that are at their work *assidui et accubui umbratiles esse coguntur.*[30] Yea, if a noble man, born in captivity or constrained through any other necessity, shall exercise any manual occupation or art, he, by the opinion of some, loseth his nobility civil, but not Christian, and shall at his return be restored. Where I said the "custom of the country" I intend thus: by law of Mahomet,[31] the Grand Seignior or Great Turk himself is bound to exercise some manual trade or occupation (for none must be idle), as Solyman the Magnificent that so threatened Vienna. His trade was making of arrowheads; Achmet the Last, horn rings for archers, and the like.

From the root and branches let us taste the fruit, which fall not like the apples of Sodom with a light touch into nothing, but are as those of Hesperides, golden and out of the vulgar reach.

First, noble- or gentlemen ought to be preferred in fees, honors, offices, and other dignities of command and government before the common people.

They are to be admitted near and about the person of the prince, to be of his council in war, and to bear his standard.[32]

---

[28] *Xenophon in Oeconomica.*   [29] *A faint and spent reason.
[30] "Are busily occupied and are forced to remain in the shadows."
[31] *Hippolyt. à Coll. in Axiomat. Nobilitatis [Principles of Nobility].
[32] *Which was the office of a baron in ancient times.

We ought to give credit to a noble or gentleman before any of the inferior sort.

He must not be arrested or pleaded against upon cozenage.

We must attend him and come to his house, and not he to ours.

His punishment ought to be more favorable and honorable upon his trial, and that to be by his peers of the same noble rank.

He ought in all sittings, meetings, and salutations to have the upper hand and greatest respect.

They must be cited by bill or writing to make their appearance.

In criminal causes noblemen may appear by their attorney or procurator.

They ought to take their recreations of hunting, hawking, etc., freely, without control, in all places.

Their imprisonment ought not to be in base manner or so strict as others.

They may eat the best and daintiest meat that the place affordeth, wear at their pleasure gold, jewels, the best apparel, and of what fashion they please, etc.

Besides, nobility stirreth up emulation in great spirits, not only of equaling others, but of excelling them, as in Cimon, the Elder Scipio Africanus, Decius the Son, Alexander, Edward, our Black Prince, and many other.

It many times procureth a good marriage, as in Germany, where a fair coat and a crest is often preferred before a good revenue.[33]

It is a spur in brave and good spirits to bear in mind those things which their ancestors have nobly achieved.

It transferreth itself unto posterity, and as for the most part we see the children of noble personages to bear the lineaments and resemblance of their parents, so in like manner for the most part they possess their virtues and noble dispositions, which

---

[33] Income.

even in their tenderest years will bud forth and discover itself.

Having discoursed of nobility in general, the division and use thereof, give me leave in a word to inveigh against the pitiful abuse thereof, which like a plague, I think, hath infected the whole world, every undeserving and base peasant aiming at nobility. Which miserable ambition hath so furnished both town and country with coats of a new list that were Democritus living he might have laughing matter for his life. In Naples such is the pride of every base groom that, though he be *di stalla*,[34] he must be termed *Signore,* and scarce will he open a note from a poor *calzolaio*[35] to whom he hath been a twelve-month indebted for his boots if *Don* be not in the superscription.

In Venice, likewise, every mechanic is a *Magnifico,* though his *magnificenza* walketh the market but with a sequin.

In France every peasant and common lackey is saluted by the name of *Monsieur* or *Sire,* the King himself having no other title, the word *Sire* immediately proceeding from Cyrus, the Persian word for a lord or great prince, as H. Stephanus[36] well noteth, or, as it pleaseth some, from κῦρος, authority, or κύριος, a lord or governor, πόλεων καὶ τόπων κύριοι.[37] Go but from Paris to Anjou and see if you find not all, from the count to the *esculière*,[38] allied either to the King, some prince of the blood, noble, peer, or other.

In the Low Countries mine old host at Arnhem in Gelderland changed his coat and crest thrice in a fortnight because it did not please his young wife. For ye must understand they are all gentlemen by a grant, they say, from Charles the Fifth, in consideration of a great sum of money they lent him in time of his wars. Come into what house soever, though *mijn heer weert*[39] be but a gardener, ropemaker, or aquavitae-seller, you shall be

[34] "From the stable." [35] "Shoemaker." [36] *In Lexico.*
[37] *Demost[henes], Olynth.* 2. ["Lords of cities and lands."]
[38] *Escuyer,* esquire. [39] "My worthy sir."

sure to have his arms, with the beaver full-faced (allowed to none but kings and princes) in his glass window, with some ingenious motto or other of his own device. I remember one Telink there gave for his coat a wild goose in the water, with this witty one: *Volans, natans;* [40] another, three hogs falling upon a dog who was lugging one of their fellows, with this: *Endracht mackt macht;* [41] another, three great drinking bowls, orbiquiers, with this truly Dutch, and more tolerable than the rest, underneath, *Quem non fecere disertum?* [42] with infinite others of like nature. Yet the ancient nobility (whereof there are many honorable families, as Hohenlohe, Egmont, Horn, Brederode, Waggenaer, Botselaer, with sundry others) keep themselves entire and, maintaining their ancient houses and reputation free from scandal of dishonor as well as we, laugh at these their boorish devices.

Some again, by altering letters or syllables or adding to their names, will insinuate themselves into noble houses and not stick many times to bear their coats.

But the most common and worst of all is in all places the purchasing of arms and honors for money, very prejudicial to true nobility and politic government. For who will hazard his person and estate to infinite dangers for honor when others at home may have it *sine sudore et sanguine* [43] only by bleeding in the *vena cava* called *marsupium?* [44] The pure oil cannot mingle with the water, no more this extracted quintessence and spirit of virtue with the dregs and subsistence of unworthiness. Euripides,[45] when his father told him he was knighted, made this reply: "Good father, you have that which every man may have for his money." And certainly virtue *dum petit ardua* [46] will not stoop to take up her reward in the street. The Frenchman is so

---

[40] "Flying, swimming." [41] *Concord makes might.
[42] "Whom have they not made eloquent?"
[43] "Without sweat and blood." [44] "Hollow vein called money-bag."
[45] *Hippolytus à Collibus. [46] "As she pursues difficult tasks."

bold as to term such intruders *gentil-vilains,* but I dare not use that word lest some that challenge the first part of it should return me the latter.

Lastly, to conclude, most pitiful is the pride of many, who, when they are nobly born, not only stain their stock with vice and all base behavior, relying and vaunting of their long pedigrees and exploits of their fathers, but, themselves living in sloth and idleness, disparage and disgrace those who by their virtuous endeavors are rising. To these and such I oppose Marius and that stout reply of his in Sallust: "They contemn me as an upstart; I scorn their sloth and baseness." Again:

What they idly hear and read at home myself hath either acted or seen. If they scorn me, let them scorn their ancestors who came by their nobility as I have done. If they envy mine honor, let them also envy my labors, mine innocence, my perils, etc. Now see how equally they deal. That which they arrogate to themselves from the virtue of others, that they deny me for mine own because I have no images, and my nobility is new, etc. Shortly after, I cannot, to prove my descent, bring forth the images of my ancestors, their triumphs, their consulships, but, if need be, I can show lances, my ensign, caparisons, and other such warlike implements, besides a number of scars upon my breast. These are my images, my nobility, not left me by descent and inheritance, etc.

And as resolute of late years was the answer of Verdugo, a Spaniard, commander in Friesland, to certain of the Spanish nobility who murmured at a great feast that the son of a hangman should take place above them (for so he was, and his name importeth): "Gentlemen," quoth he, "question not my birth or who my father was. I am the son of mine own desert and fortune. If any man dares as much as I have done, let him come and take the table's end with all my heart."

CHAPTER II

Of the Dignity and Necessity of
Learning in Princes and Nobility

Since learning, then, is an essential part of nobility, as unto which we are beholden for whatsoever dependeth on the culture of the mind, it followeth that who is nobly born and a scholar withal deserveth double honor, being both εὐγενής and πολυμαθής.[1] For hereby as an engine of the fairest colors he is afar off discerned and winneth to himself both love and admiration, heighthing with his skill his image to life, making it precious and lasting to posterity.

It was the reply of that learned King of Aragon to a courtier of his, who affirmed that learning was not requisite in princes and nobility, *Questa è voce d'un bue, non d'un huomo.*[2] For if a prince be the image of God, governing and adorning all things, and the end of all government the observation of laws, that thereby might appear the goodness of God in protecting the good and punishing the bad, that the people might be fashioned in their lives and manners and come near in the light of knowledge unto him who must protect and defend them by establishing religion, ordaining laws; by so much, as the sun from his orb of empire, ought he to outrun the rest in a virtuous race and outshine them in knowledge by how much he is mounted

---

[1] "Wellborn and learned." *Si ad naturam eximiam eruditio accesserit tum demum singulare quoddam existere solet.—Cic[ero] pro Archia Poeta.* ["When erudition is joined to exceptional natural endowments, something quite extraordinary results."]

[2] "This is the voice of an ox, not of a man."

nearer to heaven and so in view of all that his least eclipse is taken to a minute.

What, tell me, can be more glorious [3] or worthy the scepter than to know God aright, the mysteries of our salvation in Jesus Christ; to converse with God in soul, and oftener than the mere natural man to advance him in his creatures; to be able with Solomon [4] to dispute from the loftiest cedar on Libanus to the lowest hyssop upon the wall; to be the conduit pipe and instrument whereby, as in a goodly garden, the sweet streams of heaven's blessings are conveyed in piety, peace, and plenty to the nourishing of thousands and the flourishing of the most ingenious arts and sciences?

Wherefore, saith the kingly prophet, *Erudimini, Reges,*[5] etc., as if he should say: How can you kings and judges of the earth understand the grounds of your religion, the foundation and beginnings of your laws, the ends of your duties and callings, much less determine of such controversies as daily arise within your realms and circuits, define in matters of faith, public justice, your private and economic affairs, if from your cradles ye have been nursed, as Solomon's fool,[6] with ignorance, brutish Ignorance, mother of all misery,[7] that infecteth your best actions with folly, ranketh you next to the beast, maketh your talk and discourse loathsome and heavy to the hearer, as a burden upon the way,[8] yourselves to be abused by your vassals, as blind men by their boys, and to be led up and down at the will and pleasure of them whose eyes and ears you borrow?

Hence the royal Solomon above all riches of God desired wisdom and understanding, that he might govern and go before so mighty a people. And the ancient Romans,[9] when their voices

---

[3] *Nicephorus, lib. 17. cap. 40.
[4] *Regum I. cap. 4.33 [i.e., I Kings 4:33].
[5] *Psalm 2 [1634 Psalm 1. "Be wise now, therefore, O ye kings," etc.]
[6] *Prov. 15.   [7] *Plato, lib. 5. de Repub.   [8] *Ecclesiast[icus] 15.
[9] *[Flavius] Vopisc[us] in Tacit[o].

were demanded at the election of their emperor, cried with one consent, *Quis melior quam literatus?* [10] Hence the Persians would elect none for their king except he were a great philosopher, and great Alexander acknowledged his εὖ εἶναι [11] from his master Aristotle.

Rome saw her best days under her most learned kings and emperors, as Numa, Augustus, Titus, Antoninus, Constantine, Theodosius, and some others. Plutarch [12] giveth the reason: "Learning," saith he, "reformeth the manners and affordeth the wholesomest advice for the government of a commonwealth." I am not ignorant but that, as all goodness else, she hath met with her mortal enemies, the champions of ignorance, as Licinius gave for his mot or poesy: [13] *Pestes reipublicae literae,*[14] and Louis the Eleventh, King of France, would ever charge his son to learn no more Latin than this: *Qui nescit dissimulare, nescit regnat.*[15] But these are the fancies of a few, and those of ignorant and corrupted judgments.

Since learning, then, joined with the fear of God, is so faithful a guide that without it princes undergo but lamely, as Chrysostom saith, their greatest affairs, they are blind in discretion, ignorant in knowledge, rude and barbarous in manners and living, the necessity of it in princes and nobility may easily be gathered, who, however they flatter themselves with the favorable sunshine of their great estates and fortunes, are indeed of no other account and reckoning with men of wisdom and understanding than glowworms that only shine in the dark of ignorance and are admired of idiots and the vulgar for the outside, statues or huge colossuses full of lead and rubbish within, or

---

[10] "Who is better than a learned man?"   [11] "Well-being."

[12] °*Plutarch. in Coriolano.*   [13] °*Eutropius.*

[14] "Letters are the disease of the republic."

[15] "One who does not know how to dissemble does not know how to rule." Cf. below, p. 186.

the Egyptian ass [16] that thought himself worshipful for bearing golden Isis upon his back.

Sigismund,[17] King of the Romans, and son to Charles the Fourth, Emperor, greatly complained at the Council of Constance of his princes and nobility, whereof there was no one that could answer an ambassador who made a speech in Latin. Whereat Lodovic, the Elector Palatine, took such a deep disdain in himself that with tears ashamed he much lamented his want of learning, and presently hereupon returning home began, albeit he was very old, to learn his Latin tongue. Eberhard also, the first Duke of Württemberg, at an assembly of many princes in Italy who discoursed excellently in Latin while he stood still and could say nothing, in a rage struck his tutor or governor there present for not applying him to his book when he was young. I gladly allege these examples as by a public council to condemn opinion of heresy, believing to teach and teaching to believe the unnecessity of learning in nobility, an error as prejudicial to our land as sometime was that rotten chest to Ethiopia, whose corrupted air, vented after many hundreds of years, brought a plague not only upon that country but over the whole world.

I cease to urge further the necessity and dignity of learning, having, as Octavius said to Decius, a captain of Antony's, to the understanding spoken sufficient, but to the ignorant too much had I said less.[18]

[16] *Plutarch. Alciat[i] in Emblem.*
[17] *Iacob. Wimphelingus.*   [18] *Appian.*

CHAPTER III

Of the Time of Learning, Duty of Masters,
and What the Fittest Method to Be Observed

As THE spring is the only fitting seedtime for grain, setting and planting in garden and orchard, so youth, the April of man's life, is the most natural and convenient season to scatter the seeds of knowledge upon the ground of the mind. Δεῖ γὰρ εὐθὺς ἐκ νέου ὀρέχεσθαι, saith Plato,[1] "It behooveth in youth out of hand to desire and bend our minds to learning." Neither as good husbands, while time serveth, let slip one hour. For, saith he elsewhere,[2] "Our ground is hard and our horses be wild." Withal, if we mean to reap a plentiful harvest, take we the counsel of Adrastus in Euripides, "To look that the seed be good." For, "In the foundation of youth, well ordered and taught, consists," saith Plato again, "the flourishing of the commonwealth." This tender age is like water spilt upon a table, which with a finger we may draw and direct which way we list, or, like the young hop, which, if wanting a pole, taketh hold of the next hedge, so that now is the time, as wax, to work it pliant to any form.

How many excellent wits have we in this land that smell of the cask by neglecting their young time when they should have learned! Horace his *Quo semel*,[3] once fit for the best wine, since too bad for the best vinegar, who, grown to years of discretion and solid understanding, deeply bewail their misspent or mis-

---

[1] *°Plato politic.* 6.   [2] *°In Phaedro.*

[3] *Quo semel est imbuta recens, servabit odorem / testis diu:* "The jar will long keep the fragrance of what it was once steeped in when new." —*Epist.* i.2.69–70.

32

guided youth with too late wishing, as I have heard many, that they had lost a joint or half their estates, so that they had been held to their books when they were young. The most, and not without cause, lay the fault upon bad masters. To say truth, it is a general plague and complaint of the whole land, for, for one discreet and able teacher you shall find twenty ignorant and careless, who, among so many fertile and delicate wits as England affordeth, whereas they make one scholar, they mar ten.

The first and main error of masters is want of discretion when, in such variety of natures as different as their countenances, the master never laboreth to try the strength of every capacity by itself, which, as that Lesbian stone Aristotle speaketh of,[4] must have the rule fitted to it, not that brought to the rule. For, as the selfsame medicines have several operations according to the complexions they work upon, so one and the selfsame method agreeth not with all alike. Some are quick of capacity and most apprehensive, others of as dull; some of a strong memory, others of as weak; yet may that dullard or bad memory, if he be observed, prove as good, yea, in Aristotle's opinion, better than of the other. But we see, on the contrary, out of the master's carterly judgment, like horses in a team, they are set to draw all alike, when some one or two prime and able wits in the school, αὐτοδίδακτοι [5] (which he culls out to admiration if strangers come, as a costardmonger his fairest pippins), like fleet hounds go away with the game, when the rest need helping over a stile a mile behind. Hence, being either quite discouraged in themselves, or taken away by their friends, who for the most part measure their learning by the form they sit [6] in, they take leave of their books while they live.

A second oversight nigh akin to the former is indiscretion in correction, in using all natures alike, and that with immoderation or rather plain cruelty. True it is: *Quo quisque est solertior*

---

[4] *In Ethic.*   [5] "Self-taught."   [6] From 1622; 1634 set.

et ingeniosior, hoc docet iracundior.[7] But these fellows believe with Chrysippus in Quintilian [8] that there is no other method of making a scholar than by beating him, for that he understandeth not through their own fault; wherein they show themselves egregious tyrants, for correction without instruction is plain tyranny.

The noble, generous, and best natures are won by commendation, enkindled by glory, which is *fax mentis honestae*,[9] to whom conquest and shame are a thousand tortures. Of which disposition for the most part are most of our young nobility and gentlemen, wellborn, inheriting with their being the virtues of their ancestors, which even in this tender greenness of years will bewray itself as well in the school as abroad at their play and childish recreations.

Quintilian, above all others, desireth this disposition to make his orator of, and whom chiding grieveth to be tenderly dealt withal. Yet have I known these good and towardly natures as roughly handled by our *Plagosi Orbilii* [10] as by Dionysius himself taking revenge upon the buttocks of poor boys for the loss of his kingdom, and railed upon by the unmannerly names of blockheads (oft by far worse than blockheads), asses, dolts, etc., which deeply pierceth the free and generous spirit. For *Ingenuitas,* saith Seneca,[11] *non recipit contemptum:* ingenuity or the generous mind cannot brook contempt, and which is more ungentlemanly, nay, barbarous and inhuman, pulled by the ears, lashed over the face, beaten about the head with the great end of the rod, smitten upon the lips for every slight offense with the *ferula* (not offered to their fathers' scullions at home)

---

[7] *Cicero pro Rosc. comoedo.* ["The more clever and more talented one is, the more is one inclined to anger."]

[8] *Quintilian, lib. institut. 1. cap. 3.*

[9] *Virgil.* ["Torch of the fine mind."]

[10] "Orbilius' Floggers." Pupillus Orbilius, Horace's teacher and grammarian, to whom the poet applied the epithet *plagosus.*

[11] *Senec[a] de moribus.*

by these *Aiaces flagelliferi*,[12] fitter far to keep bears (for they thrive and are the fatter for beating, saith Pliny) than to have the charge of nobles and gentlemen.

In Germany the school is, and as the name importeth it ought to be, merely *ludus literarius,* a very pastime of learning, where it is a rare thing to see a rod stirring; yet I heartily wish that our children of England were but half so ready in writing and speaking Latin, which boys of ten and twelve years old will do so roundly and with so neat a phrase and style that many of our masters would hardly mend them, having only for their punishment shame and for their reward praise. *Cavendum a plagis,* saith Quintilian, *sed potius laude aut aliorum praelatione urgendus est puer;* that is, we must hold our hands, and rather bring the child forward with praise and preferring of others. Besides, there ought to be a reciprocal and a mutual affection betwixt the master and scholar, which judicious Erasmus [13] and Lodovicus Vives (sometimes teacher to Queen Mary and a Spaniard who came to England with Queen Katherine, her mother) do principally require, *patris in illum induendo affectum,* by putting on a father's affection toward him, and, as Pliny saith,[14] *Amore, non artifice docente, qui optimus magister est,* to win his heart and affection by love, which is the best master, the scholar again the contrary. So may a discreet master, with as much or more ease, both to himself and his scholar, teach him to play at tennis or shoot at rovers in the field, and profit him more in one month, besides his encouragement, than in half a year with his strict and severe usage. But instead hereof many of our masters for the most part so behave themselves that their very name is hateful to the scholar, who trembleth at their coming in, rejoiceth at their absence, and looketh his master, returned, in the face as his deadly enemy.

[12] "Whip-bearing Ajaxes."
[13] *Erasm[us] in Epi[st]. ad Christianum Lubecensem.*
[14] *Plin. epist. lib. 4.*

Some affect, and severer schools enforce, a precise and tedious strictness in long keeping the scholars by [15] the walls, as from before six in the morning till twelve or past, so likewise in the afternoon; which, besides the dulling of the wit and dejecting the spirit (for *Otii non minus quam negotii ratio extare debet* [16]), breedeth in him afterward a kind of hate and carelessness of study when he cometh to be *sui juris,* at his own liberty (as experience proveth by many who are sent from severe schools unto the universities), withal overloading his memory and taking off the edge of his invention with overheavy tasks in themes, verses, etc. To be continually poring on the book, saith Socrates, hurteth and weakeneth the memory very much, affirming learning to be sooner attained unto by the ear in discourse and hearing than by the eye in continual reading. I verily believe the same, if we had instructors and masters at hand as ready as books. For we see by experience these who have been blind from their birth to retain more by hearing than others by their eyes, let them read never so much; wherefore Fabius would have *Istud ediscendi taedium protinus a pueris devorari,* this same toil or tediousness of learning by heart to be presently swallowed or passed over by children.

Wherefore I cannot but commend the custom of their schools in the Low Countries, where for the avoiding of this tedious sitting still and irksome poring on the book all day long, after the scholar hath received his lecture he leaveth the school for an hour and walketh abroad with one or two of his fellows, either into the field or up among the trees upon the rampire,[17] as in Antwerp, Breda, Utrecht, etc., where they confer and recreate themselves till time calls them in to repeat, where perhaps they stay an hour; so abroad again, and thus at their pleasure the whole day. For true it is that Lipsius saith,[18]

---

[15] Within.

[16] °*Cicero pro Planc[io].* ["There should be reason for leisure no less than for work."]

[17] Embankment.   [18] °*Lipsius in Epist.*

ingenia vegetativa must have *suos recessus*, strong and lively wits must have their retrait [19] or intermission of exercise, and, as rams, engines of war in old time, recoil back to return with greater force; which the mind doth unto study after pause and rest, not unlike a field, which by lying fallow becometh far more fat and fruitful.

A fourth error is the contrary—for, *Stulti in contraria currunt* [20]—too much carelessness and remissness in not holding them in at all, or not giving them in the school that due attendance they ought, so that every day is playday with them, bestowing the summer in seeking birds' nests or haunting orchards, the winter in keeping at home for cold or abroad all day with the bow or the birding piece, they making as little conscience in taking as their master in giving their learning, who forgetteth belike that rumor layeth each fault of the scholar upon his neck.[21] Plato remembereth one Protagoras, a bird of the same feather, who when he had lived threescore years made his boast he had spent forty of those threescore in corrupting and undoing youth. We have, I fear, a race of those Protagor-asses even yet among our common schoolmasters in England.

But the diseases whereunto some of them are very subject are humor and folly (that I may say nothing of the gross ignorance and insufficiency of many), whereby they become ridiculous and contemptible both in school and abroad. Hence it comes to pass that in many places, especially in Italy, of all professions that of *pedanteria* [22] is held in basest repute, the schoolmaster almost in every comedy being brought upon the stage to parallel the zany or pantaloon. He made us good sport in that excellent comedy of *Pedantius,* acted in our Trinity College in Cambridge, and, if I be not deceived, in *Priscianus vapulans* [23] and many of our English plays.

---

[19] Retreat. [20] "Fools run in a contrary direction."
[21] *Plutarch. ad Trajanum.* [22] "Profession or office of a schoolmaster."
[23] *Priscian the Flogger,* a celebrated comedy by the German scholar Nicodemus Firschlin (d. 1589).

I knew one who in winter would ordinarily in a cold morning whip his boys over for no other purpose than to get himself a heat; another beat them for swearing, and all the while swears himself with horrible oaths. He would forgive any fault saving that.

I had, I remember, myself (near St. Albans in Hertfordshire, where I was born) a master who by no entreaty would teach any scholar he had farther than his father had learned before him, as, if he had only learned but to read English, the son, though he went with him seven years, should go no further. His reason was they would prove saucy rogues and control their fathers. Yet these are they that oftentimes have our hopeful gentry under their charge and tuition to bring them up in science and civility.

Besides, most of them want that good and direct method whereby in shortest time and with least labor the scholar may attain unto perfection. Some, teaching privately, use a grammar of their own making; some, again, none at all; the most, Lily's,[24] but preposterously posted over that the boy is in his quantity of syllables before he knoweth the quality of any one part of speech, for he profiteth no man more than he mastereth by his understanding. Nor is it my meaning that I would all masters to be tied to one method, no more than all the shires of England to come up to London by one highway. There be many equally alike good. And since method, as one saith,[25] is but ὁδοποιητική,[26] let every master, if he can, by pulling up stiles and hedges make a more near and private way to himself,[27] and in God's name say with the divinest of poets:

[24] The widely used elementary grammar by William Lily and John Colet.

[25] *[Joannes] Philoponus 1. Physicorum* [i.e., Philoponus' commentary on Aristotle's *Physics*, book I].

[26] "Finding a way."

[27] *See Master Doctor [Joseph] Webbe his *Appeal to Truth* [1622].

The Complete Gentleman

deserta per avia dulcis
Raptat amor, iuvat ire iugis, qua nulla priorum
Castalium molli divertitur orbita clivo.[28]

With sweet love rapt I now by deserts pass,
And over hills, where never track of yore,
Descending easily, yet remembered was
That led the way to Castalie before.

But instead of many good they have infinite bad and go stumbling from the right as if they went blindfold for a wager. Hence cometh the shifting of the scholar from master to master, who, poor boy, like a hound among a company of ignorant hunters holloing every deer they see, misseth the right, begetteth himself new labor, and at last by one of skill but well rated[29] or beaten for his pains. They cannot commonly err if they shall imitate the builder, first to provide the scholar with matter, then cast to lay a good foundation. I mean a solid understanding of the grammar, every rule made familiar and fast by short and pleasant examples. Let him bring his matter into form, and by little and little raise the frame of a strong and well-knit style both in writing and speaking. And what doth harm in all other building is here most profitable and needful; that is, translation. For I know nothing that benefiteth a scholar more than that: first, by translating out of Latin into English, which laid by for some time, let him translate out of English into Latin again, varying as oft as he can both his words and phrases.[30] Dosetus, who hath gathered all the phrases of Tully into one volume, Manutius, Erasmus his *Copia*, and Draxe his *Calliopoea*, with others, will help him much at the first. Let him after by his own reading enrich his understanding and learn *haurire ex ipsis fontibus*,[31] next exercise himself in themes and declamations, if he be able. The old method of teaching grammar, saith

---

[28] *Georgic[a]* 3.   [29] From 1622; 1634 read.
[30] Ascham's method, long used in England.
[31] "To drink from the fountains themselves."

Suetonius, was disputation in the forenoon and declamation in the afternoon. But this I leave to the discretion of the judicious master.

I pass over the insufficiency of many of them, with ill example of life (which Plato wisheth above all things to be respected and looked into), whereof as of physic and ill physicians there is many times more danger than of the disease itself, many of them being no grammarians at all, much less, as Quintilian requireth in a schoolmaster, rhetoricians to expound with proper and purest English an eloquent Latin or Greek author, unfold his invention and handling of the subject, show the form and fluency of the style, the apt disposition of figures, the propriety of words, the weight of grave and deep sentences, which are *nervi orationis,* the sinews of discourse; musicians, without which grammar is imperfect in that part of *prosodia* that dealeth only with meter and rhythmical proportions; astronomers, to understand authors who have written of the heavens and their motions, the several constellations, setting and rising of the planets, with the sundry names of circles and points, as Manilius and Pontanus; and, lastly, natural and moral philosophers, without which they cannot, as they ought, understand Tully's *Offices* or Aesop's fables, as familiar as they seem.

Far be it that I may be thought to question the worth and dignity of the painful and discreet teacher, who, if learning be needful, must be as necessary. Besides, I am not ignorant that even the greatest princes,[32] with the most reverend bishops and most profound scholars of the world, have not been ashamed of teaching the grammar; or that I inveigh in the least against the learned and worthy masters of our public schools, many of whom may be ranked with the most sufficient scholars of Europe. I inveigh against the pitiful abuse of our nation by such who by their ignorance and negligence deceive the church and

---

[32] *Augustus et Octavius Caesar. Dionysius. L. Aemilius. Aristotle. Adrian the Sixth. Erasmus. Joseph Scaliger, etc.*

commonwealth of serviceable members, parents of their money, poor children of their time, esteem in the world, and perhaps means of living all their lives after.

CHAPTER IV

Of the Duties of Parents in Their Children's Education [1]

NEITHER must all the blame lie upon the schoolmasters. Fond and foolish parents have oft as deep a share in this precious spoil, as he [2] whose cockering and apish indulgence, to the corrupting of the minds of their children, disabling their wits, effeminating their bodies, how bitterly doth Plato [3] tax and abhor! For avoiding of which the law of Lycurgus commanded children to be brought up and to learn in the country, far from the delicacy of the city. And the Brutii in Italy, a people bordering upon Lucania, following the custom of the Spartans, sent their children after the age of fourteen away, to be brought up in fields and forests among shepherds and herdsmen, without any to look unto them or to wait upon them, without apparel or bed to lie on, having nothing else than milk or water for their drink and their meat such as they could kill or catch. And hear the advice of Horace:

> *Augustam, amice, pauperim pati*
> *Robustus acri militia puer*
> *Condiscat, et Parthos feroces*

[1] For more on the same subject, see below, pp. 185 ff.
[2] From 1622; 1634 as whose.
[3] *In Gorgia* [from 1622; 1634 *In Gordia*].

Henry Peacham

Vexet eques metuendus hasta,
Vitamque sub dio, et trepidis agat
In rebus, etc.[4]

Friend, let thy child hard poverty endure,
And, grown to strength, to war himself inure,
And, bravely mounted, learn, stern cavalier,
To charge the fiercest Parthian with his spear.
Let him in fields withoutdoors lead his life,
And exercise him where are dangers rife, etc.

If any of our young youths and gallants were dieted in this manner, mercers might save some paper and city laundresses go make candles with their saffron and eggs, dicing houses and ten-shilling ordinaries let their large rooms to fencers and puppet players, and many a painted piece betake herself to a wheel[5] or the next hospital. But nowadays parents either give their children no education at all, thinking their birth or estate will bear out that; or, if any, it leaveth so slender an impression in them that, like their names cut upon a tree, it is overgrown with the old bark by the next summer. Besides, such is the most base and ridiculous parsimony of many of our gentlemen, if I may so term them, that if they can procure some poor bachelor of art from the university to teach their children to say grace and serve the cure of an impropriation,[6] who, wanting means and friends, will be content, upon the promise of ten pounds a year at his first coming, to be pleased with five, the rest to be set off in hope of the next advowson (which perhaps was sold before the young man was born), or, if it chance to fall in his time, his lady or master tells him, "Indeed, sir, we are beholden unto you for your pains. Such a living is lately fallen, but I had before made a promise of it to my butler or bailiff for his true and extraordinary service," when

---

[4] *Horat[ius] lib. 3. Ode 2.*   [5] Spinning wheel?
[6] Transfer of a benefice or ecclesiastical property to a layman.

42

the truth is he hath bestowed it upon himself for fourscore or an hundred pieces, which indeed his man two days before had hold of but could not keep.

Is it not commonly seen that the most gentlemen will give better wages and deal more bountifully with a fellow who can but teach a dog or reclaim an hawk than upon an honest, learned, and well-qualified man to bring up their children? It may be, hence it is, that dogs are able to make syllogisms in the fields when their young masters can conclude nothing at home if occasion of argument or discourse be offered at the table. "Look upon your nobility and gentry nowadays," saith a wise and grave historian,[7] "and you shall see them bred as if they were made for no other end than pastime and idleness. They observe moderation neither in talk nor apparel; good men and such as are learned are not admitted amongst them; the affairs of their estates they impose upon others," etc. "But to view one of them rightly," saith Seneca,[8] "look upon him naked, lay by his estate, his honors, and *alia fortunae mendacia*, his other false disguisements of fortune, and behold his mind, what and how great he is, whether of himself or by some borrowed greatness."

But touching parents, a great blame and imputation, how justly I know not, is commonly laid upon the mother, not only for her overtenderness, but in winking at their lewd courses, yea, more in seconding and giving them encouragement to do wrong, though it were, as Terence saith,[9] against their own fathers.

I dare not say it was long of [10] the mother that the son told his father he was a better man and better descended than he. Nor will I affirm that it is her pleasure the chambermaid

---

[7] *Philip de Commines, lib.* I.   [8] *Seneca ad Lucil[ium]. epist.* 31.

[9] *Matres omnes filiis in peccato et auxilio in paterna iniuria esse solent. Terent[ius] in Heautont[imorumenos.* 992. "All mothers help their sons in trouble and usually support them against paternal harshness."]

[10] Because of, attributable to.

should be more curious in fitting his ruff than his master in refining his manners.

Nor that it is she that filleth the cistern of his lavish expense at the university or Inns of Court, that, after four or five years spent, he returns home as wise as Ammonius his ass that went with his master every day to school to hear Origen and Porphyry read philosophy.

But albeit many parents have been diligent enough this way, and good masters have likewise done their parts, and neither want of will or ability of wit in their children to become scholars; yet, whether out of an overweening conceit of their towardness, a pride to have their sons outgo their neighbors, or to make them men before their time, they take them from school, as birds out of the nest, ere they be flidge,[11] and send them so young to the university that scarce one among twenty proveth ought. For as tender plants, too soon or often removed, begin to decay and die at the root, so these young things of twelve, thirteen, or fourteen, that have no more care than to expect the next carrier and where to sup on Fridays and fasting nights, no further thought of study than to trim up their studies with pictures and place the fairest books in openest view, which, poor lads, they scarce ever opened or understand not, that when they come to logic and the crabbed grounds of arts there is such a disproportion between Aristotle's categories and their childish capacities that what together with the sweetness of liberty, variety of company, and so many kinds of recreation in town and fields abroad, being like young lapwings apt to be snatched up by every buzzard, they prove with Homer's willow ὠλεσίκαρποι,[12] and as good go gather cockles with Caligula's people on the sand [13] as yet to attempt the difficulties of so rough and terrible a passage.

Others again, if they [14] perceive any wildness or unstaidness

[11] Fledge, feathered.
[13] See Suetonius iv.47.

[12] "To shed their fruit immaturely."
[14] From 1622; 1634 you.

in their children, are presently in despair and out of all hope
of them for ever proving scholars or fit for anything else, neither
consider the nature of youth nor the effect of "Time, the physician of all," [15] but, to mend the matter, send them either to the
court to serve as pages, or into France or Italy to see fashions
and mend their manners, where they become ten times worse.
These of all other, if they be well tempered, prove the best
metal. Yea, Tully, as of necessity, desireth some abundant rankness or superfluity of wit in that young man he would choose
to make his orator of. *Vellem,* saith he, *in adolescente aliquod
redundans et quod amputem:* [16] "I wish in a young man something to spare and which I might cut off." This taken away ere
degenerate with luxurious abundance, like that same rank vine
the prophet Jeremiah speaketh of,[17] you shall find the heart
divino satu editum,[18] and sound timber within to make Mercury of, *qui non fit ex quovis ligno,*[19] as the proverb saith.

And some of a different humor will determine, even from the
A B C, what calling their children shall take upon them, and
force them, even in despite of nature, like Lycurgus his whelps,
to run contrary courses and to undertake professions altogether
contrary to their dispositions. This, saith Erasmus, is *peccare
in genium.*[20] And certainly it is a principal point of discretion
in parents to be thoroughly acquainted with and observe the
disposition and inclination of their children, and indeed for
every man to search into the addiction of his genius, and not
to wrest nature, as musicians say, out of her key, or, as Tully
saith, to contend with her, making the spaniel to carry the ass's
load; which was well observed by the Lacedaemonians and
ancient Romans in laying forth instruments of sundry occupa-

---

[15] *Πάσης λύπης ἰατρὸς χρόνος.* [16] *2. De Oratore.*
[17] Ier. 2. 21 [Jeremiah 2:21]. [18] "Of divine origin."
[19] "Which is not made of just any sort of wood," presumably a reference
to the making of a wooden statue of Mercury, with a play upon the
name of the god.
[20] "To err against genius or inclination."

tions before their children at a certain age, they to choose what liked them best and ever after to take upon them that profession whereunto they belonged.

How many are put by worldly and covetous fathers, *invita Minerva*,[21] to the study of the laws (which study I confess to be most honorable and most deserving), who notwithstanding spend most of their time even in divinity at the Inns of Court! And how many divines have we (I appeal to the courts), heirs of their fathers', friends', or purchased advowsons, whom the buckram bag would not better beseem than the Bible, being never out of law with their parishioners, following their suits and causes from court to court, term to term, no attorney more!

In like manner I have known many commanders and worthy gentlemen, as well of our own nation as strangers, who, following the wars in the field and in their arms, have confessed unto me nature never ordained them for that profession, had they not fallen accidentally upon it either through death of friends, harshness of masters and tutors, thereby driven from the university (as an honorable friend of mine in the Low Countries hath many times complained unto me), or the most common mischief, miserableness of greedy parents, the overthrow and undoing of many excellent and prime wits, who, to save charges, marry a daughter or prefer a younger brother, turn them out into the wide world with a little money in their purses, or perhaps none at all, to seek their fortunes, where necessity dejects and besots their spirits, not knowing what calling or course to take, enforceth them desperately to beg, borrow, or to worse or baser shifts (which in their own natures they detest as hell), to go on foot, lodge in alehouses and sort themselves with the basest company till what with want and wandering so long in the circle, at last they are (upon the center of some hill) constrained to say, as Hercules between his two pillars, *non ulterius*.[22]

Much less have parents nowadays that care to take the pains

[21] "Against the grain."   [22] "No further."

to instruct and read to their children themselves, which the greatest princes and noblest personages have not been ashamed to do. Octavius Augustus Caesar read the work of Cicero and Virgil to his children and nephews himself. Anna,[23] the daughter of Alexis, the Grecian emperor, was by her father so instructed that while she was yet a young and goodly lady she wrote of herself a very learned and authentic history of the church. Aemilius Paulus, the son who so bravely ended his days at Cannae when his colleague forsook him, seeing the favor of the state not inclinable toward him, left the city and only spent his time in the country in teaching his own children their Latin and Greek, notwithstanding he daily maintained grammarians, logicians, rhetoricians, painters, carvers, riders of great horses, and the skillfulest hunters he could get to instruct and teach them in their several professions and qualities.

The three daughters of ever-famous Sir Thomas More were by their father so diligently held to their book (notwithstanding he was so daily employed, being Lord Chancellor of England) that Erasmus [24] saith he found them so ready and perfect in *Lily* [25] that the worst scholar of them was able to expound him quite through without any stop, except some extraordinary and difficult place: *Quod me,* saith he, *aut mei similem esset remoraturum.*[26] I shall not need to remember, within memory, those four sisters, the learned daughters of Sir Anthony Cooke, and rare poetesses, so skillful in Latin and Greek, besides many other their excellent qualities eternized already by the golden pen of the prince of poets of our time; [27] with many other in-

---

[23] * She is cited by Bishop Jewel in his *Apology.*

[24] *In *Farragine Epistolarum.*   [25] William Lily's Latin grammar.

[26] "That she would leave me, or one such as I, behind."

[27] *George Buchanan.* [Buchanan was known on the Continent as *huius saeculi poetarum facile princeps,* "easily the prince of poets in his time." The five daughters of Sir Anthony Cooke were Mildred, Ann, Margaret, Elizabeth, and Katherine, who married Lord Burghley, Sir Nicholas Bacon, Sir Ralph Rowlett, Sir Thomas Hoby, and Sir Henry Killigrew respectively.]

comparable ladies and gentlewomen in our land, some yet living, from before whose fair faces Time, I trust, will never draw the curtain.

Lastly, the fault may be in the scholar himself, whom nature hath not so much befriended with the gift of understanding as to make him capable of knowledge, or else more unjust, disposed him to sloth or some other worse inbred vice. Marcus Cicero, albeit he was the son of so wise, so eloquent, and so sober a father (whose very counsel and company had been enough to have put learning and regard of well-living into the most barbarous Gete) and had Cratippus, so excellent a philosopher, to his reader at Athens, yet by the testimony of Pliny he proved so notorious a drunkard that he would ordinarily drink off two gallons of wine at a time and became so debauched every way that few of that age exceeded him.[28] Sundry the like examples might be produced in our times, but one of this nature is too many. Others, on the contrary, are αὐτοδίδακτοι,[29] and have no other helps save God and their own industry. We never read of any master Virgil ever had. St. Augustine likewise saith of himself: *Se didicisse Aristotelis Categorias nemine tradente,* that he learned Aristotle's categories or predicaments, no man instructing him; which, how hard they be at the first to wade through without a guide, let the best wit of them all try. And Bede, our countryman, for his profound learning in all sciences surnamed *Venerabilis,* attained to the same within the limits of his cell in Northumberland, though it is said he was once at Rome. Joseph Scaliger taught privately many years in a nobleman's house and never made abode in any university

---

[28] *Cicero [De] Offic[iis], lib.* 1. *Marc[us] Cicero, cum pater abstinentissimus fuerat, binos congios haurire solitus est (teste Plinio). Temulentus impegit scyphum.* ["Marcus Cicero, although his father had been most abstemious, was accustomed to drink two *congii* (i.e., about six quarts), according to Pliny. The drunkard fastened upon the cup, etc."] *M. Agrippa. Valer. Max[imus]*
[29] "Self-taught."

that ever I heard of till called in his later years to Leyden in Holland. And many admirable scholars and famous men our age can produce, who never came at any university except to view the colleges or visit their friends, that are inferior to few doctors of the chair either for learning or judgment, if I may say so, *Pace matris academiae.*[30]

CHAPTER V

Of a Gentleman's Carriage in the University

HAVING hitherto spoken of the dignity of learning in general, the duty and quality of the master, of ready method for understanding the grammar, of the parent, of the child, I turn the head of my discourse, with my scholar's horse (whom methinks I see stand ready bridled), for the university.[1] And now, Master William Howard, give me leave, having passed that, I imagine, *limbus puerorum*[2] and those perilous pikes of the grammar rules, as a well-willer unto you and your studies, to bear you company part of the way and to direct henceforth my discourse wholly to yourself.

Since the university whereinto you are embodied is not untruly called the light and eye of the land, in regard from hence, as from the center of the sun, the glorious beams of knowledge disperse themselves over all, without which a chaos of blindness would repossess us again, think now that you are in public view, and, *nucibus relictis,*[3] with your gown you have put on

---

[30] "With leave of Mother Academe."

[1] Young Howard was matriculated at St. John's College, Cambridge, Easter, 1624—Cokayne, *Complete Peerage,* XII, pt. I, 188.

[2] "Borderline of youth."   [3] "The nut trees left behind."

the man, that from hence the reputation of your whole life taketh her first growth and beginning. For as no glory crowneth with more abundant praise than that which is here won by diligence and wit, so there is no infamy abaseth the value and esteem of a gentleman all his life after more than that procured by sloth and error in the universities; yea, though in those years whose innocency have ever pleaded their pardon, whereat I have not a little marveled, considering the freedom and privilege of greater places.

But as in a delicate garden kept by a cunning hand and overlooked with a curious eye, the least disorder or rankness of any one flower putteth a beautiful bed or well-contrived knot out of a square, when rudeness and deformity is born withal in rough and undressed places; so, believe it, in this paradise of the Muses the least neglect and impression of Error's foot is so much the more apparent and censured by how much the sacred arts have greater interest in the culture of the mind and correction of manners.

Wherefore, your first care, even with pulling off your boots, let be the choice of your acquaintance and company.[4] For as infection in cities in a time of sickness is taken by concourse and negligent running abroad, when those that keep within and are wary of themselves escape with more safety, so it falleth out here in the university. For this *eye* hath also her diseases as well as any other part of the body (I will not say with the physicians "more") with those whose private houses and studies, being not able to contain them, are so cheap of themselves and so pliable to good fellowship abroad that in mind and manners, the tokens plainly appearing, they are past recovery ere any friend could hear they were sick.

Entertain therefore the acquaintance of men of soundest reputation for religion, life, and learning, whose conference and

[4] For further discussion of choice of company, see below, pp. 203 ff., 218, 244.

company may be unto you μουσεῖον ἔμψυχον καὶ περιπατοῦν, "a living and a moving library." "For conference and converse was the first mother of all arts and science,"[5] as being the greatest discoverer[6] of our ignorance and increaser of knowledge, teaching and making us wise by the judgments and examples of many. And you must learn herein of Plato, φιλομαθῆ, φιλήκοον, καὶ ζητητικόν εἶναι, that is, "To be a lover of knowledge, desirous to hear much, and, lastly, to inquire and ask often."

For the companions of your recreation consort with gentlemen of your own rank and quality, for that friendship is best contenting and lasting. To be overfree and familiar with inferiors argues a baseness of spirit and begetteth contempt, for as one shall here at the first prize himself, so let him look at the same rate for ever after to be valued of others.

Carry yourself even and fairly, *tanquam in statera,*[7] with that moderation in your speech and action that you seem with Ulysses to have Minerva always at your elbow, which should they be weighed by Envy herself, she might pass them for current; that you be thought rather leaving the university than lately come thither. But hereto the regard of your worth, the dignity of the place, and abundance of so many fair precedents will be sufficient motives to stir you up.

Husband your time to the best, for "the greedy desire of gaining time is a covetousness only honest."[8] And if you follow the advice of Erasmus and the practice of Plinius Secundus, *diem in operas partiri,* to divide the day into several tasks of study, you shall find a great ease and furtherance hereby; remembering ever to refer your most serious and important studies unto the morning, which finisheth alone, say the learned, three parts of the work. Julius Caesar, having spent the whole day in the field about his military affairs, divided the night also

---

[5] *'Ομιλία ἔτεκε τέχνας. Euripides in Andromache.
[6] From 1622; 1634 discovery.   [7] "Always in balance."
[8] *Seneca de brevitate vitae. cap. 1 et 3.

for three several uses: one part for his sleep, a second for the commonwealth and public business, the third for his book and studies. So careful and thrifty were they then of this precious treasure which we as prodigally lavish out, either vainly or viciously, by whole months and years until we be called to an account by our great Creditor, who will not abate us the vain expense of a minute.

But forasmuch as the knowledge of God is the true end of all knowledge, wherein as in a boundless and immense ocean all our studies and endeavors ought to embosom themselves, remember to lay the foundation of your studies, the fear and service of God, by oft frequenting prayer and sermons, reading the Scriptures and other tractates of piety and devotion, which howsoever profane and irreligious spirits condemn and contemn, as Politian, a canon of Florence, being upon occasion asked if he ever read the Bible over, "Yes, once," quoth he, "I read it quite through, but never bestowed my time worse in all my life." [9] Believe you with Chrysostom [10] that the ignorance of the Scriptures is the beginning and fountain of all evil, that the word of God is, as our Saviour calleth it, the key of knowledge, which, given by inspiration of God, is profitable to teach, to convince, to correct, and to instruct in righteousness. And rather let the pious and good King Alphonsus [11] be a precedent unto you and to all nobility, who read over the Bible not once, nor twice, but fourteen times, with the postils of Lyra and Burgos,[12] containing thrice or four times as much in quantity,

[9] *D. Pezel. 2. Postill. Melanchthon.* [The reference may be to the second part of *A Postil* (1550) or to the *Annotations* (*Postils*) of Melanchthon.] Preferring moreover, wickedly and profanely, the odes of Pindar before the Psalms of David.

[10] *Chrysost[om] in epist. ad Coloss. cap.* 3. Luke 11:52. 2 Tim[othy] 2:3.

[11] *In vita Alphonsi.*

[12] The glosses or annotations of Nicolas de Lyra and Paul de Burgos.

and would cause it to be carried ordinarily with his scepter before him, whereon was engraven, *Pro lege et grege*.[13]

And that worthy emperor and great champion of Christendom, Charlemagne,[14] who spent his days of rest (after so many glorious victories obtained of the Saracens in Spain, the Huns, Saxons, Goths, and Vandals in Lombardy and Italy, with many other barbarous nations, whereof millions fell under his sword) in reading the Holy Scriptures and the works of the Fathers, especially St. Augustine and his books, *De civitate Dei*, in which he took much delight; whom, besides, it is recorded to have been so studious that even in bed he would have his pen and ink with parchment at his pillow ready, that nothing in his meditation might overslip his memory. And if anything came into his mind, the light being taken away, a place upon the wall next him was thinly overlaid with wax, whereon with a brazen pin he would write in the dark. And we read, as a new king was created in Israel, he had with the ornaments of his kingly dignity the Book of Law delivered him, signifying his regal authority was lame and defective except swayed by piety and wisdom contained in that book. Whereunto alludeth that device of Paradin,[15] an image upon a globe with a sword in one hand and a book in the other, with *ex utroque Caesar;* [16] and to the same purpose another of our own in my *Minerva Britanna*, which is a serpent wreathed about a sword, placed upright upon a Bible, with the word, *Initium Sapientiae*.[17]

[13] "For law and the people." [14] *Eginardus in vita Caroli magni.*
[15] Claude Paradin (d. 1573), French emblematist.
[16] "Caesar on both sides."
[17] "The beginning of wisdom." The emblem described appears in Peacham's *Minerva Britanna* (1612), p. 2.

CHAPTER VI

Of Style in Speaking and Writing
and of History

SINCE speech is the character of a man and the interpreter of his mind, and writing the image of that,[1] that so often as we speak or write, so oft we undergo censure and judgment of ourselves, labor first by all means to get the habit of a good style in speaking and writing, as well English as Latin. I call with Tully [2] that a good and eloquent style of speaking "where there is a judicious fitting of choice words, apt and grave sentences, unto matter well disposed, the same being uttered with a comely moderation of the voice, countenance, and gesture." Not that same ampullous [3] and scenical pomp, with empty furniture of phrase, wherewith the stage and our petty poetic pamphlets sound so big, which like a net in the water, though it feeleth weighty, yet it yieldeth nothing, since our speech ought to resemble plate, wherein neither the curiousness of the picture or fair proportion of letters but the weight is to be regarded; and, as Plutarch saith, when our thirst is quenched with the drink, then we look upon the enameling and workmanship of the bowl; so first your hearer coveteth to have his desire satisfied with matter ere he looketh upon the form or vinetry,[4] which many times fall in of themselves to matter well contrived, according to Horace: [5]

---

[1] *Cicero I. de Oratore.*
[3] Ampullar, turgid.
[5] *In Arte Poet[ica].*

[2] *Cic[ero] in prolog. Rhetor.*
[4] Decorations, ornaments.

The Complete Gentleman

Rem bene dispositam vel verba invita sequuntur.

To matter well disposed words of themselves do fall.

Let your style therefore be furnished with solid matter, and compact of the best, choice, and most familiar words, taking heed of speaking or writing such words as men shall rather admire than understand (herein were Tiberius, Mark Antony, and Maecenas much blamed and jested at by Augustus, himself using ever a plain and most familiar style, and, as it is said of him, *verbum insolens tanquam scopulum effugiens*); [6] then, sententious, yea, better furnished with sentences than words, and, as Tully willeth, without affectation (for, as a king [7] said, *Dum tersiori studemus eloquendi formulae, subterfugit nos clanculum apertus ille et familiaris dicendi modus*); flowing at one and the selfsame height, neither taken in and knit up too short, that like rich hangings of arras or tapestry thereby lose their grace and beauty, as Themistocles was wont to say, nor suffered to spread so far, like soft music in an open field, whose delicious sweetness vanisheth and is lost in the air, not being contained within the walls of a room. In speaking rather lay down your words one by one than pour them forth together. This hath made many men, naturally slow of speech, to seem wisely judicious and be judiciously wise, for, besides the grace it giveth to the speaker, it much helpeth the memory of the hearer and is a good remedy against impediment of speech. Sir Nicholas Bacon, sometime Lord Chancellor of England and father to my Lord of St. Albans, a most eloquent man and of as sound learning and wisdom as England bred in many ages, with the old Lord William Burghley, Lord Treasurer of England, have above others herein been admired and commended

[6] "Eschewing the unusual word like a rock in the sea."

[7] *Henricus Octavus Angliae Rex in epistola quadam ad Erasmum Roterod[ami] in Farragine Epist[olarum]*. ["While we strive for a neater rule of eloquence, that clear and familiar manner of speaking secretly eludes us."]

in their public speeches in the Parliament House and Star Chamber. For nothing draws our attention more than good matter eloquently digested and uttered with a graceful, clear, and distinct pronunciation.

But to be sure your style may pass for current, as of the richest alloy, imitate the best authors as well in oratory as history, besides the exercise of your own invention, with much conference with those who can speak well. Nor be so foolish precise as a number are, who make it a religion to speak otherwise than this or that author. As Longolius was laughed at by the learned for his so apish and superstitious imitation of Tully, insomuch as he would have thought a whole volume quite marred if the word *possibile* had passed his pen, because it is not to be found in all Tully, or every sentence had not sunk with *esse posse videatur*,[8] like a peal ending with a chime or an *Amen* upon the organs in Paul's. For, as the young virgin to make her fairest garlands gathereth not altogether one kind of flower, and the cunning painter to make a delicate beauty is forced to mix his complexion [9] and compound it of many colors, the arras worker to please the eyes of princes to be acquainted with many histories; so are you to gather this honey of eloquence, a gift of heaven,[10] out of many fields, making it your own by diligence in collection, care in expression, and skill in digestion. But let me lead you forth into these all-flowery and verdant fields where so much sweet variety will amaze and make you doubtful where to gather first.

First, Tully, in whose bosom the treasure of eloquence seemeth to have been locked up and with him to have perished, offereth himself as *pater Romani eloquii*,[11] whose words and style, that you may not be held an heretic of all the world, you must prefer above all other, as well for the sweetness, gravity, richness, and inimitable texture thereof as that his works are

[8] "It might appear to be; so it may seem," etc.   [9] Combination.
[10] *Exod[us] 4.   [11] "The father of Roman eloquence."

throughout seasoned with all kind of learning and relish of a singular and Christianlike honesty. "There wanted not in him," saith Tacitus,[12] "knowledge of geometry, of music, of no manner of art that was commendable and honest. He knew the subtlety of logic, each part of moral philosophy," and so forth. How well he was seen in the civil laws his books *De legibus* and the actions *in Verrem* [13] will show you; which are the rather worthy your reading because you shall there see the grounds of many of our laws here in England. For the integrity of his mind, though his *Offices* had lain suppressed, let this one saying among many thousands persuade you to a charitable opinion of the same: *A recta conscientia transversum unguem non oportet quenquam in omni sua vita discedere.*[14] Whereto I might add that tale of Gyges' ring in his *Offices*, which book, let it not seem contemptible unto you because it lieth tossed and torn in every school, but be precious, as it was sometime unto the old Lord Burghley, Lord High Treasurer of England, before named, who to his dying day would always carry it about him, either in his bosom or pocket, being sufficient, as one said of Aristotle's rhetorics, to make both a scholar and an honest man. Imitate Tully for his phrase and style, especially in his Epistles *Ad Atticum*, his books *De oratore*, among his orations those *Pro M. Marcello, Pro Archia Poeta, T. Annio Milone, Sext. Rosc. Amerino, Pub. Quinctio,* the first two against Catiline and the third action against Verres. These in my opinion are fullest of life, but you may use your discretion; you cannot make your choice amiss.

After Cicero I must needs bring you Caesar, whom Tully himself confesseth of all orators to have spoken the most eloquent and purest Latin. *Et hanc bene loquendi laudem,* saith

---

[12] *Tacitus in Oratore* [i.e., *De oratoribus*].

[13] "Against Verres," prosecuted on charges of extortion.

[14] *Ad Atticum. lib.* 13. ["It is wrong for anyone ever to depart from a consciousness of right."]

he,[15] *multis literis, et iis quidem reconditis et exquisitis, summaque studio et diligentia est consequutus.* And *In quo,* saith Quintilian,[16] *tanta vis, id acumen, ea concitatio, ut illum eodem animo dixisse appareat quo bellavit,* "in whom there was so great vehemency, that fine judgment, that courage and motion, that it seems he wrote with the same spirit he fought." To read him as you ought, you must bring with you an able judgment, besides your dictionary by reason of the diversity of countries, tracts, places, rivers, people, names of ancient cities and towns to be sought out in modern, strange, and unknown names; of materials in buildings, as in his bridge over the Rhine, framed *ex tignis, trabibus, fibulis, sublicis, longuriis,*[17] etc., which, except you were seen in architecture, you would hardly understand; then strange names and forms of warlike engines and weapons then in use; sundry forms of fortification, waterworks, and the like; which notwithstanding since have been made known and familiar unto us by the painful labors of those all-searching wits, Lipsius, Ramus, Giovanni de Ramellia, and others, and may be read in English excellently translated and illustrated by that learned and truly honorable gentleman, Sir Clement Edmonds, knight, clerk of his Majesty's most honorable Privy Council, my worthy friend, though many excellent works of Caesar's, as his Epistles, his Astronomy, etc., through the iniquity of envious Time are utterly lost and perished.

Now offereth himself Cornelius Tacitus, the prince of historians, of whom I may not untruly say, as Scaliger of Virgil, *E cuius ore nil temere excidit,*[18] as well for his diligence as gravity; so copious in pleasing brevity, each sentence carrying with it a kind of lofty state and majesty such as should, methink,

---

[15] *Cicero, lib. 4. de claris Oratoribus.* ["And he strove for commendation for eloquence in many exquisite and profound letters and applied himself to the most important matters with enthusiasm and diligence."]

[16] *Quintilian, lib. 10, ad filium.*

[17] "From beams, tree trunks, iron clasps, stakes, nails, and the like."

[18] "Nothing fell from his lips casually."

proceed from the mouth of greatness and command; in sense retired, deep, and not fordable [19] to the ordinary reader. He doth in part speak most pure and excellent English by the industry of that most learned and judicious gentleman [20] whose long labor and infinite charge in a far greater work have won him the love of the most learned and drawn not only the eye of Greece but all Europe to his admiration.

But there being, as Lipsius saith, *suus cuique linguae genius*,[21] let me advise you of this by the way, that no translation whatsoever will affect you like the author's own and proper language, for to read him as he spake, it confirmeth our judgments with an assured boldness and confidence of his intent and meaning, removing that scruple of jealousy we have commonly of ignorant and unfaithful pens which deal many times herein, *sublesta fide*.[22] Besides, it is an injury to the author, who hereby loseth somewhat of his value, like a piece of rich stuff in a broker's shop, only for that it is there at a second hand, though never worn, or newly translated but yesterday.

The next, Titus Livius, whom like a milky fountain you shall everywhere find flowing with such an elegant sweetness, such banquetlike variety that you would imagine other authors did but bring your mouth out of taste. In his first Decade you have the coming of Aeneas into Italy, the building of Rome, the first choice of the Senate, the religious rites of Numa, the brave combat of the Horatii and the Curiatii, the tyranny of Tarquin, the rape of Lucrece by Sextus, his son, and first consuls created.

In the third, the history of the second Punic War, Hannibal's passage against the league over the river Iberius, who after eight months' siege took Saguntum, his passage over the Pyrenean hills, his foraging of France; after descending the Alps,

[19] From 1622; 1634 forceable.
[20] Sir Henry Savile, who translated four books of the histories and the life of Agricola in 1591.
[21] "A genius for every language."
[22] "With slight fidelity." From 1622; 1634 *sublata*.

with his overthrow of the Romans with his horse troops at the river Ticino, where Scipio, after Africanus, rescued his father, being very grievously wounded; his second overthrow of the Romans at the river Trebbia, his hard passage in cruel weather and tempests over the Appenines, etc.

In the fourth is recorded the occasion of the war against Philip, King of Macedonia (concerning the coming in of two young men of Acarnania into the temple of Ceres at Athens), against whom Sulpitius was sent, by whom the Macedonians were overthrown in an horse battle; how L. Furius subdued the rebellious Gauls, overthrew Hamilcar with thirty-five thousand Carthaginians; with many other expeditions of Philip of Macedon and Sulpitius.

In the fifth, the going out of the fire in the temple of Vesta; how Titus Sempronius Gracchus subdued the Celtiberian Spaniards and built a town in Spain called Graccharis, after his name; Posthumius Albinius triumphed over the Portugals; the number of citizens of Rome reckoned by the poll, with the law of Volumnius Saxa by which no woman was to inherit, etc.

Be then acquainted with Quintus Curtius, who passing eloquently with a faithful pen and sound judgment writeth the life and acts of Alexander, in whom you shall see the pattern of a brave prince for wisdom, courage, magnanimity, bounty, courtesy, agility of body, and whatsoever else were to be wished in majesty, till, surfeiting in the best of his age on his excessive fortunes and even burdensome to himself by his overgreatness, he became ἐτώσιον ἄχθος ἀρούρης,[23] an unprofitable burden of the earth and from the darling of heaven to be the disdain of all the world.

After him, whom indeed I should have preferred before, as being honored with the title of *historiae pater*,[24] followeth Sallust, commended most for brevity, as also for richness of his speech and phrase, but wherein his brevity consisteth the

---

[23] *Iliad.* 6.   [24] "Father of history."

most are ignorant. Our grammarians imagine because his *Discourses*, as they say, are only of the matter and persons barely and nakedly described without circumstance and preparation, counsels and deliberations had before, effects and events after; which is quite contrary, as may be seen by the conspiracy of Catiline, which he might in a manner have set down in three words. But how amply and with what ado doth he describe it! What circumstances more open, more abundant, than where he saith:

The Roman soldiers, being amazed with an unwonted uproar, betook themselves to their weapons: some hid themselves, others advised their companions to stand stoutly to it. They were afraid in every place, the multitude of enemies was so great. The heaven was obscured with night and thick clouds; the peril was doubtful. And, lastly, no man knew whether it were safest for him to fly or to stay by it.

And let them now see their error who affirm his discourse to be unfurnished of counsels, deliberations, consultations, etc. Is not the reason set down why Jugurtha assaulted Cirta at the arrival of the ambassadors? the intent and preparation of the wars by Metellus, the consul, laid open in an ample manner, wherein consisteth the richness of his discourse? His brevity, indeed worthy your observation and imitation, consisteth in shutting up whole and weighty sentences in three words, fetching nothing afar or putting in more than needs, but in quick and stirring asyndetons after this manner, as the most learned have out of him observed.[25]

And since it is Tully's advice, as was his own use, as himself testifieth, *Non in philosophia solum, sed etiam in dicendi exercitatione, cum Graecis Latina coniungere*,[26] by this time acquaint yourself with that golden *Cyropaedia* of Xenophon, whom here

[25] *Scaliger Poet. lib. 4. cap. 24.*
[26] "Not only in philosophy but in the exercise of speech to join the Latin with the Greek."

you shall see a courageous and brave commander marshaling an army; there a most grave and eloquent philosopher in the person of Cyrus, shaping out unto us with ink of nectar a perfect and absolute prince (to the example of all princes and nobility) for his studies, his diet, his exercise, his carriage, and every way manner of living, insomuch as the noble Scipio Africanus, as well in his wars abroad as in peace at home, above all other held Xenophon in highest regard, ever saying he could never commend him sufficiently or read him over often enough.

Hitherto have I given you a taste, at your own choice, as well for universal history as your imitation in writing and speaking. That I account universal which treateth of the beginning, increase, government, and alterations of monarchies, kingdoms, and commonwealths, and to further you herein you may read Justin, Diodorus Siculus, Zonaras, Orosius; of more later times, Sabellicus, Carion, with some others.[27]

For special history that reporteth the affairs and government of particular estates you have the most ancient Herodotus, the noble and eloquent Thucydides, Arrianus, Halicarnassus, Polybius, Suetonius, and others.

All history divideth itself into four branches. The first spreadeth itself into and over all places, as geography; the second groweth and gathereth strength with tract of time, as chronology; the third is laden with descents, as genealogy; the fourth and last, like the golden bough Proserpina gave Aeneas,[28] is that truly called by Cicero *lux veritatis*,[29] which telleth us of things as they were done, and of all other most properly is called history. For all history in times past, saith Tully,[30] was none other than *annalium confectio*, the making of *annales*, that is, recording of what was done from year to year. But while I

[27] John Zonoras (d. 1130), Byzantine chronicler; Sabellicus (1463–1506), Italian annotator of Pliny, Livy, and others; John Carion (1499–1538), German astrologer and chronicler.

[28] *Aeneid. 6. [29] "The light of truth." From 1622; 1634 *lex*.
[30] *Cic[ero]. 2. de oratore.*

wander in foreign history, let me warn you *ne sis peregrinus domi*,[31] that you be not a stranger in the history of your own country, which is a common fault imputed to our English travelers in foreign countries, who, curious in the observation and search of the most memorable things and monuments of other places, can say, as a great peer of France told me, nothing of their own, our country of England being no whit inferior to any other in the world for matter of antiquity and rarities of every kind worthy remark and admiration. Herein I must worthily and only prefer unto you the glory of our nation, Mr. Camden,[32] as well for his judgment and diligence as the purity of sweet fluence of the Latin style; and with him the rising star of good letters and antiquity, Mr. John Selden of the Inner Temple.[33] As for Giraldus, Geoffrey, Higden, Ranulph of Chester, Walsingham, a monk of St. Albans, with the rest, they did *cum saeculo caecutire*,[34] and took upon credit many a time more than they could well answer; that I may omit Polydore Vergil, an Italian, who did our nation that deplorable injury in the time of King Henry the Eighth, for that his own history might pass for current he burned and embezzled the best and most ancient records and monuments of our abbeys, priories, and cathedral churches under color (having a large commission under the Great Seal) of making search for all such monuments, manuscript records, ledger books, etc., as might make for his purpose; yet for all this he hath the ill luck to write nothing well, save the life of Henry the Seventh, wherein he had reason

[31] *The old Lord Treasurer Burghley, if anyone came to the lords of the Council for a license to travel, he would first examine him of England; if he found him ignorant, would bid him stay at home and know his own country first.

[32] *His *Britannia*, with the life of Queen Elizabeth.

[33] *His *Jani Angl[orum]*, *Titles of Honor*, together with his *Mare clausum*, though not yet printed. [The same note appeared in the 1622 edition, indicating that P. was acquainted with *Mare clausum* at that early date. The work appeared in 1635.]

[34] "Become blind with the age."

to take a little more pains than ordinary, the book being dedicated to Henry the Eighth, his son.

No subject affecteth us with more delight than history, imprinting a thousand forms upon our imaginations from the circumstances of place, person, time, matter, manner, and the like. And what can be more profitable, saith an ancient historian,[35] than sitting on the stage of human life, to be made wise by their example who have trod the path of error and danger before us. Bodin tells us of some who have recovered their healths by reading of history; and it is credibly affirmed of King Alphonsus that the only reading of Quintus Curtius cured him of a very dangerous fever. If I could have been so rid of my late quartan ague, I would have said with the same good King: *Valeat Avicenna, vivat Curtius,*[36] and have done him as much honor as ever the Chians their Hippocrates, or the sunburned Egyptians their Aesculapius.

For morality and rules of well-living, delivered with such sententious gravity, weight of reason, so sweetened with lively and apt similitudes, entertain Plutarch, whom, according to the opinion of Gaza, the world would preserve should it be put to the choice to receive one only author (the sacred Scriptures excepted) and to burn all the rest, especially his *Lives* and *Morals*. After him, the virtuous and divine Seneca, who, for that he lived so near the times of the apostles and had familiar acquaintance with St. Paul (as it is supposed by those epistles that pass under either their names [37]) is thought in heart to have been a Christian; and certes so it seemeth to me, by that spirit wherewith so many rules of patience, humility, contempt of the world are refined and exempt from the degrees of paganism. Some say [38] that about the beginning of Nero's reign he came over hither into Britain, but most certain it is he had

---

[35] *Diodorus Siculus.

[36] "Away with Avicenna (the Arabian physician)! Long live Curtius!"

[37] From 1622; 1634 either names.   [38] *In vita Senecae.*

divers lands bestowed on him here in England, and those supposed to have lain in Essex near to Camalodunum, now Maldon.

Again, while you are intent to foreign authors and languages, forget not to speak and write your own properly and eloquently, whereof, to say truth, you shall have the greatest use, since you are like to live an eminent person in your country and mean to make no profession of scholarship. I have known even excellent scholars so defective this way that, when they had been beating their brains twenty or four and twenty years about Greek etymologies or the Hebrew roots and rabbins, could neither write true English nor true orthography. And to have heard them discourse in public or privately at a table, you would have thought you had heard Loy talking to his pigs or John de Indagine [39] declaiming in the praise of wild geese; otherwise for their judgment in the arts and other tongues very sufficient.

To help yourself herein, make choice of those authors in prose who speak the best and purest English. I would commend unto you, though from more antiquity, the life of Richard the Third, written by Sir Thomas More, the *Arcadia* of the noble Sir Philip Sidney, whom Du Bartas makes one of the four columns of our language, the *Essays* and other pieces of the excellent master of eloquence,[40] my Lord of St. Albans, who possesseth not only eloquence but all good learning, as hereditary both by father and mother. You have, then, Mr. Hooker his *Policy; Henry the Fourth,* well written by Sir John Hayward; that first part of our English kings by Mr. Samuel Daniel. There are many others I know, but these will taste you best, as proceeding from no vulgar judgment. The last Earl of Northampton in his ordinary style of writing was not to be mended. Procure, then, if you may, the speeches made in Parliament, frequent learned sermons; in termtime resort to the Star Chamber, and be present at the pleadings in other public courts, whereby

[39] Cf. McKerrow's Nashe, III, 149.
[40] °The late published life of Henry the Seventh.

you shall better your speech, enrich your understanding, and get more experience in one month than in other four by keeping your melancholy study and by solitary meditation. Imagine not that hereby I would bind you from reading all other books, since there is no book so bad, even *Sir Bevis* himself, *Owlglass*, or Nashe's *Herring*, but some commodity may be gotten by it. For as in the same pasture the ox findeth fodder, the hound a hare, the stork a lizard, the fair maid flowers, so we cannot, except we list ourselves, saith Seneca,[41] but depart the better from any book whatsoever.

And ere you begin a book, forget not to read the epistle, for commonly they are best labored and penned.[42] For as in a garment, whatsoever the stuff be, the owner for the most part affecteth a costly and extraordinary facing; and in the house of a country gentleman, the porch of a citizen, the carved gate and painted posts carry away the glory from the rest; so is it with our common authors. If they have any wit at all, they set it like velvet before, though the back, like a bankrupt's doublet, be but of poldavy[43] or buckram.

Affect not, as some do, that bookish ambition to be stored with books and have well-furnished libraries yet keep their heads empty of knowledge. To desire to have many books and never to use them is like a child that will have a candle burning by him all the while he is sleeping.

Lastly, have a care of keeping your books handsome and well bound, not casting away overmuch in their gilding or stringing for ostentation sake, like the prayer books of girls and gallants, which are carried to church but for their outsides. Yet for your own use spare them not for noting or interlining, if they be printed, for it is not likely you mean to be a gainer by them when you have done with them; neither suffer them through

---

[41] *Seneca Epist.* 109.
[42] *The epistles of books ofttimes the best piece of them.
[43] A coarse canvas or sacking.

negligence to mold and be moth-eaten or want their strings and covers.

King Alphonsus, about to lay the foundation of a castle at Naples, called for Vitruvius his book of architecture. The book was brought in very bad case, all dusty and without covers, which the King observing said, "He that must cover us all must not go uncovered himself," then commanded the book to be fairly bound and brought unto him. So say I. Suffer them not to lie neglected who must make you regarded, and go in some coats who must apparel your mind with the ornaments of knowledge above the robes and riches of the most magnificent princes.

To avoid the inconvenience of moths and moldiness, let your study be placed and your windows open, if it may be, toward the east, for where it looketh south or west, the air being ever subject to moisture, moths are bred and darkishness increased, whereby your maps and pictures will quickly become pale, losing their life and colors or, rotting upon their cloth or paper, decay past all help and recovery.

CHAPTER VII

Of Cosmography

THAT, like a stranger in a foreign land, ye may not wander without a guide, ignorant of those places by which you are to pass and stick amused—amazed in the labyrinth of history—cosmography, a second Ariadne bringing lines enough, is come to your delivery, whom imagine standing on a fair hill and with one hand pointing and discoursing unto you of the celestial sphere, the names, uses, and distinctions of every circle, whereof it consisteth, the situation of regions according to the same, the reason of climates, length and shortness of days and nights, motion, rising and setting as well of fixed stars as erratic, elevation of the pole, parallels, meridians, and whatsoever else respecteth that celestial body. With the other hand downward she showeth you the globe of the earth, distinguished by seas, mountains, rivers, rocks, lakes, and the like.

The subject of geography which, defined according to Ptolemy and others, is an imitation of the face, by draught and picture, of the whole earth and all the principal and known parts thereof, with the most remarkable things thereunto belonging. A science at once both feeding the eye and mind with such incredible variety and profitable pleasure that even the greatest kings and philosophers have not only bestowed the best part of their time in the contemplation hereof at home, but to their infinite charge and peril of their persons have themselves traveled to understand the situation of far countries, bounds of seas, qualities of regions, manners of people, and the like.

So necessary for the understanding of history, as I have said, and the fables of poets, wherein no small part of the treasure of human learning lieth hid, that without it we know not how the most memorable enterprises of the world have been carried and performed; we are ignorant of the growth, flourish, and fall of the first monarchies, whereat history taketh her head and beginning; we conceive nothing of the government and commodities of other nations; we cannot judge of the strength of our enemies, distinguish the limits between kingdom and kingdom, names of places from names of people. Nay, with Monsieur Gaulart we doubt at Paris whether we see there the same moon we have at London or not. On the contrary, we know this and much more without exposing, as in old time, our bodies to a tedious travel, but with much more ease, having the world at will, or, as the saying is, the world in a string in our own chamber. How prejudicial the ignorance of geography hath been unto princes in foreign expeditions against their enemies, unfortunate Cyrus will tell you, who, being ignorant of Oaxis and the straits, was overthrown by Tomyris, the Scythian queen, and of two hundred thousand Persians in his army not one escaped through his unskillfulness herein, as Justin reporteth.

And at another time what a memorable victory to his perpetual glory carried Leonidas from the Persians, only for that they were unacquainted with the straits of Thermopylae.[1]

And the foul overthrow that Crassus received by the Parthians was imputed to nothing else than his ignorance of that country and the passages thereof.

Alexander, therefore, taking any enterprise in hand, would first cause an exact map of the country to be drawn in colors, to consider where were the safest entrance, where he might pass this river, how to avoid that rock, and in what place most commodiously to give his enemy battle.

Such is the pleasure, such is the profit of this admirable knowledge, which account rather in the number of your recreations than severer studies, it being besides quickly and with much ease attained unto. Prince Henry of eternal memory was herein very studious, having for his instructor that excellent mathematician and, while he lived, my loving friend, Master Edward Wright.

To the attaining of perfection herein, as it were your first entrance, you are to learn and understand certain geometrical definitions which are first: *punctum,* or a prick; a line; a superficies either plain, convex, or concave; your angles right, blunt, and sharp; figures, circles, semicircles; the diameter; triangles, squares of all sorts; parallels and the like, as Master Blundeville [2] in his first book of the sphere will show you; for

---

[1] *Thermopylae, that long hill of Greece through which is a strait and a narrow passage environed with a rough sea and deep fen; so called from the wells of hot waters which are there among the rocks.

[2] Thomas Blundeville's *Exercises* (1599 and later eds.), a widely read book on cosmography, astronomy, geography, and navigation.

you shall have use of many of these to the understanding thereof. Cosmography containeth astronomy, astrology, geography, and chorography. Astronomy considereth the magnitude and motions of the celestial bodies.[3]

The celestial bodies are the eleven heavens and spheres.

The eleventh heaven is the habitation of God and his angels.

The tenth, the first mover.

The ninth, the crystalline heaven.

The eighth, the starry firmament.

Then the seven planets in their order, which you may remember in their order by this verse.

Post Sim S V M sequitur, ultima L U N A subest:

Would you count the planets soon,
Remember S I M S V M and the Moon.

The first letter S for Saturn, I for Iupiter, M for Mars, S for the Sun, V, Venus, M, Mercury, lastly, the Moon.

The empyreal heaven is immovable, most pure, immense in quantity, and clear in quality.

The tenth heaven or first mover is also most pure and clear, and maketh his revolution in four and twenty hours, carrying with the swiftness the other heavens violently from east to west, from their proper revolutions, which is from west to east.

The ninth, or crystalline, heaven moveth by force of the first mover, first from east to west, then from west to east upon his own poles, and accomplisheth his revolution in 36,000 years. And this revolution being finished, Plato was of opinion that the world should be in the same state as it was before. I should live and print such a book again and you read it in the same apparel and the same age you are now in.

Two scholars in Germany, having lain so long in an inn that they had not only spent all their money but also ran into debt

---

[3] *Vide Clevian in Sacrobosco, edit. ult.* [i.e., see Clevian (Clavius?) in the latest edition of Sacro Bosco's *Sphaera*.]

some two hundred dollars, told their host of Plato's great year, and how that time six and thirty thousand years the world should be again as it was and they should be in the same inn and chamber again, and desired him to trust them till then. Quoth mine host, "I believe it to be true, and I remember six and thirty thousand years ago you were here and left just such a reckoning behind to pay. I pray you, gentlemen, discharge that first and I will trust you for the next."

The eighth heaven or glorious starry firmament hath a three-fold motion, viz., from east to west in four and twenty hours, *secundum primum mobile;* [4] then from west to east according to the motion of the ninth heaven; then sometimes to the south and sometimes toward the north, called *motus trepidationis.* [5]

Touching the motions of the planets, since you may have them in every almanac, I willingly omit them.

The sphere of the world consisteth of ten circles: the equinoctial, the zodiac, the two colures, the horizon, the meridian, the two tropics, and the two polar circles.

The equinoctial is a circle dividing the world, as in the midst equally distant from the two poles. It containeth three hundred and sixty degrees, which, being multiplied by sixty, the number of miles in a degree, make one and twenty thousand and six hundred miles, which is the compass of the whole earth. The third part of which, being the diameter, about seven thousand and odd miles, is the thickness of the same. Those who dwell under the equinoctial having no latitude either to the north or south but their days and nights always of an equal length.

The zodiac is an oblique circle, dividing the sphere athwart the equinoctial into points, viz., the beginning of Aries and Libra, in the midst whereof is the ecliptic line; the utmost limits thereof are the two tropics, Cancer and Capricorn; the length thereof is three hundred and sixty degrees, the breadth, sixteen. It is divided into twelve signs, six northerly and six

[4] "According to the prime mover."   [5] "Motion of trepidation."

southerly. The northern are Aries, Taurus, Cancer, Gemini, Leo, Virgo; the southern, Libra, Scorpio, Sagittarius, Capricorn, Aquarius, Pisces. He turneth upon his own poles from west to east.

The two colures are two great movable circles passing through both the poles of the world, crossing one another with right spherical angles, so that, like an apple cut into four quarters, they divide into equal parts the whole sphere. The one passeth through the equinoctial points and poles of the world and is called the equinoctial colure; the other passeth through the solstitial points and is called the solstitial colure.

The horizon is a circle immovable which divideth the upper hemisphere or half part of the world from the nether. It hath the name ὁρίζω, which is *termino* or to bound or limit, because, imagine you stood upon Highgate or the Tower Hill at Greenwich. So far as you may see round about as in a circle, where the heaven seemeth to touch the earth, that is called the horizon, the poles whereof are the point just over your head, called zenith in Arabian, and the other under your feet, passing by the center of the world, called nadir.

The meridian is an immovable circle passing through the poles of the world. It is called the meridian of *meridies,* noontide, because when the sun rising from the east toucheth this line with the center of his body, then it is noon to those over whose zenith that circle passeth and midnight to their antipodes, or those who are just under them in the other world.

The number of meridians are 180, allowing two to every degree in the equinoctial, which all concenter in either pole and are the utmost bounds of longitude.

By the meridian the longitude of all places is gathered and what places lie more easterly or westerly from either.

The longitude of any place is the distance you find upon the equinoctial between the meridian of the place whose longitude you desire and the first meridian, which directly passeth over the Canary or Fortunate Islands; which distance or space you must account by the degrees purposely set upon the brazen circle, or, if you please, by miles, allowing sixty to every degree. Longitude is only taken east and west.

Latitude is the distance of the meridian between the vertical point or pole of the horizon and the equinoctial, being ever equal to the height or elevation of the pole above the horizon; or, more plainly, the distance of any place, either north or south, from the equinoctial, which you are to take upon the standing globe by the degrees of the brazen meridian, that country or place whose latitude you desire being turned directly under it.

The Tropic of Cancer is an imaginary circle betwixt the equinoctial and the Arctic Circle, which the sun maketh about the thirteenth day of June, declining at his farthest from the equinoctial and coming northerly to usward. Then are our days at the longest and nights shortest. Capricorn the like to the Antarctic Circle, making our days the shortest about the twelfth of December.

The Arctic Circle, anciently accounted the horizon of Greece, is a small circle, the center whereof is the North Pole of the world, which is invisible. It is so called from *Arctos*, the Bear or Charles's Wain, the Northern Star being in the tip of the tail of the said Bear.

The Antarctic, which is near to the South Pole and answering the other under us.

But I had rather you learned these principles of the sphere by demonstration and your own diligence, being the labor but of a few hours, than by mere verbal description, which profiteth not so much in mathematical demonstrations.

We will therefore descend to geography, which is more easy and familiar. The definition I gave you before. I come to the subject, the terrestrial globe, which is composed of sea and land.

The sea is a mighty water, ebbing and flowing continually

about the whole earth, whose parts are diversely named according to the places whereupon they bound. In the East it is called the Indian Sea; in the West, the Atlantic, so named from the Mount Atlas in Mauretania; in the North, the Hyperborean; in the South, the Meridional or South Sea, commonly called *Mar-del-sur*.[6]

The Mediterranean Sea is that which stretcheth itself by the midst of the earth from west to east, dividing Europe, Asia, and Africa.

Sinus or a gulf is a part of the sea, insinuating and embosoming itself within the land or between two several lands, as the Gulf of Venice, the Persian Gulf, the Red Sea, *Sinus Mexicanus, Vermilius, Gangeticus*.[7]

Fretum or a strait is a narrow passage between two lands, as the Strait of Magellan, Anian, Gibraltar, etc.

An haven is the entrance of the sea within the land at the mouth of some river or creek where ships may ride at anchor.

A lake is a great and wide receptacle of water, ever standing still, and not moving out of the place, as the Lake Asphaltites,[8] Lacus Larius or Lago di Como, Lausanne by Geneva, etc.

The earth is either continent or island. A continent is the land continued without any division of sea, as the Low Countries to Germany, that to Austria, Austria to Hungary, etc.

An island, called *insula, quasi in salo*,[9] is a land encompassed round with the sea, as Great Britain, Ireland, Corsica, Candia, etc.

An isthmus or *chersonesus* is a strait or neck of land between two seas: *Cimbrica, Chersonesus Taurica, Aurea*, and *Archaica*.[10]

---

[6] Sp., "South Sea."

[7] Gulf of Mexico, Vermilion Bay (an arm of the preceding), and the Bay of Bengal.

[8] The Dead Sea.

[9] Erroneous derivation of *insula* from *in salo* (in the sea).

[10] Jutland, the Crimea, Malacca, and Achaia respectively.

Peninsula (*quasi paene insula*) [11] is a land environed with the sea, except at some narrow place or entrance, as that vast continent of Peru and Brazil in America were an island but for the strait or neck of land between Panama and Nombre di Dios, which Philip the Second, King of Spain, was once minded to have cut for a shorter passage for ships into the South Sea, but upon better deliberation he gave over his project.

A cape or head of land is the utmost end of a promontory or highland standing out into the sea, as the Cape de Buona Speranza, Cape Mendocino, St. Vincent, Cape Verde, the great Cape St. Augustine in America, etc.[12]

Proceeding now to understand the several parts and regions of the world, with their situation (as it is meet, dwelling in an house, you shall know all the rooms thereof), you may, if you please, observe Ptolemy's method, beginning first with Europe; and herein with our northern islands of Great Britain, Ireland, the Orcades,[13] and Thule, which are the contents of his first table, and so forth into Europe. But he was erroneous in his descriptions, obscure by reason of his antiquity, the names of places since changed, navigation by the benefit of the loadstone perfected, the want whereof heretofore hath been occasion of infinite errors among the ancients as well divines as historiographers and geographers, as Lactantius and St. Augustine could never be persuaded that there were antipodes or people going feet to feet under us, the contrary whereof experience hath taught us. Arrianus, that much esteemed Greek author, affirmed the situation of Germany to be very near the Ionian Sea. Stephanus also, another countryman of his, saith that Vienna was a

[11] "As though almost an island."
[12] Cape of Good Hope, Cape Mendocino (westermost point of California), Cape St. Vincent (west coast of Madagascar or southeast extremity of Portugal), Cape Verde (westermost point of Africa), Cape St. Augustine (on the coast of Pernambuco, Brazil).
[13] Ancient name for the Orkney Islands.

city of Galilee. Strabo saith that Danubius hath his head near to the Adriatic Sea, which indeed, being the greatest river of Europe, riseth out of the hill Arnoba in Germany and by Hungary and many other countries runneth into Slavonia, receiving threescore other rivers into his channel. It is therefore far more safe to follow our later writers.

In every country, to give one instance for all, in your observation you are to follow this method: first, to know the latitude, then the longitude of the place; the temperature of the climate; the goodness or barrenness of the ground; the limits of the country, how it is bounded by sea or land or both, by east, west, north, or south; into what provinces it is divided within itself; the commodities it affordeth, as what mines, woods, or forests, what beasts, fowls, fishes, fruits, herbs, plants; what mountains, rivers, fountains, and cities; what notable matter of wonder or antiquity; the manners, shape, and attire of the people; their building, what ports and havens; what rocks, sands, and suchlike places of danger are about the place; and, last of all, the religion and government of the inhabitants.

You shall have drawn upon your globe or map, upon the vastest seas, where most room is to be spared, a round figure representing the mariner's compass, with the two and thirty winds, from every of which there runneth a line to the land, to some famous city, haven, or either, to show you in that sea and place what course you are to keep to go thither, whether full north, northeast, south, or southwest, and so forth. These winds of the Spaniards are called *rombes;* and for that Columbus and Vesputius, Italians, with others, first discovered the East and West Indies, the eight principal winds are commonly expressed in the Italian. This compass hath the needle in manner of a flower-de-luce which pointeth still to the north.

I could wish you now and then to exercise your pen in drawing and imitating cards and maps, as also your pencil in washing and coloring small tables of countries and places, which at your leisure you may in one fortnight easily learn to do. For the practice of the hand doth speedily instruct the mind and strongly confirm the memory beyond anything else. Nor think it any disgrace unto you, as I have showed heretofore; also many of our young nobility in England exercise the same with felicity.

I have seen French cards to play withal, the four suits changed into maps of several countries of the four parts of the world, and exactly colored for their numbers, the figures, 1, 2, 3, 9, 10, and so forth set over the heads; for the kings, queens, and knaves, the portraits of their kings and queens in their several country habits; [14] for the knave, their peasants or slaves; which ingenious device cannot be but a great furtherance to a young capacity and some comfort to the unfortunate gamester when that he hath lost in money he shall have dealt him in land or wit.

CHAPTER VIII

Observations in Survey of the Earth

FIRST, how Almighty God by his divine providence so disposed the earth in the first creation, not falling out by chance, as some have thought, that one country in one place or other is so nearly joined to the next that, if after it might happen to be overpeopled, as well man as beast by some small strait or passage might easily be provided of a new habitation; which Acosta hath well observed, resolving us that doubt how wild beasts, as wolves, foxes, bears, and other harmful beasts should swim over so vast seas and breed in islands.

Secondly, how the wit, disposition, yea, devotion and strength of man followeth the quality and temperature of the climate

[14] The special dress of their country.

77

and many times the nature of the soil where he lives, as we see the eastern people of the world very quick in their inventions, superstitious unto idolatry, as in China, Calcutta, Java, and other places. On the contrary, those as far north in Lapland, Iceland, and other places as dull and in a manner senseless of religion, whereupon they are held the most notorious witches of the world.

We see those that inhabit mountains and mountainous places to be far more barbarous and uncivil than those that live in the plains. Witness the inhabitants of the huge hills, Sierras and the Andes in America, the mountainous north part of Nova Francia, the Navarrois in Spain, and the highland men in Scotland.

We see and find it by experience that where the soil is dry and sandy the air is most pure, and, consequently, the spirits of the inhabitants active and subtle above those who inhabit the fens and marshes.

Thirdly, consider the wonder of wonders, how the ocean, so far distant, holdeth motion with the moon, filling our shores to the brim from the time of her appearing above the horizon until she has ascended the meridian, then decreasing as much until she toucheth the line of midnight, making her tide twice in four and twenty hours and odd minutes; how the Atlantic or Western Ocean is most rough and dangerful, the South Sea or Del Sur, albeit of infinite vastness, on the contrary, so calm and quiet that you seem rather to sail upon dry land than water.[1]

How in the sea of Calcutta it is high water but at every full moon, in the sea by the shore of Indus but at every new moon; how in the main ocean the current runs from east to west, toward the Strait of Magellan, but from west to east in the Mediterranean.

---

[1] *And so swift that from Malabar to Madagascar (or the Isle of St. Laurence) they may come in twenty days, but are not able to return in three months. So from Spain into America in thirty days, but cannot return in three months.

Fourthly, how in one place the north wind, as upon the coast of Scythia near the mouth of the great river Dvina, bloweth in a manner perpetually so that the west or southwest winds are scarce known.

In another, the East: in the Indian Sea the winds keep their turns, obscuring the course of the sun, which, being in Aries and Libra, the western winds blow perpetually.[2]

Neither less admirable are the inland floods and fresh waters for their properties, as Nilus, who only by his overflowing maketh Egypt fertile where it never raineth; Euripus, an arm of the sea by Euboea, an island of the Sporades in the Aegean Sea, which ebbeth and floweth seven times a day. Likewise, much may be said of our lakes and fountains in England, Scotland, and Ireland, of turning wood into stone, iron, and the like.

Fifthly, it is worthy the consideration how the divine wisdom for the behoof of mankind hath set an enmity between birds and beasts of prey and rapine, who accompany not by herds, as lions, bears, dogs, wolves, foxes, eagles, kites, and the like; which if they should do, they would undo a whole country; whereas, on the contrary, those which are necessary and needful for mankind live *gregatim*, in herds and flocks, as kine, sheep, deer, pigeons, partridges, geese, etc.

Sixthly, how nature hath provided for the creatures of the northern parts of the world, as bears, dogs, foxes, etc., not only thick skins but great store of hair or feathers to defend them from the extremity of the cold there. On the other side, to those in Guinea, by reason of the extreme heat, none at all, as you may see by the Guinea dogs which are daily brought over.

Seventhly, how God hath so disposed the rivers that by their crookedness and winding they might serve many places.

Let us then consider how the most fruitful places and beautiful cities have become the dwellings and the homes of the most slaves, as Spain overrun by the Moors, Italy by the Goths

[2] *Jul[ius] C. Scaliger. exerc[itationes]* 37.

and Vandals, and at this day a great part of Europe by the Turk.

How the earth like an aged mother is become less fruitful, as we see by the barrenness of sometime the most fertile places, the decay of the stature and strength of men within these few years.[3]

It is also worthy observation to see how the earth hath been increased by the access of islands and again been diminished by inundation and gulfs breaking again into the same.

The islands of the Echinades [4] were cast up by the river Achelous and the greatest part of Egypt by Nilus; so were Rhodes and Delos. Of lesser islands beyond Melos, Anaphe, between Lemnos and the Hellespont, Nea, as one would say, and elsewhere Alone, Thera, Therasia, and Hiera, which also from the event was called Automate.

And that sundry goodly countries on the contrary have been eaten up by the sea, our neighbor Zeeland and many other places will give lamentable testimony. Besides, the face of the earth hath since the creation been much altered by avulsion or division of the sea, as Sicily was divided and severed from Italy, Cyprus from Syria, Euboea from Boetia, Atlas and Macris from Euboea, Bebycus from Bithynia, Leucosia from the promontory of the Syrenes, and, as some suppose, Lesbos from Ida, Prochyta and Pithecusa from Misenio, and, which is more, Spain from Barbary, as Strabo is of opinion.[5]

Again, it is affirmed by Volscus that our Great Britain hath been one continent with France and that tract between Dover and Calais hath been gained by the sea, there called Mare Gessoriacum.

Excellent is that contemplation to consider how nature (rather the Almighty Wisdom) by an unsearchable and stupendous work showeth us in the sea the likeness and shapes, not only

---

[3] Cf. below, pp. 235 ff.
[4] Curzolari Islands on the southwest coast of Acarnania, Greece.
[5] *Strabo. lib.* I.

of land creatures, as elephants, horses, dogs, hogs, calves, hares, snails, etc., but of fowls in the air, as hawks, swallows, vultures, and a number the like. Yea, it affordeth us men and women, and among men even the monk. But hereof see Junius in his *Batavia*,[6] and, if you please, Alex. ab Alexandro, with some others.[7]

Moreover, what inestimable wealth it affordeth in pearls, coral, amber, and the like!

By reading you shall also find what strange earthquakes, removing of whole towns, hills, etc., have been upon the face of the earth, raising of it in one place, leaving gulfs and vastity in another. And Lucius Marcius and Sextus Julius being consuls in Rome, in the country of Mutinum two mountains met and joined themselves together.

In the reign of Nero, Vectus Marcellus being overseer of Nero's affairs and steward of his court, meadows and olive trees were removed from a common highway side and placed a good way off on the contrary side; so whereas they stood before on the right hand, as one traveled they were now on the left hand. The like happened within these few years to Pleurs, a town of the Grisons among the Alps.

Lastly, let us take a view of the earth itself, which, because it was divided with the sea, rivers, marshes, etc., yet making one absolute circle, Homer calleth it ἀπείρονα,[8] and for this cause Numa Pompilius dedicated a temple to Vesta in a round form. The roundness of it is proved of mathematicians by shadows of dials and the eclipses; also by descent of all heavy things to the center, itself being the center of the universe, as Aristotle and Ptolemy affirm.[9]

Now, in respect of heaven, it is so small a point that the least

[6] The Dutch poet and naturalist, Adrian Junius, author of *Phallus Batavius*.

[7] *See Olaus Magnus his description of the northern parts of the world. At Swartwale near Brill in Holland is to be seen a mermaid's dead body hanging up.

[8] "Limitless."

[9] *Arist[otle] lib. Meteor. 1. cap. 4. Ptolom. cap. 6. Alphragano disert. 14.

star is not darkened with the shadow thereof. For if the smallest star, albeit in judgment of our sense, seemeth but a prick or point yet far exceedeth the body of the earth in greatness, it followeth in respect of heaven that the earth must seem as little.

Besides, if the earth were of any quantity in respect of the higher orbs, the stars should seem bigger or less in regard of those *hypsomata* (altitudes) or the climes. But it is certain that at the selfsame time sundry astronomers find the same bigness and elevation of the selfsame star observed by their calculation to differ no whit at all. Whereby we may see if that distance of place which is on the earth, in respect of the heavenly orbs, exceedeth all sense, it follows that the earth, poor little point as it is, seems the like, if it be compared with heaven. Yet this is that point which with fire and sword is divided among so many nations, the matter of our glory, our seat. Here we have our honors, our armies, our commands; here we heap up riches at perpetual war and strife among ourselves, who, like the toad, shall fall asleep with most earth in his paws, never thinking how of a moment of time well spent upon this poor plot or dunghill common to beasts as well as ourselves dependeth eternity and fruition of our true happiness in the presence of Heaven and court of King of Kings for ever and ever.[10]

Now I must take leave of our common mother, the earth, so worthily called in respect of her great merits of us; for she receiveth us being born, she feeds and clotheth us brought forth, and lastly, as forsaken wholly of nature, she receiveth us into her lap and covers us until the dissolution of all and the Last Judgment.

Thus have I only pointed at the principles of cosmography, having as it were given you a taste and stopped up the vessel again, referring the rest to your own diligence and search. And herein you shall have your helps: Master Blundeville in his treatise of cosmography and the sphere, Doctor Dee, Master

[10] *Augustine.

Cooke in his principles of geometry, astronomy, and geography, Gemma Frisius, Ortelius, Copernicus, Clavius the Jesuit, Joannes de Monte Regio, Mercator, Munster, Hunter, and many others; [11] of ancient writers Ptolemy, Dionysius Halicarnassus. For maps I refer you wholly unto Ortelius and those set last forth by Hondius, being later than Plancius and more perfect by reason of the late discovery made by Schouten unto the 57 and 58 degrees of southerly latitude beyond the Strait of Magellan, and of late Master Henry Hudson to the 61 or 62 to the northwest beyond Terra de Labrador. To omit that terrible voyage of Barents and his company for the discovery of the northeast passage by the backside of Nova Zembla, which out of a Dutch translation you may read in English.

CHAPTER IX

Of Geometry

SINCE Plato would not suffer any to enter his school which was ἀγεωμέτρητος, or not entered into geometry, and Zenocrates turned away his auditors if unfurnished with geometry, music, and astronomy, affirming they were the helps of philosophy,[1] I am also bound by the love I bear to the best arts and your studies to give it you also in charge. Philo the Jew calleth it the princess and mother of all sciences, and excellently was it said of [2] Plato that God did always γεομετρεῖν,[3] but more divinely of Solomon [4] that God did dispose all his creatures according

---

[11] *M. Hughes de usu Globi,* pr[inted] at Frankford, Amsterdam, and turned into French. M. *Edward Wright, de usu Sphaerae.*

[1] *Laertius lib.* 4.   [2] By.   [3] "Geometrize."

[4] *Wisdom [of Solomon], chap. 12.

to measure, number, and weight; that is, by giving the heavens their constant and perpetual motion, the elements their places and predominance according to lightness or gravity, and every creature its number and weight, without which it were neither able to stand upright or move. To the consideration of which depth of wisdom let us use the help of this most ingenious and useful art, worthy the contemplation and practice of the greatest princess, a science of such importance that without it we can hardly eat our bread, lie dry in our beds, buy, sell, or use any commerce else whatsoever.[5]

The subject of geometry is the length, breadth, and height of all things, comprised under the figures of triangles, squares, circles, and magnitudes of all sorts, with their terms or bounds.[6]

It hath properly the name for measuring the earth, being first found in Egypt; for when the Nilus with his overflowing drowned and confounded the limits of their fields, certain of the inhabitants more ingenious than the rest, necessity compelling, found out the rules of geometry, by the benefit whereof, after the fall of the water, every man had his own portion of ground lotted and laid out to him, so that from a few poor and weak principles at the first it grew to that height that from earth it reached up to the heavens, where it found out their quantities as also of the elements and the whole world beside.[7]

Out of Egypt Thales brought it into Greece, where it received that perfection we see it now hath.

For by means hereof are found out the forms and drafts of all figures, greatness of all bodies, all manner of measures and weights, the cunning working of all tools with all artificial instruments whatsoever.

[5] *Petrarch. de regno. lib. 2. cap.* 14. [I can find no such work by Petrarch. *De republica bene administranda* may have been intended, and perhaps the erroneous reference to book and chapter was picked up from the next note.]

[6] *Proclus in Euclid. lib. 2. cap.* 14.

[7] *Martianus Capella in Geom. Proclus in Euclid. lib. 2. cap.* 4.

All engines of war, for many whereof, being antiquated, we have no proper names, as exosters, sambukes, catapults, testudos, scorpions, etc., petards, grenades, great ordnance of all sorts.[8]

By the benefit, likewise, of geometry we have our goodly ships, galleys, bridges, mills, chariots and coaches (which were invented in Hungary [9] and there called *cotzki,* some with two wheels, some with more), pulleys, and cranes of all sorts.

She also with her ingenious hand rears all curious roofs and arches, stately theaters, the columns simple and compounded, pendant galleries, stately windows, turrets, etc., and first brought to light our clocks and curious watches (unknown to the ancients), lastly, our kitchen jacks,[10] even the wheelbarrow, besides whatsoever hath artificial motion either by air, water, wind, sinews, or cords, as well all manner of musical instruments, waterworks, and the like.

Yea, moreover, such is the infinite subtlety and immense depth of this admirable art that it dares contend even with nature's self in infusing life as it were into the senseless bodies of wood, stone, or metal. Witness the wooden dove of Archytas, so famoused not only by Agellius [11] but many other authors beyond exception, which, by reason of weights equally peised [12] within the body and a certain proportion of air (as the spirit of life enclosed), flew cheerfully forth as if it had been a living dove.

Albeit Julius Caesar Scaliger [13] accounteth this dove no great piece of workmanship when he saith he is able to make of his own invention with no great labor a ship which shall swim and steer itself, and by the same reason that Archytas his dove was made; that is, by taking the pith of rushes covered over with

[8] Exosters (*exostrae*) and sambukes (*sambucae*) were bridges used in assaulting city walls; *testudos* were protective roofs against falling stones; and scorpions were engines for throwing stones.

[9] *See the Hungarian history. Whence "coach" had the name.

[10] Devices for turning spits.

[11] *Agellius lib.* 10, *cap.* 12 [Agellius, more correctly Aulus Gellius].

[12] Balanced.   [13] *Scaliger Exercit. 326. ad Cardanum.*

bladders or those thin skins wherein goldbeaters beat their leaves, and wrapped about with little strings of sinews, where, when a semicircle shall set one wheel on going, it moving others, the wings shall stir and move forward. This Archytas was a most skillful mathematician, as it may be gathered out of Horace,[14] who calleth him *mensorem,* a measurer,

Et maris et terrae numeroque carentis arenae,

Of sea and land and number-wanting sand.

And not inferior to the aforesaid dove of Archytas was that wooden eagle which mounted up into the air and flew before the emperor to the gates of Nuremberg, of which, as also of that iron fly that flew about a table, Saluste, Lord of Bartas, maketh mention.[15] Ramus attributeth the invention of either of these, in the preface of his second book of [16] his mathematical observations, to Joannes Regiomontanus.

Callicrates, if we may credit Pliny,[17] made ants and other suchlike small creatures of ivory, that their parts and joints of their legs could not be discerned.

Myrmecides Milesius, also, among other monuments of his skill made a coach or wagon with four wheels, which together with the driver thereof a fly could easily hide and cover with her wings; besides, a ship with her sails, which a little bee could overspread. Varro [18] teacheth how small pieces of this nature and subtlest workmanship may be discerned; that is, saith he, by laying close about them black horsehairs. Of later times Hadrian Junius [19] tells us that he saw with great delight and admiration, at Mechlin in Brabant, a cherry stone cut in the

---

[14] *°Horat. lib.* 1. *Carm*[ina], ode 28.

[15] *°Bartas, le* 6. *jour du* 1. *Semain*[e] [Bartas, the 6th day of the first week of *Le création*].

[16] From 1622; 1634 by.   [17] *°Plin*[ius] *lib.* 7. *cap.* 21 *et lib.* 36. *cap.* 5.

[18] *°Varro de lingua Latin*[a]. *lib.* 6.   [19] *°Iunius lib. animad. cap.* 6.

form of a basket, wherein were fifteen pair of dice distinct, each with their spots and number very easily of a good eye to be discerned.

And that the *Iliad* of Homer written was enclosed within a nut,[20] Cicero tells us he saw it with his eyes, though Alexander thought it worthy of a far better case, the rich cabinet of Darius. By the statue of Homer the ancients usually set a nightingale, as by Orpheus a swan, for the manifold variety and sweetness of his voice or the continuance or holding out to the last the same sweetness. For some are of opinion that the perfection of musical sounds are to be discerned in the nightingale's notes. Pliny [21] reckoneth up sixteen several tunes she hath, and fitteth them to Latin words very properly as unto ditties, which the translator of Pliny hath nothing near so well fitted in the English, which might surely have been as well done, as I have observed in their notes. But to return, Scaliger,[22] whether in jest or earnest I know not, tells Cardanus of a flea he saw with a long chain of gold about his neck, kept very daintily in a box and, being taken forth, could skip with his chain and sometime suck his mistress' white hand and, his belly being full, get him to his lodging again. But this same ματαιοτεχνίαν [23] Alexander wittily scoffed when he gave a fellow only a bushel of peas for his pains of throwing every time a pease upon a needle's point standing a pretty way off.

Archimedes, to the wonder of all the world, framed a brazen heaven, wherein were the seven planets with their motions. Hereof Claudian wrote a witty epigram. Sapor, King of Persia, as Du Bartas in the sixth day of his *Divine Week* mentioneth, has an heaven of glass, which, proudly sitting in his estate, he trod upon with his feet, contemplating over the same as if he had been Jupiter, and upon this occasion calling himself brother

[20] *Plin[ius]* *lib.* 7. *cap.* 12.
[22] *Exercitat.* 326.
[21] *Plin. lib.* 10. *cap.* 29.
[23] "Useless kind of art."

to the sun and moon and partner with the stars. For in his letter to the Emperor Constantine he beginneth thus: *Rex regum, Sapor, particeps syderum, frater solis et lunae, etc.*[24]

Nor must I forget that heaven of silver sent by Ferdinand, the emperor, to Solyman, the Great Turk, wherein the motions kept their true courses with those of the heavens, the stars arising and setting, the planets keeping their oblique motion, the sun eclipsed at his just time, and the moon duly changing every month with the same in the heaven.[25] By these see the effects of this divine knowledge, able to work wonders beyond all belief, insomuch as Archimedes affirmed [26] he would move the whole earth, might a place be given him whereon to stand. But I rather believe him who saith, "The foundation thereof shall never be moved." [27] Much was it that with his left hand only he could by his skill draw after him the weight of five thousand bushels of grain and devise, at the cost of Hiero, those rare engines which shot small stones at hand but great ones afar off; by benefit of which device only, while the stones fell as thick as hail from heaven among the enemies, Syracuse was preserved from the fury of Marcellus, ready to enter with a resolute and powerful army. The oracle of Apollo, being demanded when the war and misery of Greece should have an end, replied, if they would double the altar in Delos, which was cubic form; which they tried by adding another cube unto it, but that availed nothing. Plato, then taking upon him to expound this riddle, affirmed the Greeks were reproved by Apollo because they were ignorant of geometry. Nor herein can I blame them, since the doubling of the cube in solids and quadrature of the circle in plane hath ever since so troubled our greatest geometricians that, I fear, except Apollo himself ascend from

[24] *Cael[ius] Rhodigin[us] lib. 8. cap. 3.

[25] *P. Jovius et Sabellicus in Supplement. Hist., lib. 24.* This heaven was carried by twelve men before Solyman and taken to pieces and set up again by the maker.

[26] *Plutarch in Marcello.*   [27] *Psal. 24.

hell to resolve his own problem, we shall not see it among our ordinary stonecutters effected.

But in brief, the use you shall have of geometry will be in surveying your lands, affording your opinion in building anew, or translating; [28] making your mills as well for grinding of corn as throwing forth water from your lower grounds; bringing water far off for sundry uses; seeing the measure of timber, stone, and the like (wherein gentlemen many times are egregiously abused and cheated by such as they trust), to contrive much with small charge and in less room. Again, should you follow the wars—as who knows the bent of his fate?—you cannot without geometry fortify yourself; take the advantage of hill or level; fight; order your battalia [29] in square, triangle, cross (which form the Prince of Orange hath now late taken up), crescent-wise (and many other forms Jovius showeth); level and plant your ordnance; undermine; raise your half-moons, bulwarks, casemates, rampires, ravelins, [30] with many other means as of offense and defense, by fortification. So that I cannot see how a gentleman, especially a soldier and commander, may be accomplished without geometry, though not to the height of perfection, yet at the least to be grounded and furnished with the principles and privy rules hereof. The authors I would commend unto you for entrance hereinto are, in English: Cooke's *Principles,* and *The Elements of Geometry,* written in Latin by P. Ramus and translated by Mr. Dr. Hood, sometime mathematical lecturer in London; Master Blundeville; Euclid, translated into English. [31] In Latin you may have the

[28] Furthering your opinion in building anew, or moving from one place to another.

[29] Order of battle.

[30] Half-moons: two embankments in a fortification forming an angle.

[31] Francis Cooke's edition of *The Principles of Geometry* (1591) from George Heinsch's work. Dr. Thomas Hood's translation of Ramus appeared in 1590, and Sir Henry Billingsley's translation of Euclid—the first in English—appeared in 1570. "Master Blundeville" refers to Thomas Blundeville's *Exercises* (1594).

learned Jesuit Clavius, Melanchthon, Frisius, Valturius his geometry military. Albert Duerer hath excellently written hereof in high Dutch; and in French, Forcadell upon Euclid, with sundry others.

CHAPTER X

Of Poetry

To SWEETEN your severer studies by this time vouchsafe poetry your respect, which howsoever censured and seeming fallen from the highest stage of honor to the lowest stair of disgrace, let not your judgment be infected with that pestilent air of the common breath to be an infidel, in whose belief and doer of their contrary actions is to be religious in the right and to merit if it were possible by good works.

The poet, as that laurel Maia dreamed of, is made by miracle from his mother's womb, and, like the diamond, only polished and pointed of himself, disdaining the style and midwifery of foreign help.

Hence Tully was long ere he could be delivered of a few verses, and those poor ones too; and Ovid so backward in prose that he could almost speak nothing but verse. And experience daily affordeth us many excellent young and growing wits, as well from the plow as palace, endued naturally with this divine and heavenly gift, yet not knowing, if you should ask the question, whether a metaphor be flesh or fish.

If bare saying poetry is an heavenly gift be too weak a prop to uphold her credit with those buzzardly poor ones, who, having their feathers moulted, can creep no farther than their own puddle, able only to envy this imperial eagle for fight and flight,[1] let them, if they can, look back to all antiquity, and they shall find all learning by divine instinct to breathe from her bosom, as both Plato and Tully in his *Tusculanes* affirm.[2]

Strabo saith poetry was the first philosophy that ever was taught, nor were there ever any writers thereof known before Musaeus, Hesiod, and Homer, by whose authority Plato, Aristotle, and Galen determine their weightiest controversies and confirm their reasons in philosophy. And what were the songs of Linus, Orpheus, Amphion, Olympus, and that ditty Iopas sang to his harp at Dido's banquet, but natural and moral philosophy, sweetened with the pleasance of numbers that rudeness and barbarism might the better taste and digest the lessons of civility? According to Lucretius, Italianized by Ariosto and Englished by Sir John Harington,

> *Sed veluti pueris absynthia tetra medentes*
> *Cum dare conantur, prius oras pocula circum*
> *Contingunt mellis dulei flavoque liquore,*
> *Ut puerorum aetas improvida ludificetur,* etc.

> As leeches when for children they appoint
> Their bitter wormwood potions, first the cup
> About the brim with honey sweet they noint,
> That so the child, beguiled, may drink it up, etc.[3]

Neither hath human knowledge been the only subject of this divine art, but even the highest mysteries of divinity. What are the Psalms of David (which St. Hilary [4] so aptly compareth

---

[1] *°Plato in Phaedro.*   [2] *°Καλὴ καὶ θεία ἡ ὁρμή in Parmenide.*

[3] The reference is to *Lucretius de rerum natura* (i. 936–939) and, presumably, to a passage in Harington's translation of *Orlando Furioso* (1591), although I have been unable to locate it. Harington expresses a similar idea in his preface (sig. ¶ij verso), but the citation is a stanza from Tasso's *Gierusalemme liberata* on the same theme of making medicine palatable to a sick child.

[4] *°Hil. in Prologo Psalm.*

to a bunch of keys in regard of the several doors whereby they give the soul entrance either to prayer, rejoicing, repentance, thanksgiving, etc.) but a divine poem, going sometime in one measure, sometime in another? What lively descriptions are there of the majesty of God, the estate and security of God's children, the miserable condition of the wicked! [5] What lively similitudes and comparisons, as the righteous man to a bay tree, the soul to a thirsty hart, unity to ointment and the dew of Hermon! [6] What excellent allegories, as the vine planted in Egypt, what epiphonemas, prosopopoeias, and whatsoever else may be required to the texture of so rich and glorious a piece!

And the Song of Solomon, which is only left us of a thousand, is it not a continued allegory of the mystical love betwixt Christ and His church? Moreover, the apostles themselves have not disdained to allege the authority of the heathen poets, Aratus, Menander, and Epimenides, as also the fathers of the church, Nazianzen, St. Augustine, Bernard, Prudentius, with many other. Besides the allowance they have given of poetry they teach us the true use and end thereof, which is to compass the songs of Sion and address the fruit of our invention to His glory who is the author of so goodly a gift, which we abuse to our loves, light fancies, and basest affections.

And if mechanical arts hold their estimation by their effects in base subjects, how much more deserveth this to be esteemed that holdeth so sovereign a power over the mind, can turn brutishness into civility, make the lewd honest (which is Scaliger's opinion of Virgil's poem), turn hatred to love, cowardice into valor, and, in brief, like a queen command over all affections.

Moreover, the Muse, Mirth, Graces, and perfect health have ever an affinity each with either. I remember Plutarch telleth us of Telesilla, a noble and brave lady who, being dangerously sick and imagined past recovery, was by the oracle advised to apply her mind to the Muse and poetry, which she diligently

[5] *Psalm 80. Psalm 90.   [6] *Psalm 1. Psalm 104.

observing, recovered in a short space and withal grew so sprightly courageous that, having well fortified Argos with divers companies of women only, herself with her companions, sallying out, entertained Cleomenes, King of the Lacedaemonians with such a camisado that he was fain to show his back, leaving a good part of his people behind to fill ditches, and then by plain force of arms drove out Demaratus, another king who lay very strong in garrison within.

Alexander by the reading of Homer was especially moved to go through with his conquests.

Leonidas also, that brave King of the Spartans, being asked how Tirtaeus, who wrote of war in verse, was esteemed among poets, replied, "Excellently, for my soldiers," quoth he, "moved only with his verses, run with a resolute courage to the battle, fearing no peril at all."

What other thing gave an edge to the valor of our ancient Britons but their bards, remembered by Athenaeus, Lucan, and sundry other, recording in verse the brave exploits of their nation and singing the same unto their harps at their public feasts and meetings, amongst whom Taliesin, a learned bard and master to Merlin, sung the life and acts of King Arthur?

Hence hath poetry never wanted her patrons, and even the greatest monarchs and princes, as well Christian as heathen, have exercised their invention herein, as that great glory of Christendom, Charlemagne, who, among many other things, wrote his nephew Roland's epitaph after he was slain in a battle against the Saracens among the Pyrenean Hills.[7] Alphonsus, King of Naples,[8] whose only delight was the reading of Virgil; Robert, King of Sicily; and that thrice-renowned and learned

---

[7] *The place to this day is called "Rowland's Valley," and was in times past a great pilgrimage, there being a chapel built over the tomb and dedicated to our Lady, called commonly, but corruptly, "Our Lady of Rencevall."

[8] *Panormitan[us] *lib.* 1. *de gestis Alphonsi* [i.e., *De dictis et factis regis Alphonsi* (Pisa, 1485)].

French king, who, finding Petrarch's tomb without any inscription or epitaph, wrote one himself, which yet remaineth, saying: "Shame it was that he who sung his mistress' praise seven years before her death and twelve years after his own should [9] want an epitaph." Among the heathen eternized for their skill in poesy, Augustus Caesar Octavius, Adrian, Germanicus.

Every child knoweth how dear the works of Homer were unto Alexander, Euripides to Amyntas, King of Macedon, Virgil to Augustus, Theocritus to Ptolemy and Berenice, King and Queen of Egypt, the stately Pindar to Hiero, King of Sicily, Ennius to Scipio, Ausonius to Gratian, who made him proconsul; in our own country Chaucer to Richard the Second,[10] Gower to Henry the Fourth, with others I might allege.

The Lady Anne of Bretagne, who was twice French queen,[11] passing through the presence in the court of France, espying Chartier, the King's secretary and a famous poet, leaning upon his elbow at a table's end fast asleep, she, stooping down and openly kissing him, said: "We must honor with our kiss the mouth from whence so many sweet verses and golden poems have proceeded."

But some may ask me how it falleth out that poets nowadays are of no such esteem as they have been in former times. I answer, because virtue in our declining and worser days generally findeth no regard. Or, rather, more truly with Aretine, being demanded why princes were not so liberal to poesy and other good arts as in former times: "Because the conscience telleth them how unworthy they are of their praises given them by poets. As for other arts, they make no account of that they know not."

But since we are here, having before overrun the champaign and large field of history, let us awhile rest ourselves in the

---

[9] From 1661; 1662 and 1634 twelve years should.

[10] *Who gave him, it is thought, his manor of Ewelme in Oxfordshire.

[11] *To Charles the Eighth and Louis the Twelfth.

garden of the Muses and admire the bounty of heaven in the several beauties of so many divine and fertile wits.

We must begin with the King of Latin Poets, whom nature hath reared beyond imitation, and who above all other only deserveth the name of a poet. I mean Virgil. In him you shall at once find, not elsewhere, that prudence, efficacy, variety, and sweetness which Scaliger requireth in a poet and maketh his prime virtues. Under prudence is comprehended out of general learning and judgment that discreet, apt-suiting, and disposing as well of actions as words in their due place, time, and manner, which in Virgil is not observed by one among twenty of our ordinary grammarians, "Who," to use the words of the Prince of Learning [12] hereupon, "only in shallow and small boats glide over the face of the Virgilian sea." How divinely, according to the Platonics, doth he discourse of the soul! how properly of the nature, number of winds, seasons of the year, qualities of beasts, nature of herbs! What insight into ancient chronology and history! In brief, what not worthy the knowledge of a divine wit! To make his Aeneas a man of extraordinary aspect and comeliness of personage, he makes Venus both his mother and lady of his horoscope. And forasmuch as grief and perpetual care are inseparable companions of all great and noble achievements, he gives him Achates *quasi* ἄχος ἄτης, "his faithful companion." What immoved constancy when no tears or entreaty of Eliza could cause him stay! What piety, pity, fortitude beyond his companions! See how the divine poet gave him leave to be wounded, lest his valor in so many skirmishes might be questioned, and that afar off, not at hand, that rather it might be imputed to his fortune than his [13] rashness or weakness; then by one who could not be known, to give the enemy occasion rather of fear than of challenging the glory. And whereas he bringeth in Camilla, a courageous lady, and invincible at the

---

[12] *[Scaliger] in Poetic. lib. 3. qui et Idea. cap. 25.
[13] From 1622; 1634 this.

sword's point in encountering other, yet he never bringeth her to try her valor with Aeneas.[14] Again, that Tarchon and she might show their brave deeds, he makes Aeneas absent; as also when Turnus so resolutely broke into his tents. Lastly, what excellent judgment showeth he in appropriating the accidents and histories of his own times to those of the ancient, as where he bringeth in Venulus, plucked by force from his horse and carried away with full speed! The like Caesar confesseth to have happened to himself. Aeneas with his right arm naked commands his soldiers to abstain from slaughter. The like did Caesar at the battle of Pharsalia, and with the same words. But thus much out of the heap and most judicious observations of the most learned Scaliger.

Efficacy is a power of speech which representeth a thing after an excellent manner, neither by bare words only, but by presenting to our minds the lively *ideas* or forms of things so truly as if we saw them with our eyes; as the places in hell, the fiery arrow of Acesta, the description of Fame, the flame about the temples of Ascanius; but of actions more open and with greater spirit, as in that passage and passion of Dido preparing to kill herself.[15]

> *At trepida et coeptis immanibus effera Dido,*
> *Sanguineam volvens aciem, maculique trementes*
> *Interfusa genas, et pallida morte futura,*
> *Interiora domus irrumpit limina, et altos*
> *Conscendit furibunda rogos, ensemque recludit*
> *Dardanium, etc.*

Which for my English readers' sake I have after my manner translated, though assured all the translations in the world must come short of the sweetness and majesty of the Latin.

> But she, amazed and fierce by cruel plots,
> Rolling about her bloody eye, her cheeks

---

[14] *°Aeneid.* 11.　　　　　　　[15] *°Aeneid.* 4.

All-trembling and arising, full of spots,
And pale with death at hand, perforce she breaks
Into the inmost rooms.—
Enraged then she climbs the lofty pile,
And out of sheath the Dardane sword doth draw,
Ne'er for such end ordained, when awhile
The Trojan garments and known couch she saw,
With trickling tears herself thereon she cast
And, having paused a little, spake her last.
Sweet spoils, while fates and heavens did permit,
Receive this soul and rid me of my cares.
What race my fortune gave I finished, etc.

Moreover, that lively combat between Nisus and Volscens, with many other of most excellent life.

A sweet verse is that which, like a dish with a delicate sauce, invites the reader to taste even against his will. The contrary is harshness. Hereof I give you an example in the description of young Pallas (whom imagine you see laid forth, newly slain, upon a bier of crab tree and oaken rods covered with straw and arched over with green boughs), than which no nectar can be more delicious.

Qualem virgineo demessum pollice florem,
Seu mollis violae, seu languentis hyacinthi,
Cui nec fulgor adhuc, nec dum sua forma recessit,
Non iam mater alit tellus viresque ministrat, etc.[16]

Even as the flower by maiden's finger mown,
Of th' drooping hy'cinth or soft violet,
Whose beauty's fading, yet not fully gone,
Now mother earth no more doth nourish it, etc.

The like of fair Euryalus breathing his last.

Purpureus veluti cum flos succisus aratro,
Languescit moriens, lassove papavera collo
Demisere caput, pluvia cum forte gravantur.[17]

---

[16] *Aeneid. 11.   [17] *Aeneid. 9.

Henry Peacham

Look how the purple flower which the plow
Hath shorn in sunder, languishing, doth die;
Or poppies down their weary necks do bow
And hang the head, with rain when laden lie, etc.

This kind Plutarch [18] termeth "flowery," as having in it a beauty and sweet grace to delight, as a flower.

Variety is various and the rules of it so difficult that to define or describe it were as to draw one picture which should resemble all the faces in the world, changing itself like Proteus into all shapes; which our divine poet so much and with such excellent art affecteth that seldom or never he uttereth words or describeth actions spoken or done after the same manner, though they be in effect the same. Yea, though the conclusion of all the books of his *Aeneides* be tragical, save the first, yet are they so tempered and disposed with such variety of accidents that they bring admiration to the most divine judgments, among them all not one like another, save the ends of Turnus and Mezentius.[19] What variety in his battles, assailing the enemy's camp, besieging cities, broils among the common people, set battles in fields, aids of horse and foot! etc. Never the same wounds, but given with divers weapons, as here one is wounded or slain with a piece of a rock, a flint, firebrand, club, halberd, long pole; there another with a drinking bowl or pot, a rudder, dart, arrow, lance, sword, balls of wildfire,[20] etc. In divers places, as the throat, head, thigh, breast, hip, hand, knee; before, behind, on the side, standing, lying, running, flying, talking, sleeping, crying out, entreating. Of place, as in the field, in the tents, at sacrifice, upon the guard, in the daytime, in the night. To proceed further were to translate Virgil himself; therefore, hitherto of variety. I forbear his most lively descriptions of per-

[18] *'Ανθηρόν κάλλος έχον καὶ χάριν εἰς τὸ τέρπειν καὶ ἥδειν ὥσπερ ἄνθος.*
[19] *Vide Scal[iger] lib. 3. Poet. cap. 27.*
[20] *Phalaricae [falaricae,* "missiles wrapped with tow and pitch, set on fire, and thrown by a catapult."—*Harper's Latin Dict.*]

98

sons, times, places, and manners; his most sweet and proper similitudes, as where he resembleth Aeneas, who could not be moved by any entreaty or tears of Dido or her sister Anna, to a stubborn oak, after this manner.

> *At veluti annosam valido cum robore quercum,*
> *Alpini Boreae, nunc hinc nunc flatibus illinc,*
> *Eruere inter se certant: it stridor et alte*
> *Consternunt terram concusso stipite frondes,* etc.[21]

> As when the Alpine winds with each contend
> Now this way, now that way, with their furious might
> Some aged oak up by the roots to rend,
> Loud whistling's heard, the earth bestrewed quite
> (The body reeling) all about with leaves,
> While it stands firm and, irremoved, cleaves
> Unto the rock; for look how high it heaves
> The lofty head to heavenward, so low
> The stubborn root doth down to hellward grow.

Again, that elegant comparison of Aruns (having cowardly slain the brave Lady Camilla and retired himself for fear into the body of his army) to a wolf that had done a mischief and durst not show his head.

> *At velut ille prius quem tela inimica sequantur*
> *Continuo in montes sese avius abdidit altos*
> *Occiso pastore, lupus, magnove iuvenco,*
> *Conscius audacis facti, caudamque remulcens*
> *Subiecit pavitantem utero, sylvasque petivit,* etc.[22]

> And as a wolf that hath the shepherd slain,
> Or some great beast, before the country rise,
> Knowing him guilty, through byways amain
> Hath got the mountains, leering where he lies,
> Or clapt his tail betwixt his legs, in fear
> Ta'en the next coppice till the coast be clear.

---

[21] *Aeneid.* [4.]   [22] *Aeneid.* 11.

After Virgil I bring you Ovid, as well because they lived in one time (yet Ovid confesseth he saw Virgil but once in all his life) as that he deserveth to be second in imitation for the sweetness and smooth current of his style, everywhere seasoned with profound and antique learning. Among his works his epistles are most worthy your reading, being his neatest piece, everywhere embellished with excellent and wise sentences, the numbers smoothly falling in and borrowing their luster and beauty from imitation of native and antique simplicity. That of Acontius is somewhat too wanton; those three of Ulysses, Demophon, and Paris to Oenone are suspected, for the weakness of conceit in regard of the other, to be none of Ovid's.

Concerning his books *Amorum* and *De arte amandi,* the wit, with the truly ingenuous and learned, will bear out the wantonness, for with the weeds there are delicate flowers in those walks of Venus. For the argument of his *Metamorphosis* he is beholden to Parthenius and divers others, and those who long before wrote of the same subject.

About the year 1581,[23] when the King of Poland made war in Moscovia, certain Polonian ambassadors traveling into the inmost places of Moscovia, as far as Podolia and Kiovia, they passed the great River Boristhenes. Having in their company a certain young gentleman, very well seen in the Latin, Greek, and Hebrew tongues, withal an excellent poet and historian, he persuaded the Polonians to well horse themselves and ride with him a little further. For he would, said he, show them Ovid's sepulcher, which they did. And when they were gone six days' journey beyond Boristhenes, through most vast and desolate places, at last they came into a most sweet and pleasant valley, wherein was a clear running fountain, about which the grass growing very thick and high, with their swords and falchions they cut it down till at last they found a stone chest

---

[23] *Vide Surium in Commentario rerum in orbe gestarum. An.* 1581. *fol.* 1026.

or coffin, covered over with sticks and shrubs, whereon, it being rubbed and cleansed from moth and filth, they read Ovid's epitaph, which was this:

> Hic situs est vates quem Divi Caesaris ira
> Augusti, Latia cedere jussit humo.
> Saepe miser voluit patriis occumbere terris
> Sed frustra. Hunc illi fata dedere locum.[24]

This his sepulcher, saith mine author, remaineth upon the borders of Greece, near to the Euxine Sea, and is yet to be seen.

Of lyric poets, as well Greek as Latin, hold Horace in highest account as the most acute and artificial[25] of them all, having attained to such height that to the discreet judgment he hath cut off all hope of equalizing him. His style is elegant, pure, and sinewy, with most witty and choice sentences, neither *humili contentus stylo,* as Quintilian saith of him, *sed grandiloquo et sublimi.*[26] Yea, and if we believe Scaliger, more accurate and sententious than Pindar. His *Odes* are of most sweet and pleasant invention, beyond all reprehension, everywhere illustrated with sundry and rare figures and verses, so fluent that the same Scaliger protesteth he had rather be composer of the like than be king of whole Aragon.[27] In his satires he is quick, round, and pleasant, and as nothing so bitter, so not so good as Juvenal. His *Epistles* are neat, his *Poetica* his worst piece, for while he teacheth the art, he goeth unartificially to work even in the very beginning.

Juvenal of satirists is the best, for his satires are far better than those of Horace, and though he be sententiously tart, yet is his phrase clear and open.

[24] "Here lies the poet whom the wrath of Divine Augustus commanded to leave his native Latium. Often miserable, he wished to die in his fatherland. The Fates gave him a place here."—The tomb and epitaph are, of course, an imposition.

[25] Artful.

[26] "Not striving for a low style, . . . but for the grand and sublime."

[27] *Scalig[er] Poet. lib. 6. Totius Terraconensis Rex.*

Persius—I know not why we should so much affect him, since with his obscurity he laboreth not to affect us; yet in our learned age he is now discovered to every schoolboy. His style is broken, forward, unpleasing, and harsh.

In Martial you shall see a divine wit with a flowing purity of the Latin tongue, a true epigrammatist. His verse is clear, full, and absolute good, some few too wanton and licentious being winked at.

Lucan breathes with a great spirit; wherefore, some of our shallow grammarians have attempted to equal him with Virgil. But his error is, while he doth *ampullare* [28] with big-sounding words and a conceit unbounded, furious, and ranging, and cannot with Virgil contain himself within that sweet, humble, and unaffected moderation, he incurreth a secret envy and ridiculous contempt, which a moderate and well-tempered style avoideth.

Seneca for majesty and state yieldeth not to any of the Grecians whosoever, *cultu et nitore*,[29] to use Scaliger's words, far excelling Euripides, albeit he borrowed the argument of his tragedies from the Grecians. Yet the spirit, loftiness of sound, and majesty of style is merely [30] his own.

Claudian is an excellent and sweet poet, only overborne by the meanness of his subject, but what wanted to his matter he supplied by his wit and happy invention.

Statius is a smooth and sweet poet, coming nearest of any other to the state and majesty of Virgil's verse, and, Virgil only excepted, is the Prince of Poets as well Greek as Latin. For he is more flowery in figures and writeth better lines than Homer. Of his works his *Sylvae* are the best.

Propertius is an easy, clear, and true elegiac, following the tract of none save his own invention.

Among comic poets, how much antiquity attributed to Plautus for his pleasant vein (to whom Volcatius giveth the place next

[28] "Speak bombastically."   [29] "In refinement and brilliance."
[30] Entirely.

to Caecilius, and Varro would make the mouth of the Muses), so much do our times yield to Terence for the purity of his style. Wherefore Scaliger willeth to admire Plautus as a comedian but Terence as a pure and elegant speaker.

Thus have I in brief comprised for your behoof the large censure of the best of Latin poets, as it is copiously delivered by the Prince of all Learning and Judge of Judgments, the divine Julius Caesar Scaliger. But while we look back to antiquity let us not forget our later and modern times (as imagining Nature hath heretofore extracted her quintessence and left us the dregs), which produce as fertile wits as perhaps the other, yea, and in our Britain.

Of Latin poets of our times, in the judgment of Beza and the best learned, Buchanan is esteemed the chief, who, albeit in his person, behavior, and fashion he was roughhewn, slovenly, and rude, seldom caring for a better outside than a rug gown girt close about him, yet his inside and conceit in poesy was most rich, and his sweetness and facility in a verse unimitably excellent, as appeareth by that masterpiece, his *Psalms,* as far beyond those of B. Rhenanus as the stanzas of Petrarch the rimes of Skelton, but deserving more applause, in my opinion, if he had fallen upon another subject. For I say with one, *Mihi spiritus divinus eiusmodi placet quo seipsum ingessit a patre, et illorum piget qui David Psalmos suis calamistris inustos sperarant efficere plausibiliores.*[31] And certain in that boundless field of poetical invention it cannot be avoided but something must be distorted beside the intent of the divine inditer.

His tragedies are lofty, the style pure; his epigrams not to be mended save here and there, according to his genius, too broad and bitter.

---

[31] **Jul. Caes. Scaliger.* ["His divine spirit pleases me when it has proceeded from the Father, and they annoy me who expect David to produce through the use of excessive ornamentation perfect psalms quite worthy of praise."]

But let us look behind and we shall find one English-bred whose glory and worth, although *cineri supposta doloso,*[32] is inferior neither to Buchanan or any of the ancients, and so much the more to be valued by how much the brighter he appeared out of the fogs of barbarism and ignorance in his time. That is Joseph of Exeter, who lived under Henry the Second and Richard the First, who wrote that singular and stately poem of the Trojan War after the history of Dares Phrygius, which the Germans have printed under the name of Cornelius Nepos. He died at Bordeaux in France, where he was archbishop, where his monument is yet to be seen.[33]

After him (all that long tract of ignorance until the days of Henry the Eighth, which time Erasmus calleth the Golden Age of Learning in regard of so many famously learned men it produced more than ever heretofore) flourished Sir Thomas More, sometime Lord Chancellor of England, a man of most rich and pleasant invention, his verse fluent, nothing harsh, constrained, or obscure, wholly composed of conceit and inoffensive mirth, that he seemeth *ad lepores fuisse natum.*[34] How wittily doth he play upon the archcuckold Sabinus, scoff at Frenchified Lalus, and Hervey, a French cowardly captain, beaten at the sea by our English and his ship burned, yet his victory and valor, to the English disgrace, proclaimed by Brixius, a German poetaster![35] What can be more lofty than his gratulatory verse to King Henry upon his coronation day, more witty than that epigram upon the name of Nicolaus, an ignorant physician that had been the death of thousands, and Abingdon's epitaph, more sweet than that nectar epistle of his to his daughters Margaret, Elizabeth, and Cicely! But as these ingenious

[32] "Hidden beneath treacherous ashes."

[33] Joseph of Exeter, or Josephus Iscanus (fl. 1190), "a miracle of the age in classical composition" (Warton), wrote *De bello Troiano,* first published at Basel in 1558. He was never Archbishop of Bordeaux.

[34] "To have been born to agreeableness and pleasantry."

[35] From 1661; 1622 Pot-aster; 1634 Pot aster.

exercises bewrayed in him an extraordinary quickness of wit and learning, so his *Utopia* his depth of judgment in state affairs, than which, in the opinion of the most learned Budaeus in a preface, before it our age hath not seen a thing more deep and accurate. In his younger years there was ever a friendly and virtuous emulation for the palm of invention and poesy between William Lily, the author of our grammar, and him, as appeareth by their several translations of many Greek epigrams and their invention tried upon one subject, notwithstanding they loved and lived together as dearest friends. Lily also was, besides an excellent Latin poet, a singular Grecian, who, after he traveled all Greece over and many parts of Europe besides and lived some four or five years in the Isle of the Rhodes, he returned home and by Dean John Colet, dean of Paul's, was elected master of Paul's School which he had newly founded.

Shortly after began to grow eminent, as well for poesy as all other general learning, Sir Thomas Chaloner, knight (father to the truly honest and sometime lover of all excellent parts, Sir Thomas Chaloner, who attended upon the late prince), born in London, brought up in Cambridge, who, having left the university and followed the court a good while, went over with Sir Henry Knyvet, ambassador to Charles the Fifth, as his friend and companion; what time the emperor being preparing a mighty fleet against the Turks in Algiers, the English ambassador, Sir Thomas Chaloner, Henry Knowles, Mr. Henry Isam, and others went in that service as voluntaries with the Emperor. But the galley wherein Sir Thomas was, being cast away by foulness of weather, after he had labored by swimming for his life as long as he was able, and the strength of his arms failing him, he caught hold upon a cable thrown out from another galley, to the loss and breaking of many of his teeth, and by that means saved his life. After the death of King Henry the Eighth he was in the battle of Musselburgh and knighted

by the Duke of Somerset. And in the beginning of the reign
of Queen Elizabeth he went over ambassador into Spain, where
at his hours of leisure he compiled ten elegant books in Latin
verse, *De Repub. Anglorum instauranda,* supervised after his
death by Malim and dedicated to the old Lord Burghley, Lord
Treasurer. Being sent for home by her Majesty, he shortly after
died in London and was buried in Paul's, near to the steps of
the choir, toward the south door, under a fair marble; but the
brass and epitaph written by Doctor Haddon by sacrilegious
hands is since torn away. But the Muses and eternal fame have
reared him a monument more lasting and worthy the merit of
so excellent a man.

Of English poets of our own nation esteem Sir Geoffrey
Chaucer the father. Although the style for the antiquity may
distaste you, yet as under a bitter and rough rind there lieth
a delicate kernel of conceit and sweet invention. What examples, similitudes, times, places, and, above all, persons with
their speeches and attributes do, as in his *Canterbury Tales*—
like the threads of gold, the rich arras—beautify his work quite
through! And albeit divers of his works are but merely translations out of Latin and French, yet he hath handled them so
artificially [36] that thereby he hath made them his own, as his
Troilus and Cressid. The Roman of the Rose was the invention
of Jean de Meung, a French poet, whereof he translated but
only the one half. His *Canterbury Tales* without question were
his own invention, all circumstances being wholly English. He
was a good divine and saw in those times without his spectacles,
as may appear by the Plowman and the Parson's Tale; withal
an excellent mathematician, as plainly appeareth by his discourse of astrolabe to his little son Lewis. In brief, account him
among the best of your English books in your library.

Gower, being very gracious with King Henry the Fourth,
in his time carried the name of the only poet, but his verses,

[36] Artfully.

to say truth, were poor and plain, yet full of good and grave morality, but while he affected altogether the French phrase and words, made himself too obscure to his reader; besides, his invention cometh far short of the promise of his titles. He published only, that I know of, three books, which at St. Mary Overies in Southwark upon his monument lately repaired by some good benefactor lie under his head; which are *Vox clamantis, Speculum meditantis,* and *Confessio amantis.* He was a knight, as also was Chaucer.[37]

After him succeeded Lydgate, a monk of Bury, who wrote that bitter satire of *Piers Plowman.*[38] He spent most part of his time in translating the works of others, having no great invention of his own. He wrote for those times a tolerable and smooth verse.

Then followed Hardyng,[39] and after him Skelton, a poet laureate, for what desert I could never hear. If you desire to see his vein and learning, an epitaph upon King Henry the Seventh at Westminster will discover it.

In the latter end of King Henry the Eighth, for their excellent faculty in poesy were famous the right noble Henry, Earl of Surrey (whose *Songs and Sonnets* yet extant are of sweet conceit) and the learned, but unfortunate, Sir Thomas Wyatt.

In the time of Edward the Sixth lived Sternhold, whom King Henry, his father, a little before had made groom of his chamber for turning of certain of David's Psalms into verse; and merry John Heywood, who wrote his epigrams, as also Sir Thomas More his *Utopia,* in the parish wherein I was born, where either of them dwelt and had fair possessions.

About Queen Mary's time flourished Doctor Phaer, who in part translated Virgil's *Aeneids,* after finished by Arthur Golding.

[37] Chaucer was no divine, nor was either he or Gower ever knighted.
[38] There is no evidence that Lydgate wrote *Piers Plowman.*
[39] John Hardyng (1378–1465?), author of a *Chronicle* in stanzaic verse.

In the time of our late Queen Elizabeth, which was truly a golden age (for such a world of refined wits and excellent spirits it [40] produced whose like are hardly to he hoped for in any succeeding age), above others who honored poesy with their pens and practice (to omit her Majesty, who had a singular gift herein) were Edward, Earl of Oxford; the Lord Buckhurst; Henry, Lord Paget; [41] our phoenix, the noble Sir Philip Sidney; Mr. Edward Dyer; Mr. Edmund Spenser; Mr. Samuel Daniel, with sundry others, whom, together with those admirable wits yet living and so well known, not out of envy, but to avoid tediousness, I overpass. Thus much of poetry.

CHAPTER XI

Of Music

MUSIC, a sister to poetry, next craveth your acquaintance, if your genius be so disposed. I know there are many who are *adeo* ἄμουσοι [1] and of such disproportioned spirits that they avoid her company, as a great cardinal in Rome did roses at their first coming in, that, to avoid their scent, he built him an house in the champaign far from any town; or as with a rose not long since, a great lady's cheek in England, their ears are ready to blister at the tenderest touch thereof. I dare not pass so rash a censure of these as Pindar doth, or the Italian, having fitted a proverb to the same effect: Whom God loves not, that man loves

---

[40] From 1622; 1634 is.
[41] If Henry, Lord Paget (1537?–1568) wrote any verse, nothing is known of it.
[1] "So unmusical."

not music. But I am verily persuaded they are by nature very ill-disposed and of such a brutish stupidity that scarce anything else that is good and favorable to virtue is to be found in them. Never wise man, I think, questioned the lawful use thereof, since it is an immediate gift of heaven bestowed on man, whereby to praise and magnify his Creator, to solace him in the midst of so many sorrows and cares wherewith life is hourly beset; and that by song, as by letters, the memory of doctrine and the benefits of God might be forever preserved, as we are taught by that song of Moses and those divine Psalms of the sweet singer of Israel, who with his psaltery[2] so loudly resounded the mysteries and innumerable benefits of the Almighty Creator and the service of God advanced, as we may find in II Samuel 6:5, Psalm 33, 21, 43, and 4, 108, 3, and in sundry other places of Scripture which for brevity I omit.

But, say our sectaries, the service of God is nothing advanced by singing and instruments, as we use it in our cathedral churches; that is, by antiphony, rests, repetitions, variety of moods and proportions, with the like.

For the first, that it is not contrary but consonant to the Word of God so in singing to answer either, the practice of Miriam, the prophetess and sister of Moses, when she answered the men in her song will approve. For repetition, nothing was more usual in the singing of the Levites, and among the Psalms of David the 136th is wholly compounded of those two most graceful and sweet figures of repetition, symploce and anaphora.

For resting and proportions the nature of the Hebrew verse, as the meanest Hebrician knoweth, consisting many times of uneven feet, going sometime in this number, sometimes in that, one while, as St. Jerome saith, in the numbers of Sappho, another while of Alcaeus, doth of necessity require it. And wherein doth our practice of singing and playing with instruments in

[2] *Deut. 32. It was an instrument threesquare, of 72 strings, of incomparable sweetness.

his Majesty's chapel and our cathedral churches differ from the practice of David, the priests, and Levites? Do we not make one sign in praising and thanking God with voices and instruments of all sorts? [3] *Donec,* as St. Jerome saith, *reboet laquear templi,* the roof of the church echoeth again, and which, lest they should cavil at as a Jewish ceremony, we know to have been practiced in the ancient purity of the church. But we return where we left.

The physicians will tell you that the exercise of music is a great lengthener of the life by stirring and reviving of the spirits, holding a secret sympathy with them. Besides, the exercise of singing openeth the breast and pipes. It is an enemy to melancholy and dejection of the mind, which St. Chrysostom [4] truly calleth "the Devil's Bath." Yea, a curer of some diseases: in Apulia, in Italy, and thereabouts it is most certain that those who are stung with the tarantula are cured only by music. Besides the aforesaid benefit of singing, it is a most ready help for a bad pronunciation and distinct speaking, which I have heard confirmed by many great divines. Yea, I myself have known many children to have been holpen of their stammering in speech only by it.

Plato [5] calleth it "a divine and heavenly practice," profitable for the seeking out of that which is good and honest.

Homer [6] saith "musicians are worthy of honor and regard of the whole world"; and we know, albeit Lycurgus imposed most strait and sharp laws upon the Lacedaemonians, yet he ever allowed them the exercise of music.

Aristotle [7] averreth music to be the only disposer of the mind to virtue and goodness; wherefore he reckoneth it among those four principal exercises wherein he would have children instructed.

---

[3] *Chron. 2. cap. 5. vers. 12 et 13 [i.e., II Chron. 5:12–13].
[4] *In lib. de Augore animi.   [5] *'Δαιμόνιον πρᾶγμα.
[6] Τεμῆς ἔμμορί εἰσι καὶ αἰδοῦς. *Odyss.* 8.   [7] *Arist[otle] Politic.

Tully [8] saith there consisteth in the practice of singing and playing upon instruments great knowledge and the most excellent instruction of the mind, and for the effect it worketh in the mind he termeth it *stabilem thesaurum, qui mores instituit, componitque, ac mollit irarum ardores, etc.*, a lasting treasure, which rectifieth and ordereth our manners and allayeth the heat and fury of our anger, etc.

I might run into an infinite sea of the praise and use of so excellent an art, but I only show it you with the finger because I desire not that any noble or gentleman should, save at his private recreation and leisurable hours, prove a master in the same or neglect his more weighty employments, though I avouch it a skill worthy the knowledge and exercise of the greatest prince.

King Henry the Eighth could not only sing his part sure but of himself compose a service of four, five, and six parts, as Erasmus [9] in a certain epistle testifieth of his own knowledge.

The Duke of Venosa, an Italian prince, in like manner of late years hath given excellent proof of his knowledge and love to music, having himself composed many rare songs, which I have seen.

But above others who carrieth away the palm for excellency, not only in music, but in whatsoever is to be wished in a brave prince, is the yet-living Maurice, Landgrave of Hesse, of whose own composition I have seen eight or ten several sets of motets and solemn music set purposely for his own chapel, where, for the great honor of some festival, and many times for his recreation only, he is his own organist. Besides, he readily speaketh ten or twelve several languages. He is so universal a scholar that, coming, as he doth often, to his University of Marburg, what questions soever he meeteth with set up, as the manner is in the German and our universities, he will extempore dispute an hour or two, even in boots and spurs, upon them with

[8] *Cicero. Tusc. quaest. lib. 1.*   [9] *Erasm. in Farragine epist.*

their best professors. I pass over his rare skill in chirurgery, he being generally accounted the best bonesetter in the country. Who have seen his estate, his hospitality, his rich-furnished armory, his brave stable of great horses, his courtesy to all strangers, being men of quality and good parts, let them speak the rest.

But since the natural inclination of some men driveth them, as it were, perforce to the top of excellency, examples of this kind are very rare; yea, great personages many times are more violently carried than might well stand with their honors and necessity of their affairs; yet were it to these honest and commendable exercises savoring of virtue, it were well. But many, neglecting their duties and places, will addict themselves wholly to trifles and the most ridiculous and childish practices: As Europus, King of Macedonia, took pleasure only in making of candles; Domitian his recreation was to catch and kill flies, and could not be spoken with many times in so serious employment; Ptolomaeus Philadelphus was an excellent smith and a basketmaker; Alphonse Atestino, Duke of Ferrara, delighted himself only in turning and playing the joiner; Rodolph, the late emperor, in setting of stones and making watches; which and the like much eclipse state and majesty, bringing familiarity and, by consequence, contempt with the meanest.

I desire no more in you than to sing your part sure and at the first sight withal to play the same upon your viol or the exercise of the lute, privately, to yourself.

To deliver you my opinion whom among other authors you should imitate and allow for the best, there being so many equally good, is somewhat difficult. Yet as in the rest herein you shall have my opinion.

For motets and music of piety and devotion as well for the honor of our nation as the merit of the man, I prefer above all other our phoenix, Mr. William Byrd, whom in that kind I know not whether any may equal. I am sure none excel, even by the judgment of France and Italy, who are very sparing in the commendation of strangers in regard of that conceit they have of themselves. His *Cantiones sacrae,* as also his *Gradualia,* are mere angelical and divine, and, being of himself naturally disposed to gravity and piety, his vein is not so much for light madrigals or canzonets, yet his *Virginellae* [10] and some others in his first set cannot be mended by the best Italian of them all.

For composition I present next Ludovico de Victoria, a most judicious and a sweet composer. After him, Orlando di Lasso, a very rare and excellent author, who lived some forty years since in the court of the Duke of Bavaria. He hath published as well in Latin as French many sets; his vein is grave and sweet. Among his Latin songs his seven penitential Psalms are the best, and that French set of his wherein is *Susanna un jour,* upon which ditty many others have since exercised their invention.

For delicious air and sweet invention in madrigals Luca Marenzio excelleth all other whosoever, having published more sets than any other author else whosoever, and, to say truth, hath not an ill song, though sometime an oversight, which might be the printer's fault, of two eighths or fifths escaped him, as between the tenor and bass in the last close of "I must depart all hapless," ending according to the nature of the ditty most artificially [11] with a minim rest. His first, second, and third parts of *Thyrsis,* "Veggo dolce mio ben chi fae hoggi mio sole cantava," or "sweet singing Amaryllis" [12] are songs the Muses themselves might not have been ashamed to have had com-

[10] Byrd's *Psalms, Sonnets, and Songs of Sadness and Piety* (1588), no. xxiv, beginning "La virginella è simil' alla rosa."

[11] Artfully.

[12] "The proper titles of these, which are given in the above confused manner . . . are—'Tirsi morir, volea' (a5); 'Veggo dolce mio bene' (a4); 'Che fa hogg' il mio sole' (a5) and 'Cantava la più vaga' (a5), the English words 'Sweete Singing Amaryllis' being adapted to the music of the last."—Grove's *Dict. of Music,* V (1954), 576 n.

posed. Of stature and complexion he was a little and black man; he was organist in the Pope's chapel at Rome a good while; afterward he went into Poland, being in displeasure with the Pope for overmuch familiarity with a kinswoman of his; whom the Queen of Poland sent for by Luca Marenzio afterward, she being one of the rarest women in Europe for her voice and the lute, but, returning, he found the affection of the Pope so estranged from him that hereupon he took a conceit [13] and died.

Alphonso Ferrabosco, the father, while he lived, for judgment and depth of skill (as also his son yet living) was inferior unto none. What he did was most elaborate and profound and pleasing enough in air, though Master Thomas Morley censureth him otherwise. That of his, "I saw my lady weeping," and "The Nightingale," upon which ditty Master Byrd and he in a friendly emulation exercised their invention, cannot be bettered for sweetness of air or depth of judgment.

I bring you now mine own master, Horatio Vecchi of Modena, besides goodness of air most pleasing of all other for his conceit and variety, wherewith all his works are singularly beautified, as well his madrigals of five and six as those his canzonets printed at Nuremburg, wherein for trial sing his "Vivo in fuoco amoroso Lucretia mia," where upon "Io catenato moro," with excellent judgment, he driveth a crotchet through many minims, causing it to resemble a chain with the links. Again, in "S'io potessi raccor'i mei Sospiri," the breaking of the word *Sospiri* with crotchet and crotchet-rest into sighs, and that "fa mi un Canzone," etc., to make one sleep at noon, with sundry other of like conceit and pleasant invention.

Then that great master,[14] and master not long since of St. Mark's chapel in Venice, second to none for a full, lofty, and sprightly vein, following none save his own humor, who while he lived was one of the most free and brave companions of

---

[13] Took sick. [14] *Giovanni Croce.*

the world. His penitential Psalms are excellently composed and for piety are his best.

Nor must I here forget our rare countryman, Peter Philips, organist to their *altezzas* [15] at Brussels and now one of the greatest masters of music in Europe. He hath sent us over many excellent songs, as well motets as madrigals. He affecteth altogether the Italian vein.

There are many other authors very excellent, as Boschetto [16] and Claudio Monteverdi, equal to any before named; Guionnani Ferreti, Stephano Felis, Guilio Renaldi, Phillipe de Monte, Andrea Gabrieli, Cyprian de Rore, [Benedetto] Pallavicino, Geminiano,[17] with others yet living whose several works for me here to examine would be overtedious and needless. And for me please your own ear and fancy. Those whom I have before mentioned have been ever, within these thirty or forty years, held for the best.

I willingly, to avoid tediousness, forbear to speak of the worth and excellency of the rest of our English composers, Master Doctor Dowland, Thomas Morley, Master Alphonso, Master Wilbye, Master Kirby, Master Weelkes, Michael East, Master Bateson, Master Deering, with sundry others inferior to none in the world, how much soever the Italian attributes to himself, for depth of skill and richness of conceit.

Infinite is the sweet variety that the theoric of music exerciseth the mind withal, as the contemplation of proportion, of concords and discords, diversity of moods and tones, infiniteness of invention, etc. But I dare affirm there is no one science in the world that so affecteth the free and generous spirit with a more delightful and inoffensive recreation, or better disposeth the mind to what is commendable and virtuous.

[15] Highnesses.
[16] *Boschetto his motets of 8 parts, printed in Rome, 1594.
[17] I am unable to identify a musician of this name before Peacham's time of writing.

The commonwealth of the Cynethenses in Arcadia, falling from the delight they formerly had in music, grew into seditious humors and civil wars, which Polybius [18] took especially note of. And, I suppose, hereupon it was ordained in Arcadia that everyone should practice music by the space of thirty years.

The ancient Gauls in like manner, whom Julian [19] termed barbarous, became most courteous and tractable by the practice of music.

Yea, in my opinion, no rhetoric more persuadeth or hath greater power over the mind. Nay, hath not music her figures, the same which rhetoric? What is a revert but her antistrophe? her reports but sweet anaphoras? her counterchange of points, antimetaboles? her passionate airs but prosopopoeias? with infinite other of the same nature.

How doth music amaze us, when of sound discords she maketh the sweetest harmony! And who can show us the reason why two basins, bowls, brass pots, or the like of the same bigness, the one being full, the other empty, shall, stricken, be a just diapason in sound one to the other, or that there should be such sympathy in sounds that two lutes of equal size being laid upon a table and tuned unison, or alike in *Gamma, G sol re ut,* or any other string, the one stricken, the other shall answer it?

But to conclude, if all arts hold their esteem and value according to their effects, account this goodly science not among the number of those which Lucian placeth without the gates of hell as vain and unprofitable, but of such which are πηγαί τῶν καλῶν, the fountains of our lives' good and happiness. Since it is a principal means of glorifying our merciful Creator, it heightens our devotion, it gives delight and ease to our travails, it expelleth sadness and heaviness of spirit, preserveth people in concord and amity, allayeth fierceness and anger, and, lastly, is the best physic for many melancholy diseases.

[18] *Polyb[ius] *lib. 4. cap. 7.*   [19] *Julian Imperat. in Epist. ad Antioch.*

CHAPTER XII

Of Antiquities [1]

OUT of the treasury and storehouse of venerable antiquities I have selected these three sorts: statues, inscriptions, and coins, desiring you to take a short view of them ere you proceed any further.

The pleasure of them is best known to such as have seen them abroad in France, Spain, and Italy, where the gardens and galleries of great men are beautified and set forth to admiration with these kinds of ornaments. And indeed the possession of such rarities, by reason of their dead costliness, doth properly belong to princes or rather to princely minds. But the profitable necessity of some knowledge in them will plainly appear in the handling of each particular. Sure I am that he that will travel must both heed them and understand them if he desire to be thought ingenious and to be welcome to the owners. For next men and manners there is nothing fairly more delightful, nothing worthier observation, than these copies and memorials of men and matters of elder times, whose lively presence is able to persuade a man that he now seeth two thousand years ago. Such as are skilled in them are by the Italians termed *virtuosi*, as if others that either neglect or despise them were idiots or rakehells. And to say truth, they are somewhat to be excused if they have all *Leefhebbers*, as the Dutch call them, in so high estimation, for they themselves are so great lovers of them (*et similis simili gaudet* [2]) that they

---

[1] This chapter appeared for the first time in the edition of 1634.
[2] "Like pleases like."

purchase them at any rate and lay up mighty treasures of money in them. Witness that exchequer of metals in the cabinets of the great Duke of Tuscany, for number and rarity absolutely the best in the world, and not worth so little as 100,000 pound. For proof whereof do but consider the number of those which Peter de Medici lost at Florence upon his banishment and departure thence, namely, a hundred thousand pieces of gold and silver and brass, as Philip de Commines reporteth, who mentioneth them as an infinite treasure. And yet Peter was but a private man and not to be any way compared with the dukes of his house that have been since, all of them great and diligent gatherers of all manner of antiquities. And for statues, the Diana of Ephesus in the marble chamber at Paris, Laocoön and Nilus in Belvedere at Rome, and many more are pieces of inestimable value. But the matchless and never-too-much admired Toro in Cardinal Farnese's garden outstrippeth all other statues in the world for greatness and workmanship. It comprehendeth a great bull and, if my memory fail me not, seven or eight figures more as great as the life, all of one entire piece of marble, covered with a house made of purpose and estimated at the wealth of a kingdom, as the Italians say, or all other statues put together.

And now to spend a few lines on statues in general. I began with them because I suppose them of greater standing and antiquity than either inscriptions or coins. For, not to speak of inscriptions, but of the *genius* of them, writing and letters, they seem to be so much the later invention of the two (I mean in regard of statues), as it was more obvious and easier for man to figure and represent his outward body than his inward mind. We hear of Laban's idols long before the two tables of the commandments, and they are the first of either kind mentioned in the Holy Scriptures. And in the stories of the East and West Indies we find idols among those savages that had neither writing nor money. Coins I place in the rear because they are made up of both the other. For most commonly they consist (I speak not of the material but formal part) either of an inscription or an image or both, so that the other two may justly claim precedency of coins, seeing they are the ingredient simples that compound them. It is true that we read in Genesis that Abraham bought the field of Machpelah for 400 shekels, and that, you may say, is long before we hear either of idols or writings. But withal it is said there, not that he told out so much money to Ephron, but that (*appendit*) he weighed it, so that 400 shekels there are to be taken for so much in weight, not in coin, *pecunia numerata*.[3] At Rome, Servius was the first (as Remeus thinks and Snellius is persuaded) or Numa Pompilius (as Suidas out of Suetonius allegeth and Isidore believeth) that first stamped money. But their Penates were far more ancient, which their poets (and particularly Virgil) say Aeneas brought with him from Troy. I will leave this point with this by-observation: that if the story of Aeneas be true, the coins that some antiquaries have of Priamus and Troy may very well be suspected of forgery. For it is not likely that they that had time enough to bring away their household gods should be forgetful as to leave all their money behind them, and so negligent withal as, after their settling in Italy, never to put in practice a thing so useful and necessary as coined money is till Servius' or Numa's time.

To return to our statues. They, I propound, are chiefly Greek and Roman, and both these either of deities or mortals. And where should the magazine of the best of these be but where the seat of the last empire was? Even at Rome, where, though they be daily found and digged for, yet are they so extremely affected and sought after that it is, as with jennets in Spain, felony to convey them thence without special license. But in Greece and other parts of the Grand Seignior's dominions (where sometime there were more statues standing than men living,

---

[3] "Money counted."

so much had art outstripped nature in these days) they may be had for the digging and carrying. For by reason of the barbarous religion of the Turks, which alloweth not the likeness or representation of any living thing, they have been for the most part buried in ruins or broken to pieces, so that it is a hard matter to light upon any there that are not headless and lame, yet most of them venerable for their antiquity and elegancy. And here I cannot but with much reverence mention the every-way Right Honorable Thomas Howard, Lord High Marshal of England, as great for his noble patronage of arts and ancient learning as for his birth and place; to whose liberal charges and magnificence this angle of the world oweth the first sight of Greek and Roman statues, with whose admired presence he began to honor the gardens and galleries of Arundel House about twenty years ago, and hath ever since continued to transplant old Greece into England. King Charles also, ever since his coming to the crown, hath amply testified a royal liking of ancient statues by causing a whole army of old foreign emperors, captains, and senators all at once to land on his coasts, to come and do him homage and attend him in his palaces of St. James and Somerset House. A great part of these belonged to the late Duke of Mantua, and some of the old Greek marble bases, columns, and altars were brought from the ruins of Apollo's Temple at Delos by that noble and absolutely complete gentleman, Sir Kenelm Digby, knight. In the garden at St. James there are also half a dozen brass statues, rare ones cast by Hubert Le Sueur, his Majesty's servant now dwelling in St. Bartholomew's, London, the most industrious and excellent statuary,[4] in all materials, that ever this country enjoyed.

The best of them is the Gladiator, molded from that in Cardinal Borghese's villa by the procurement and industry of

[4] Sculptor.

120

ingenious Master Gage. And at this present the said Master Sueur hath divers other admirable molds to cast in brass for his Majesty, and among the rest that famous Diana of Ephesus above named. But the great horse with his Majesty upon it, twice as great as the life, and now well-nigh finished, will compare with that of the New Bridge at Paris or those others at Florence and Madrid, though made by Sueur his master, Jean Bologne, that rare workman who not long since lived at Florence. At York House, also, the galleries and rooms are ennobled with the possession of those Roman heads and statues which lately belonged to Sir Peter Paul Rubens, knight, that exquisite painter of Antwerp. And the garden will be renowned so long as Jean Bologne's Cain and Abel stand erected there, a piece of wondrous art and workmanship. The King of Spain gave it his Majesty at his being there, who bestowed it on the late Duke of Buckingham. And thus have we of late years a good sample of this first sort of antiquities accompanied with some novelties which, nevertheless, cannot but fall short of those in other countries where the love and study of them is far ancienter and the means to come by them easier.

It is not enough for an ingenuous gentleman to behold these with a vulgar eye, but he must be able to distinguish them and tell who and what they be. To do this, there be four parts: First, by general learning in history and poetry, whereby we are taught to know Jupiter by his thunderbolt, Mars by his armor, Neptune by his trident, Apollo by his harp, Mercury by his wings on his cap and feet or by his caduceus, Ceres by a handful of corn, Flora by her flowers, Bacchus by his vine-leaves, Pomona by her apples, Hercules by his club or lion's-skin, Hercules Infans by his grasping of snakes, Comedy by a vizard in her hand, Diana by a crescent, Pallas by her helmet and spear, and so generally of most of the deities. Some mortals also are known by their cognizances, as Laocoön by his snakes stinging him to death, Cleopatra by a viper, Cicero by his wart, and a great many more.

But because all statues have not such properties and badges, there is a second way to discern them, and that is by their coins. For if you look upon them sideways and consider well their half-faces, as all coins show them, you will easily know them. For this is certain (which also witnesseth the exquisite diligence of ancient works), that all the faces of any one person, whether on old coins or stones, in greater or less volume, are all alike. Insomuch as if you bring an old, rusty coin to any reasonable antiquary, if he can see but a nose upon it or a piece of the face, he will give you a shrewd guess at him, though none of the inscription be to be seen.

A third and very good way to distinguish them is by the book of collection of all the principal statues that are now to be seen at Rome, printed there with the title, *Icones statuarum quae hodie visuntur Romae.*[5]

He that is well acquainted with this book will easily discover at first sight a great many of them. For there are a number of statues of one and the same person, and he that knows one of them knows all the rest.

The fourth and last help, and without which the rest are weak, is to visit them in company of such as are learned in them and by their help to grow familiar with them and so practice their acquaintance.

Now besides the pleasure of seeing and conversing with these old heroes (whose mere presence, without any further consideration, reared on their several pedestals and ranked decently either *sub dio,*[6] where they show best, or in a stately gallery, cannot but take any eye that can but see), the profit of knowing them redounds to all poets, painters, architects, and generally to such as may have occasion to employ any of

[5] "Images of statues which are to be seen at Rome."
[6] "Out of doors."

these and, by consequent, to all gentlemen. To poets for the presentation of comedies, tragedies, masques, shows, or any learned scene whatsoever, the properties whereof can neither be appointed nor judged of but by such as are well seen in statue-craft. To painters for the picturing of some exquisite arm, leg, torso, or wreathing of the body, or any other rare posture, whether smooth or forced.

Besides, "rounds" (so painters call statues and their fragments) may be had when the life cannot, and have the patience to stand when the life will not. And this is a maxim among artists in this kind, that a round is better to draw by and comes nearer the life than any flat or painting whatsoever. And if a painter will meddle with history, then are old statues to him the only life itself. I call Rubens to witness, the best story painter of these times, whether his knowledge in this kind hath not been his only making. But his statues before named and his works do testify it for him. Yea, while he is at work, he useth to have some good historian or poet read to him, which is rare in men of his profession, yet absolutely necessary. And as for architects, they have great use of statues for ornaments for gates, arches, friezes, and cornices for tombs and divers other buildings.

And therefore I may justly conclude that the study of statues is profitable for all ingenuous gentlemen, who are the only men that employ poets, painters, and architects, if they be not all these themselves. And if they be not able to judge of their works, they well deserve to be cozened.

Inscriptions follow, wherein I will be shorter, because I can address you to better helps in them than in the former. For of the discovery of statues I know not any that have written so much as hath been now delivered, but as for inscriptions divers authors have unfolded them. I will name you one for all, and that is Lipsius, who hath set forth the collections of another and many of his own besides. This book of inscriptions is in folio and printed at Antwerp, *ex officina Plantiniana Raphelengii,*[7] where in the very beginning he bestoweth a leaf or two in deciphering unto us and explaining the sense of old characters or short writing, as that D. M. stands for *Diis Manibus,* which you usually find upon urns; L. M. Q. for *Lubens Meritoque;* D. D. D. for *Dat, Dicat, Dedicat;* D. S. P. for *De Suo Posuit;*[8] and so for the rest which I leave that I may not be a plagiary verbatim.

And because inscriptions are not only of stones, as of urns, altars, vessels, gates, aqueducts, etc., such as Lipsius handleth, but of coins also, I will give you two or three examples of these with which and some practice you may easily unriddle the rest. *M. Durmius III. VIR. A. A. A. F. F.* Read it thus: *Marcus Durmius triumvir, auro argento aere flando feriundo.*[9] Again, *Imp. Caes. Trajano. aug. ger. dac. P. M. tr. p. Cos. vi. P. P.* Express it thus: *Imperatori Caesari Trajano Augusto, Germanico, Dacico, Pontifici Maximo, tribunitiae potestatis, Consuli sextum. Patri Patriae.*[10] Where, by the way, I must commend a learned note of Stephen Pasquier in his *Recherches de la France,* that the word *Papa* comes from an old mistake of *Pater Patriae,* written thus: Pa. Pa., as we have it in many coins. If it be demanded how we know that these characters are to be thus read, I answer, by divers other inscriptions where they are written at large. I must not forget to tell you that Arundel House is the chief English scene of ancient inscriptions, which Master John Selden, the best and learnedest antiquary in this

[7] "From the Plantin shop of Raphelengius."

[8] "In divine hands; willingly and justly; he gives, he devotes, he dedicates; he gave from his own."

[9] "Gold, silver, and bronze, cast and stamped in the triumvirate of M. Durmius."

[10] "Emperor Caesar Trajan Augustus Germanicus Dacicus, Pontifex Maximus, for the sixth time consul with power of the tribuneship, father of his country."

kingdom, hath collected together under the title of *Marmora Arundeliana*.[11] You shall find all the walls of the house inlaid with them and speaking Greek and Latin to you. The garden especially will afford you the pleasure of a world of learned lectures in this kind.

The use of these old memorials tends to the illustration of history and of the antiquity of divers matters, places, and cities which otherwise would be obscure, if not altogether unknown, unto us. I will give you the next at hand for example. Upon a reverse of Nerva we find a team of horses let loose with this inscription: *Vehiculatione per Italiam remissa*. Whereby we learn, which no historian remembers, that the Roman emperors did command all the carriages of the country everywhere, that Nerva did remit that burden and acquitted them of it, and that this grievance was so heavy that coins were stamped in remembrance of the emperor's goodness that eased them of it.

I come to the last of our select antiquities, coins. They are much easier to come by than either statues or inscriptions. First, in regard of their numerous quantity and, secondly, by reason of their small bulk, which make the purchase cheaper and the carriage lighter. Those I intend to handle are Hebrew, Greek, and Latin. Of these divers learned men have treated, chiefly, Budaeus, Agricola, Alciati, Carolus Molinaeus, Hotomannus, Didacus Covarruvius, Willebrordus Snellius, and Edowardus Brerewood. These authors treat of the several species or kinds of old coins, and of their weight and value in moneys of these times. There are others that have collected and represented the stamps, that is, the figures and inscriptions of all the individual or several pieces that ever they saw or read of. Such are Goltzius for Greek pieces, Fulvius Ursinus for consulars, Occo for imperials, and for the rates at which they are now bought and sold in Germany, Hulsius. To these I add

[11] I.e., "the marbles of Arundel House."

Savot his *Discours des medailles*,[12] which excels for the material part or metal of old coins. And for anything omitted by the rest I will deliver the sum of what these have of the several species of these old moneys, but the study of individuals I will leave to your own reading and handling.[13]

.   .   .   .   .

Thus may you reduce all other sums in any old author to what species or kind of money you please.

And by this time you may perceive that without this money-learning you must be forced to balk [14] the most material passages of ancient history. For what is there in the affairs and occurrences of this world that can be thought more material or worthier our pause and consideration than money, the price of all things, and the chief commander in wars or peace?

Finally there is also much learned pleasure and delight in the contemplation of the several figures stamped on each side of these antique coins. I will let pass the content a man has to see and handle the very same individual things which were in use so many ages ago. For books and histories and the like are but copies of antiquity, be they never so truly descended unto us, but coins are the very antiquities themselves. But would you see a pattern of the *rogus,* or funeral pile, burnt at the canonization of the Roman emperors? would you see how the augur's hat and *lituus* [15] were made? would you see true and undoubted models of their temples, altars, deities, columns, gates, arches, aqueducts, bridges, sacrifices, vessels, *sellae curules*,[16] ensigns and standards, naval and mural crowns, amphitheaters, circi,

---

[12] More correctly, Louis Savot, *Discours sur médailles antiques* (Paris, 1627).

[13] Here are omitted from the text pages 113–123, which are concerned solely with the worth of ancient Hebrew, Greek, and Roman coins in English money.

[14] Pass by.   [15] "Wand."

[16] "Curule chairs," the official seats of consuls, praetors, etc.

baths, chariots, trophies, *ancilia*,[17] and a thousand things more? Repair to old coins and you shall find them, and all things else that ever they did, made, or used, there shall you see them excellently and lively represented. Besides, it is no small satisfaction to an ingenuous eye to contemplate the faces and heads, and in them the characters of all these famous emperors, captains, and illustrious men whose actions will be ever admired, both for themselves and the learning of the pens that writ them.

CHAPTER XIII

Of Drawing, Limning, and Painting, with the Lives of the Famous Italian Painters

SINCE Aristotle numbereth *graphice*, generally taken, for whatsoever is done with the pen or pencil (as writing fair, drawing, limning, and painting) among those his παιδεύματα, or generous practices of youth in a well-governed commonwealth, I am bound also to give it you in charge for your exercise at leisure, it being a quality most commendable and so many ways useful to a gentleman. For should you, if necessity required, be employed for your country's service in following the war, you can describe no plot, manner of fortification, form of *battalia*,[1] situation of town, castle, fort, haven, island, course of river, passage through wood, marsh, over rock, mountain, etc. (which a discreet general doth not always commit to the eye of another), without the help of the same. In all mathematical demonstrations nothing is more required in our travel in foreign regions. It bringeth home with us from the farthest part of the world

[17] "Shields." [1] "Order of battle."

in our bosoms whatsoever is rare and worthy of observance, as the general map of the country, the rivers, harbors, havens, promontories, etc., within the landscape; of fair hills, fruitful valleys; the forms and colors of all fruits, several beauties of their flowers; of medicinable simples never before seen or heard of; the orient colors and lively pictures of their birds, the shape of their beasts, fishes, worms, flies, etc. It presents our eyes with the complexion, manner, and their attire. It shows us the rites of their religion, their houses, their weapons, and manner of war. Besides, it preserveth the memory of a dearest friend or fairest mistress. And since it is only the imitation of the surface of nature, by it as in a book of golden and rare-limned letters, the chief end of it, we read a continual lecture of the wisdom of the Almighty Creator by beholding even in the feather of a peacock [2] a miracle,[3] as Aristotle saith.

And that you should not esteem basely of the practice thereof, let me tell you that in ancient times painting was admitted into the first place among the liberal arts, and throughout all Greece taught only to the children of noblemen in the schools, and altogether forbidden to be taught to servants or slaves.

In no less honor and esteem was it held among the Romans, as we find in Pliny and many others, who everywhere advance the professors, and the dignity of the practice thereof nothing base or servile, since one of the most noble families in Rome, the Fabii, thought themselves much honored by the addition of that surname *Pictor*. For the first of that name, although he was most honorably descended, honored with many titles, consulships, and triumphs, excellently learned in the laws, and besides accounted in the number of the orators of his time, yet he thought his skill in painting added to these honors, and his memory would hear the better of posterity for that he was endued with so excellent a quality. For after with his own hand he had painted the temple of Salus round about within and

[2] *Iob 29:16 [error for 39:13]   [3] *Τι θαυμαστόν.

finished his work, he wrote in fair letters in an eminent place *Quintus Fabius pinxi.*[4]

Neither was it the exercise of nobility among the ancients only, but of late days and in our times we see it practiced by the greatest princes of Europe without prejudice to their honors. Francis the First, King of France, was very excellent with his pencil, and the virtuous Margaret of Navarre, besides her excellent vein in poesy, could draw and limn excellently. The like is reported of Emmanuel, Duke of Savoy.[5]

Nor can I overpass the ingenuity and excellency of many nobles and gentlemen of our own nation herein, of whom I know many, but none in my opinion who deserveth more respect and admiration for his skill and practice herein than Master Nathaniel Bacon of Brome in Suffolk (younger son to the most bountiful-minded Sir Nicholas Bacon, knight and eldest baronet), not inferior, in my judgment, to our skillfulest masters. But certainly I know not what favorable aspect of heaven that right noble and ancient family hath which produceth, like delicate fruits from one stem, so many excellent in several qualities that no one name or family in England can say the like.

Painting is a quality I love, I confess, and admire in others, because ever naturally from a child I have been addicted to the practice hereof. Yet when I was young I have been cruelly beaten by ill and ignorant schoolmasters when I have been taking, in white and black, the countenance of some one or other (which I could do at thirteen or fourteen years of age, besides the map of any town according to geometrical proportion, as I did of Cambridge when I was of Trinity College and a junior sophister), yet could they never beat it out of me. I remember one master I had (and yet living not far from St. Albans) took me one time drawing out with my pen that pear tree and boys throwing at it at the end of my Latin grammar;

[4] "I, Quintus Fabius, painted this."   [5] *Lomazius.*

which he, perceiving, in a rage struck me with the great end of the rod and rent my paper, swearing it was the only way to teach me to rob orchards; besides, that I was placed with him to be made a scholar of and not a painter, which I was very likely to do; when, I well remember, he construed unto me the beginning of the first ode in Horace, "*Edite,* set ye forth, *Maecenas,* the sports, *atavis regibus,* of our ancient kings." But leaving our ingenious master, to our purpose.[6]

. . . . .

CHAPTER XV

Of Armory, or Blazon of Arms, with the Antiquity and Dignity of Heralds

IT IS meet that a noble or gentleman who beareth arms and is well descended be not only able to blazon his own proper coat, derive by pedigree the descent of his family from the original, know such matches and allies as are joined to him in blood, but also of his prince, the nobility, and gentry where he liveth; which is not of mere ornament, as the most suppose, but diversely necessary and of great consequence; as, had I fortuned to have lived in those times when that fatal difference of either R O S E was to be decided by the sword, with which party in equity and conscience could I have sided had I been ignorant

[6] Those pages (127–154) of the 1634 edition which give specific information on how to draw and paint, and which set forth the sketchy notices of Italian painters, have been omitted. Also omitted is the chapter following, XIV, "Of Sundry Blazons, both Ancient and Modern" (pp. [154–160], no pagination 154–159, 160 mispaginated 154).

of the descent and pedigree royal and where the right had been by inheritance of blood, match, or alliance?

How should we give nobility her true value, respect, and title without notice of her merit? And how may we guess her merit without these outward ensigns and badges of virtue which have anciently been accounted sacred and precious, withal discern and know an intruding upstart, shot up with the last night's mushroom, from an ancient-descended and deserved gentleman whose grandsires have had their shares in every foughten field by the English since Edward the First, or myself a gentleman know mine own rank, there being at this instant the world over such a medley (I had almost said motley) of coats, such intrusion by adding or diminishing into ancient families and houses, that had there not been within these few years a just and commendable course taken by the Right Honorable the Earl Marshals for the redress of this general and unsufferable abuse, we should, I fear me, within these few years see yeomen as rare in England as they are in France?

Besides, it is a contemplation full of pleasing variety and, for the most part, sympathizing with every noble and generous disposition; in substance the most refined part of natural philosophy, while it taketh the principles from geometry, making use almost of every several square and angle. For these and other reasons I desire that you would bestow some hours in the study of the same. For a gentleman honorably descended to be utterly ignorant herein argueth in him either a disregard of his own worth, a weakness of conceit, or indisposition to arms and honorable action, sometime mere idiotism, as Seigneur Gaulart, a great man of France, and none of the wisest, inviting on a time many great personages and honorable friends to his table, at the last service a marchpane was brought in, which being almost quite eaten, he bethought himself and said: "It was told me that mine arms were bravely set out in gold and colors upon this marchpane, but I have looked round about it and cannot see them." "Your lordship," said one of his men, "ate them up yourself but now." "What a knave," quoth Monsieur Gaulart, "art thou! Thou didst not tell me before I ate them, that I might have seen what they were!"

The dignity and place of an herald among the ancient Romans was very great, that same *Ius Feciale*, or Law of Arms, being first instituted by Ancus Martius, as Livy testifieth,[1] though some ascribe it to Numa Pompilius, who ordained a college of heralds.

The office of an herald was to see that the Romans made not war unjustly with any of their confederates, to determine of war, peace, leagues, agreements, wrongs taken or offered by them on their enemies, and the like.[2]

Now if the enemy had offered them wrong or taken away anything from them by violence, they first sent messengers to demand their right and the restoring of that they had taken away; which was done in a solemn form, and the words pronounced distinctly and with a loud voice. And this manner of delivering their message was called *clarigatio*. The form was this: *Iovem ego testem facio, si ego impie iniusteque illas res dedier populo Romano mihique exposco, tunc patriae compotem nunquam sinas esse.*[3] If they refused their demands or to make restitution, first all league and friendship, if any were betwixt them, being renounced and broken, after thirty days which they solemnly observed, they proclaimed open war and with fire and sword invaded the enemy's country and by force recovered their own.

Neither was it lawful for either consul or senate or any of the common people to take up arms against an enemy without the consent and approbation of the heralds.

---

[1] *Lib. 1.   [2] *Dionysius Halicarnass. antiquit. Rom. lib. 1.*
[3] "I make Jove my witness that if I unjustly and against religion demand the surrender of those things to myself and the people of Rome, let me never again enjoy my fatherland."—Livy i.32.

Amongst the heralds there was one, the chief and above the rest, whom they called *Pater Patratus,* and he was chosen one who was to have children, and his own father alive. Him one of the inferior heralds, crowning his head and temples with vervain, made him the chief or king, either in concluding peace or denouncing war.[4]

The most ancient form of denouncing war is set down at large by Livy. The Tiburians are reported to have been so just in their making war and defiance of their enemies that they would never meet them but first they would send them word of the day, place, yea, the very hour they meant to fight.[5]

Moreover, if any complaint by the enemy were made of breach of the league, the heralds examined the truth and, having found out the authors, they delivered them up to the enemy to do with them as he listed. Or if any without the consent of the people, senate, and heralds either fought or made peace, entered league, etc., the Romans freed themselves again by delivering up the authors to their enemies. So were the Consuls T. Veturius and Sp. Postumius for their error at Candium and making peace with the Samnites contrary to the will of the people and the senate, together with T. Numitius and Q. Aemilius, tribunes, delivered to the enemy. The words of Postumius himself, who made request that himself with the rest who had offended might be delivered to the enemy, are thus recorded by Livy: *Dedamur per feciales nudi vinctique; exolvamus religione populum, si qua obligavimus, ne quid divini humanive obstet quo minus justum piumque de integro ineatur bellum.* The form and words on their delivery to the enemy's hands were these: *Quandoquidem hisce homines iniussu populi Romani Quiritum foedus ictum iri sposponderunt atque*

---

[4] *Baltasar Ayala de jure et officiis Bell. lib.* 1. [Denouncing is equivalent to declaring.]

[5] *Liv[y] lib.* 1 *et* Gel[lius] *lib.* 16. *cap.* 4 *et Dion. Halicarn. lib.* 2. *antiquit. Rom.*

*ob rem noxam nocuerunt, ob rem quo populus ROMANUS
scelere impio sit solutus hosce homines vobis dedo.*[6] And so
many years after was C. Mancinus delivered to the Numantines,
with whom he had entered into league contrary to the will and
without the knowledge of the senate.[7]

Heralds also examined and determined of wrongs and in-
juries done unto ambassadors, and punished them by delivering
up in like manner the parties offending unto the nation or state
offended.

They looked also to the strict observing of every branch of
the league or truce. In brief, their authority was comprised in
these few words: *Belli, pacis, foederum, induciarum, oratorum,
feciales iudices sunto.*[8]

Spurius Fusius was the first herald that ever was created
among the Romans and had the name of *Pater Patratus* in the
war which Tullus Hostilius made against old Latins.

Their privileges were great and many and too long for me
to reckon up. And to conclude, for farther search of their in-
stitution, privileges, and office, I refer you to Jean Le Féron,
a French author.

I purpose not here to enter into a large field and absolute
discourse of blazonry, with all the laws and terms thereof,
having been already prevented by Bara, Upton, Gerrard Leigh,

---

[6] *Livius lib.* 9. [The two passages are translated thus by B. O. Foster:
(1) "Let us be given up, I propose, by the fetials, stripped and bound;
let us release the people from their religious obligation, if in any such we
have involved them, that no obstacle, divine or human, may block the
way to a just and righteous renewal of the war." (2) "Whereas these men,
unbidden by the Roman People of the Quirites, have guaranteed that a
treaty should be ratified, and by so doing have committed an injury; to
the end that the Roman People may be absolved of heinous guilt, I deliver
up these men to you."]

[7] *Cicero Offic. lib. 3. Flor. lib. 2. cap. 18. Vide Nonium Marcellum,
lib. 3.*

[8] *Cicero lib 2. de legibus.* ["The fetials shall be judges of war, peace,
leagues, truces, orators."]

Master Ferne, Master Guillim (late Portcullis pursuivant) in his methodical *Display of Heraldry,* with sundry others. So that, in a manner, more cannot be said than hath been—myself, besides, having written something of this subject heretofore [9] —but only to point unto you as a stranger upon the way the fairest and shortest cut unto your journey's end in this art.[10]

.   .   .   .   .

CHAPTER XVI

Of Exercise of the Body

I now from your private study and contemplation bring you abroad into the open fields for exercise of your body by some honest recreation, since Aristotle requireth the same in the education of nobility and all youth, since the mind from the ability of the body gathereth her strength and vigor.[1] Anciently by the civil law these kinds of exercises were only allowed of,[2] that is, πυγμαχία, δίσκος, δρόμος, δίαλμα, and πάλη which are the exercise of arms by single combat, as running at tilt-barrians,[3] etc., quoiting, throwing the hammer, sledge, and suchlike, running, jumping, leaping, and, lastly, wrestling. For the first, it is the most noble; those epithets of ἱπποχάρμης and ἱππόδαμος [4]

[9] See the third book of Peacham's *Graphice* (1612)—variant title: *The Gentleman's Exercise.*

[10] The remainder of the chapter, pages 158 (for 164) to 207 (for 213), which deals with the practice of blazonry, is here omitted.

[1] For other comments on exercises and recreation, see *The Worth of a Penny,* ed. 1669, pp. 30–32.

[2] *In L. Soloni ff. de Alea lusu et Aleator.* [1622 *In Solent. ff. de Aleae lusu et Aleator.*]

[3] Barriers; all eds. barrians.   [4] "Horseman and tamer of horses."

have been the attributes of kings and princes, whose delight in ancient times was to ride and manage great horses. Hereby you are enabled for command and the service of your country. "And what," saith Tully, "can be more glorious than to be able to preserve and succor our country when she hath need of our help?" It is the only commendation that Sallust gives to Jugurtha, "who did not," saith he, "give himself over to be corrupted by sloth and riot" (as many of our gallants nowadays do), "but as it is the custom of that nation exercised himself by riding, throwing the dart, and running with his equals. And though he excelled all other in the height of glory, notwithstanding, he was held dear and beloved of all men," [5] etc. And Caesar used the exercise of riding so much and hereby became so active and skillful that, laying his hands behind him, he would put his horse to his full career, make him on the sudden take hedge or ditch, and stop him, put him into a ring, and the like. And Marius, after he had been seven times consul and fourscore years of age, exercised himself daily in the field of Mars with the Roman youth, instructing them to handle their weapon, to ride, etc. The like also did Pompey even to his last expedition. And Virgil, speaking, I take it, of the Spartan youth, saith:

> *Venatu invigilant pueri, sylvasque fatigant,*
> *Flectere ludis* [6] *equos et spicula tendere cornu,* etc.

And at this day it is the only exercise of the Italian nobility, especially in Naples, as also of the French, and great pity that it is no more practiced among our English gentry.

Running at the tilt is a generous and a martial exercise, but hazardous and full of danger; for many hereby, even in sport, have lost their lives, that I may omit Henry, the French king,

[5] Sallust vi.

[6] From 1622; 1634 *jugis.* "The boys give great attention to hunting and tire the forests; they wheel their horses in games and shoot shafts from the bow."

with many other princes and noble personages of whom history is full.

Tilting and tournaments were invented by Manuel Comnenus, Emperor of Constantinople, as saith Nicetas,[7] who wrote about the year 1214. Before his time we read not anywhere that this exercise was used under the Roman Empire.

The same Nicetas reporteth of solemn jousts or tournaments which the said Manuel Comnenus showed unto the Latins at Antioch, what time they went to make war in the Holy Land. For, the Latins making a brave show in their rich armor, well horsed with their lances, and presenting themselves before the Emperor, the Emperor, to show them that the Grecians were nothing inferior unto them in bravery or courage, appointed a day when they and the Latins for the glory of either empire should so many to so many—and with lances without points—encounter either, bravely mounted, and made one of the number with his Grecians, who, saith Nicetas, so bravely carried himself that he unhorsed two Latin commanders, casting them from the saddle to the ground.

In our lances nowadays, of what wood soever they are made of, there is nothing so much danger as hath been in times past; neither in our modern practice of war have they almost any use at all. The Prince of Orange hath abandoned them, having not a lance in his whole army, but hath carbines in their room. Spinola hath some troops of them, yet not many, as I observed. Those of Hertogenbosch under Grobbendoncke are esteemed the best horse Spinola hath.

For throwing and wrestling, I hold them exercises not so well beseeming nobility, but rather soldiers in a camp or a prince's guard. Neither have I read or heard of any prince or general commended for wrestling save Epaminondas Achmat, the last Grand Seignior and Emperor of Turkey, who took great delight

---

[7] *Guido Panciroli in lib. de reb. noviter repertis, tit.* 20. [So 1634; 1622 *Pancirillo*. 1622 adds *Nicetas. lib.* 3.]

in throwing the hammer and was so strong that he overthrew his stoutest Janizaries, there being reared in Constantinople, for one extraordinary cast which none could come near, two great pillars of marble.

Running and agility of body have been esteemed most commendable in the greatest princes and commanders that ever lived. And the old Romans, next after trial made of their strength and view of their limbs and person, chose their soldiers by running. For it is an old custom among them to assault the enemy by running all close together in gross to the charge. And Caesar [8] tells us that strokes are surer laid on and the soldiers made more nimble and ready in running and by motion. Homer gave Achilles (which perhaps some of our great-feathered gallants would disdain, yet haply better deserve) the epithet of ὠκύπους, or swift-footed. And Alexander,[9] we read, excelled all his court in running. Sertorius, a brave commander under Caesar, could nimbly run up the most steep mountains, leap broken and unpassable rocks, and like invious [10] places, insomuch as Metellus being sent with a powerful army against him, he knew neither where to find him nor how to come by him, by reason of his nimble footmanship. Thereupon he sent his colleague Pompey, who, being by Sertorius overthrown at the first encounter, escaped very narrowly, for, being unhorsed and having received a great wound, while the soldiers were busied in striving, some for his horse, others for the most rich furniture (his caparison, bridle, saddle, stirrups being in a manner all of gold and shining with precious stones of inestimable value), watching his opportunity, by swiftness of foot escaped from them all and returned safe to his quarter.

Leaping is an exercise very commendable and healthful for

[8] *C. Caesar in Epistolis.*

[9] *To cure the smallness of his voice, he would usually run up a hill— a fit emblem for such as when they have ascended the height of preferment both look and speak big.

[10] Without roads, trackless.

the body, especially if you use it in the morning, as we read Alexander and Epaminondas did. Upon a full stomach or to bedward it is very dangerous and in no wise to be exercised.

The skill and art of swimming is also very requisite in every noble and gentleman, especially if he looketh for employment in the wars, for hereby, besides the preserving of his own life upon infinite occasions, he may many ways annoy his enemy. Horatius Cocles [11] only by the benefit of swimming saved his country, for when himself alone had long defended and made good the bridge over Tiber against the Etruscans, the Romans broke it down behind him, wherewith in his armor he cast himself into the river and, notwithstanding a shower of darts and arrows were sent after him, swam with safety into the city, which rewarded him with a statue erected in the market place and as much land as he could encompass with a plow in a day.

And as desperate was the attempt of a number of Roman gentlemen in the first Carthaginian War, who, leaping in a night from the hatches of their ships into the sea, by main force thrust and drew the Carthaginian ships into the haven and delivered them to Luctatius, their general.

And as resolute was that attempt, no whit inferior to the former, of Gerrard and Harvey, two gentlemen of our own nation, who in '88 in the fight at sea swam in the nighttime and pierced with augers or suchlike instruments the sides of the Spanish galleons and returned back safe to the fleet.

Scaevola, a man of inestimable courage, and who came with Caesar in his expedition for Britain, after he had made good a whole day together a mighty rock or passage against the Britons, in the nighttime, loaden with double arms and an heavy shield, cast himself into the deep and swam safe to Caesar and his fleet.

Neither is it to be wondered at that the Romans were so skillful in swimming, for they were daily exercised in the same

[11] *Liv. lib.* 2. *Decad.* 1.

after their other exercises and had a place in the river of Tiber appointed unto them for the same purpose, adjoining to the Field of Mars, and another of great depth, rough and full of whirlpits on purpose to exercise their horses in.

Shooting also is a very healthful and commendable recreation for a gentleman. Neither do I know any other comparable unto it for stirring every part of the body. For it openeth the breast and pipes, exerciseth the arms and feet with less violence than running, leaping, etc. Herein was Emperor Domitian so cunning that, let a boy a good distance off hold up his hand and stretch his fingers abroad, he would shoot through the spaces without touching the boy's hand or any finger.

And Commodus, saith Herodian, had so good an aim that he would fix on the brow of a deer two shafts as evenly and spreading in distance as if they had been his own horns.

But for the further excellence and use of this exercise [12] I refer you to that excellent book of Mr. Ascham's entitled *Toxophilus,* wherein you shall find whatsoever is requisite to be known of a complete archer.

Hawking and hunting are recreations very commendable and befitting a noble or gentleman to exercise. Hunting especially, which Xenophon commendeth to his Cyrus, calling it a gift of the gods bestowed first upon Chiron for his uprightness in doing justice, and by him taught unto the old heroes and princes, by whose virtue and prowess, as enabled by this exercise, their countries were defended, their subjects and innocents preserved, justice maintained. For there is no one exercise that enableth the body more for the war than hunting, by teaching you to endure heat, cold, hunger, thirst, to rise early, watch late, lie and fare hardly. And Eusebius is of opinion that wild beasts were of purpose created by God that men by chasing

[12] "Excellence and use of this exercise" from 1622; 1634 edition is misprinted "excellence book of Mr. Ascham's; I refer you to that excellent book of Mr. Ascham's."

and encountering them might be fitted and enabled for warlike exercises. Hereupon Alexander, Cyrus, and the old kings of Persia employed themselves exceeding much herein, not to purchase venison and purvey for the belly, but to maintain their strength and preserve their health by increasing and stirring up the natural heat within, which sloth and sitting still wastes and decays; to harden the bodies by labor against the enemy; and, withal, to search out the natures of wild beasts, which known, they might leave the same recorded to their posterity.[13] And the famous physician Quercetan [14] above all other exercises commendeth this as most healthful and keepeth the body sound and free from disease.

The old Lord Gray, our English Achilles, when he was deputy of Ireland, to insure his sons for the war, would usually in the depth of winter, in frost, snow, rain, and what weather soever fell, cause them at midnight to be raised out of their beds and carried abroad on hunting till the next morning, then, perhaps, come wet and cold home, having for a breakfast a brown loaf and a moldy cheese, or, which is ten times worse, a dish of Irish butter. And in this manner the Spartans and Laconians dieted and brought up their children till they came unto man's estate.

Hawking was a sport utterly unknown to the ancients, as Blondinus and P. Jovius in the second book of his history, where he entreateth of the Muscovitish affairs, witnesseth, but was invented and first practiced by Frederick Barbarossa when he besieged Rome. Yet it appeareth by Firmicus [15] that it was known twelve hundred years since, where he speaketh of falconers and teachers of other birds. And indeed beyond him I think it can nowhere be found that falconry was known. There have been many who have written of falconry: Frederick the

---

[13] **Langius, lib. 2. Epist. 59.*
[14] **Quercetan in Diaetetico polyhist. sect. 2. cap. 11.*
[15] **Iul. Firmicus lib. 5. cap. 8.*

Second, Emperor of Germany (whom Melanchthon [16] worthily commendeth and equaleth to the ancient heroes for his many victories achieved by his valor, his skill in all learning, being able to speak fourteen several languages, his liberality, magnificence, affability, mildness, etc., insomuch that in him alone, saith he, ended and died the remainder of ancient majesty) wrote hereof two excellent books which Joachim Camerarius, having by him the first copy in a manuscript, published together with a treatise of Albertus Magnus of the nature of hawks, and printed it at Nuremberg. Budaeus [17] hath also written a large discourse of hunting and hawking, part whereof is annexed to the latter end of Henry Estienne's French and Latin dictionary. In English, Master Blundeville's book [18] is the best that I know.

By the canon law [19] hawking was forbidden unto clergymen, as afterward hunting, by reason the exercise and instruments wherewith beasts are slain are military and not so well agreeing, as they give the reason, with spiritual warfare. But I cannot see but that they, many of them being great princes and pillars of the church, daily employed and pressed with the weight of state affairs, may have their recreations as well as others. But to prevent their pastime there is such an order taken with their parks that many of our best bishoprics can nowadays scarce show one of ten or twenty. Norwich had thirteen parks and of all other was most unjustly dealt withal. If they had taken away twelve and left the odd [20] one, it had been indifferent, but to rob the church of all was more than too much.

But as we allow not altogether that severe education of the old Spartans in their children, hazarding many times the healths of young and tender bodies by some tedious ague, yea, also

[16] *Melanchthon lib.* 5, *Cronic.* folio 789.
[17] *Budaeus de venatione et Aucupio.*
[18] Thomas Blundeville's *Exercises* (1594 and later eds.)
[19] *Concil. Aurel. cap.* 4. *Agathensi.* 55. *Epaunensi.* 3. 44. *Extr. de Clerico venatore.*
[20] From 1622; 1634 old.

their lives by the mischance of a leap or stumbling of their horse, so as much do I detest the effeminacy of the most that burn out day and night in their beds and by the fireside, in trifles, gaming, or courting their yellow mistresses all the winter in a city, appearing but as cuckoos in the spring one time in the year to their tenants, leaving the care of keeping good houses at Christmas to the honest yeomen of the country.

Some again are so intent on their pleasure that they never care for keeping within, as sometime was Mithridates, that it is reported of him: "For seven years' space together he never came within house, neither in city nor in the country." And Barnaby,[21] Viscount of Milan, was so carried away with the love of hunting that he made a law: whosoever should kill any wild boar or had killed any in five years before that his statute was enacted (contrary to ancient edict) or were privy to the eating of any at any gentleman's table should be imprisoned and tortured after a grievous manner. Besides, he afflicted the country marvelously by dispersing many thousands of dogs to be kept and brought up in villages and among the peasants to their infinite trouble and charge. Mahomet,[22] son to Amurath, on the contrary, when he made war in Caramania, turned out of service seven hundred of his father's falconers and caused as many of old huntsmen to follow arms and his camp instead of the kennel.

[21] *Volatteran. lib. 7. antiqu. Jovius in Barnaba.*
[22] *Chalcondylas lib. 7.*

CHAPTER XVII

Of Reputation and Carriage in General

THERE is no one thing that setteth a fairer stamp upon nobility than evenness of carriage and care of our reputation, without which our most graceful gifts are dead and dull, as the diamond without his foil. For hereupon as on the frontispiece of a magnificent palace are fixed the eyes of all passengers and hereby the height of our judgments (even ourselves) is taken. According to that of the wise man, "by gait, laughter, and apparel, a man is known what he is." [1] Wherefore I call it the crown of good parts and loadstone of regard. The principal means to preserve it is temperance and that moderation of the mind wherewith as a bridle we curb and break our rank and unruly passions, keeping, as the Caspian Sea, ourselves ever at one height without ebb or reflux. And albeit true it is that Galen saith, we are commonly beholden for the disposition of our minds to the temperature of our bodies, yet much lieth in our power to keep that fount from empoisoning by taking heed to ourselves, and, as good Cardinal Pole once said, to correct the malignity of our stars with a second birth. For certainly under grace it is the root of our reputation and honest fame, without the which, as one saith, "We are dead long before we are buried."

For moderation of the mind and affections, which is the ground of all honesty, I must give you that prime receipt the kingly prophet doth to a young man, teaching him wherewith to cleanse his way; that is, "by keeping," saith he,[2] "O Lord, thy

[1] *Ecclesiastic. [Cf. below, p. 198.]   [2] *Psal. 119:9.

statutes," meaning the fear of God in general, without which (he ever first striking at the head) our judgments are depraved and, left to ourselves, we are not able to give anything his true esteem and value. Therefore, first to be truly honest is to be truly religious, for if the fear of men be a great motive to keep ourselves within compass, much more will the fear of God recall us from our lusts and intemperance. Hereby the mind getteth the dominion and upper hand, wisely governing that goodly kingdom nature hath allotted her. And if it was sometime said of Fabius, *Citius solem e sua sphaera divelli quam Fabium ab honestate potuisse,*[3] how heedfully ought a Christian, who carrieth the lantern in his hand, look to his feet, when an heathen could go so directly in the dark only by the glimpse of nature and without stumbling?

Moreover, since the civil end of our life is, *ut in honore cum dignitate vivamus,*[4] you shall find withal good learning and the arts to confer a great help and furtherance hereunto, being a polisher of inbred rudeness and our informity,[5] and a curer of many diseases our minds are subject unto. For we learn not to beg to ourselves admiration from other, or boastingly to lay to view so rich and precious furniture of our minds, but that we may be useful to others, but first to ourselves, lest, as some precious receipt, while we keep that in a box which can cure another, ourselves lie lame and diseased.

The first use, then, hereof (I mean your learning) as an antidote against the common plague of our times: let it confirm and persuade you that as your understanding is by it ennobled with the richest dowry in the world, so hereby learn to know your own worth and value and in the choice of your companions[6] to entertain those who are religious and learned. For, as

---

[3] "The sun could more quickly have been torn from its orbit than Fabius from honesty."
[4] "That we may live in honor with dignity."
[5] Want of form; deformity.   [6] See also below, pp. 203 ff., 218, 244.

I said heretofore, converse of old was the mother of skill and all virtuous endeavors, so say I now, of all vices and baseness, if regard be not had. Therefore, hold friendship and acquaintance with few, and those I could wish your betters, at the least of your own rank, but endear yourself to none: *gaudebis minus, minus dolebis.*[7] The best natures I know delight in popularity and are pliable to company-keeping, but many times buy their acquaintance at overdear a rate, by being drawn either into base actions and places of which they are ashamed forever after, or to needless expense by laying out or lending to importunate base and shameless companions, gaining loss of their moneys, time, sorrow, and grief of friends, the disrepute of the better, and, lastly, contempt of the vilest among the common vulgar.

Antiochus Epiphanes, King of Asia, for his popularity and delight in company was surnamed "The Mad."[8] And likewise for the same Appius Claudius was deprived of his office and, fearing besides shame the hatred of the senate, counterfeiting blindness, forever after kept himself at home.[9] We read also of a certain King of the Goths who, making his soldiers his drinking companions, was for his free and kind heart at the last drowned by them in a tub of ale.[10]

Nor mistake me that I swerve so much on this side that I would deny a prince or gentleman the benefit of discourse and converse with the meanest, for majesty and greatness cannot always stand so bent but that it must have the remission and relaxation sometime to descend from the court to the cottage, which cannot choose but give it the better taste and relish. Adrian, the Emperor, would most courteously confer with the meanest, detesting those his high-minded courtiers who, under a color of preserving his estate and honor, envied him this

---

[7] "You will have less fun, but you will have less grief."
[8] °*Athenaeus lib.* 5. *cap.* 4.   [9] °*Diodorus lib.* 20.
[10] °*I. Magnus lib.* 7. *cap.* 7.

sweetness of humility and privacy.[11] Vespasian in like manner was wont not only to salute the chief senators of Rome, but even private men, inviting them many times to dine and sup with him, himself again going unto their houses.[12] Philopoemen was so courteous and went so plain that his hostess in Megara took him for a servingman.[13] And certainly this affability and courtesy in greatness draweth our eyes, like flowers in the spring, to behold and with admiration to love it wheresoever we find it.

There is no better sign, saith one,[14] in the world of a good and virtuous disposition than when a prince or gentleman maketh choice of learned and virtuous men for his companions, for presently he is imagined to be such a one as those to whom he joineth himself. Yea, saith Aristotle, it is a kind of virtuous exercise to be conversant with good and understanding men.

Whom, then, you shall entertain into the closet of your breast, first sound their religion; then look into their lives and carriage, how they have been reckoned of others; lastly, to their quality, how or wherein they may be useful unto you, whether by advice and counsel, direction, help in your studies, or serviceable in your exercise and recreations.

There is nothing more miserable than to want the counsel of a friend and an admonisher in time of need; [15] which hath been and is daily the bane of many of our young gentlemen, even to the utter ruin of themselves and their posterity forever, who, when like Alciati's figtree upon the high and inaccessible rock they are out of reach and cannot be come unto by men who would dress and preserve them, espied afar off, are only preyed upon and haunted by vultures and daws. And while one addeth fuel to the fire of his expense, for the which he is like to pay twenty for two at twenty and one,[16] another sootheth him in

---

[11] *Erasm. *lib. 6. Apotheg. ex Spartian.*   [12] * *Xiphilinus.*
[13] *Plutarch. in Philopoem[en].*   [14] *Philip Commines, cap.* 34.
[15] *Ludovic. Vives.*

[16] Perhaps the meaning is "to pay twenty pounds for two at a game of twenty and one."

play, knowing the best fishing is in troubled waters; another
tendereth him a match of light stuff.[17] All at once preying for
themselves, these green things of sixteen or eighteen are quite
devoured before they are ripe.

Wherefore I must next commend unto you frugality, the
mother of virtues,[18] a virtue which holdeth her own, layeth out
profitably, avoideth idle expenses, superfluity, lavish bestowing
or giving, borrowing, building, and the like, yet, when reason
requireth, can be royally bountiful, a virtue as requisite in a
noble or gentleman as the care of his whole estate and preserva
tion of his name and posterity, yet as greatly wanting in many
as they come short of the reputation and entire estates of their
forefathers, who account thrift the object of the plow or shop
too base and unworthy their consideration, while they impose
their fair estates and most important business upon a cheating
steward or crafty bailiff, who in a few years, like the young
cuckoo, are ready to devour their feeder, and themselves, like
sleepy pilots, having no eye to the compass or sounding their
estates, are run on ground ere they be aware.

First, then, as soon as you shall be able, look into your estate,
laboring not only to conserve it entire, but to augment it either
by a wise forethought, marriage, or by some other thrifty means.
And think the more ye are laden with abundance, the more, like
a vine, ye have need of props and your soundest friends to advise you. Neither do I imagine you will be so rash as to give
no ear to good counsel, to your ruin, as Caesar did when he
refused a book of a poor soldier wherein the intended plot
against him was discovered.

Marcus Cato, who was so victorious in war, so prudent in
peace, so eloquent in the oratory, learned in the laws, neglected
not thereby his estate, but looked, as Livy saith of him, even into

[17] Provides him with a paramour?

[18] *Iustine.* [For other passages on frugality and thrift, see *The Worth
of a Penny*, ed. 1669, pp. 8–9, 17 ff.]

his husbandry himself. And Plutarch [19] writeth of Philopoemen, a great and famous commander, that notwithstanding his great affairs and employments he would every morning be stirring by break of day and either to dressing of his vines, digging, or following his plow. And Cicero, to heighten the honor of King Deiotarus, reporteth thus of him: *In Deiotaro sunt regiae virtutes, quod te, Caesar, ignorare non arbitrer, sed praecipue singularis et admiranda frugalitas.*[20] And the Romans had a law: [21] He who could not look into his own estate and employ his land to the best should forfeit the same and be held for a fool or a madman all his life after. Aristides,[22] albeit he was an excellent man otherwise, yet herein he was so careless that at his death he neither left portion for his daughters nor so much as would carry him to the ground and defray the charge of his funeral.

Be thrifty also in your apparel and clothing [23] lest you incur the censure of the most grave and wisest censor, *Cui magna corporis cultus cura, ei magna virtutis incuria.*[24] And Henry the Fourth, last King of France, of eternal memory, would oftentimes merrily say by the outside only he could sound the depth of a courtier, saying, "Who had least in them made the fairest show without, inviting respect with gold lace and great feathers, which will not be won with toys." [25] Neither, on the contrary, be so basely parsimonious or frugal, as is written of one of the Kings of France in whose accounts in the exchequer are yet remaining: item, so much for red satin to sleeve the King's old

---

[19] *Plutarch in Philopoemen.*

[20] *Cic[ero] pro Deiotaro.* ["Deiotarus possesses the royal virtues—a fact, Caesar, of which you are not ignorant, but especially the virtue of a singular and admirable frugality."]

[21] *Iulianus ff. de cura furio[sa].*   [22] *Plutarch in Aristide.*

[23] Cf. below, pp. 198 ff., "Of Following the Fashion," and *The Worth of a Penny*, ed. 1669, pp. 26 ff.

[24] "Excessive attention to the body results in great neglect of virtue."

[25] Cf. below, p. 198.

149

doublet; item, a halfpenny for liquor for his boots, and so forth. Or to be known by a hat or a doublet ten or twenty years, then with some miserable usurer curse the maker for the lightness of his felt or stuff, murmuring it will not last to see the revolution of the first mover. But using that moderate and middle garb which shall rather lessen than make you bigger than you are; which hath been and is yet observed by our greatest princes, who in outside go many times inferior to their grooms and pages. That glory and champion of Christendom, Charles the Fifth, would go, except in time of war, as plain as any ordinary gentleman, commonly in black or sad stuff without lace or any other extraordinary cost, only his Order of the Golden Fleece about his neck in a ribband, and was so naturally frugal, not out of parsimony, being the most bountiful-minded prince that ever lived, that, as Guicciardini reporteth of him, if any one of his points had chanced to break, he would tie it of a knot and make it serve again.[26] And I have many times seen his Excellence, the Prince of Orange that now is, in the field in his habit as plain as any country gentleman, wearing commonly a suit of hair-colored slight stuff of silk, a plain gray cloak and hat with a green feather, his hatband only exceeding rich. And Ambrose Spinola, general for the Archduke, when he lay in Wesel at the taking of it in, one would have taken but for an ordinary merchant in a plain suit of black. And the plainness of the late Duke of Norfolk derogated nothing from his esteem. So that you see what a pitiful ambition it is to strive to be first in a fashion, and a poor pride to seek your esteem and regard from worms, shells, and tailors, and buy the gaze of the staring multitude at a thousand or fifteen hundred pounds, which would apparel the Duke and his whole Grande Consiglio of Venice. But if to do your prince honor at a tilting, employed in embassage, coming in of some great stranger, or you are to give entertainment to princes or noble personages at your

[26] Cf. below, pp. 198.

houses, as did Cosmo de Medici, or haply ye command in the wars, spare not to be brave with the bravest. Philopoemen caused his soldiers to be spare in apparel and diet, saith Plutarch,[27] and to come honorably armed into the field; wherefore he commanded in goldsmiths' shops to break in pieces pots of gold and silver, and to be employed in the silvering of bits, gilding of armors, inlaying of saddles, etc. "For the sumptuous cost upon warlike furniture doth encourage and make great a noble heart, but in other sights it carrieth away men's minds to a womanish vanity and melting the courage of the mind, as Homer saith it did Achilles when his mother laid new arms and weapons at his feet." The Spaniard when he is in the field is glorious in his cassock and affecteth the wearing of the richest jewels; the French, huge feathers, scarlet and gold lace; the English, his arms rich and a good sword. The Italian's pride is in his Neapolitan courser; the Germans and Low Dutch, to be daubed with gold and pearl, wherein, say they, there is no loss except they be lost. But herein I give no prescription.

I now come to your diet,[28] wherein be not only frugal for the saving of your purse, but moderate in regard of your health, which is impaired by nothing more than excess in eating and drinking (let me also add tobacco-taking). Many dishes breed many diseases, dulleth the mind and understanding, and not only shorten but take away life. We read of Augustus that he was never curious in his diet, but content with ordinary and common viands. And Cato the Censor, sailing into Spain, drank of no other drink than the rowers or slaves of his own galley. And Timotheus, Duke of Athens, was wont to say (whom Plato invited home to him to supper) they found themselves never distempered.[29] Contrary to our feastmakers, who suppose the glory of entertainment and giving the best welcome to consist in needless superfluities and profuse waste of good creatures,

---

[27] * In Philopoem[en]. [28] * Seneca. Rhet. 7. Cicero pro Caelio.
[29] *Plutarch de Sanitate tuenda.

as Scylla made a banquet that lasted many days, where there was such excessive abundance that infinite plenty of victuals were thrown into the river and excellent wine above forty years old spilt and made no account of. But by surfeiting and banqueting at last he got a most miserable disease and died full of lice.[30]

And Caesar, in regard of his Libyan triumph, at one banquet filled two and twenty thousand rooms with guests and gave to every citizen in Rome ten bushels of wheat and as many pounds of oil and, besides, three hundred pence in money.[31]

We read of one Smyndirides who was so much given to feasting and his ease that he saw not the sun rising nor setting in twenty years. And the Sybarites forbade all smiths and knocking in the streets and what thing soever that made any noise to be within the city walls, that they might eat and sleep; whereupon they banished cocks out of the city and invented the use of chamberpots and bade women a year before to their feasts that they might have leisure enough to make themselves fine and brave with gold and jewels.[32]

Above all, learn betimes to avoid excessive drinking,[33] than which there is no one vice more common and reigning and ill-beseeming a gentleman, which, if grown to a habit, is hardly left; remembering that hereby you become not fit for anything, having your reason degraded, your body distempered, your soul hazarded, your esteem and reputation abased, while you sit taking your unwholesome healths—*ut iam vertigine tectum ambulet et geminis exsurgat mensa lucernis*—

> until the house about doth turn
> And on the board two candles seem to burn.[34]

[30] * Sabell[icus] Ennead[es]. 2.

[31] * Suetonius. Every Roman penny was about sevenpence halfpenny. C. Rhodigin. lib. 6. cap. 35.

[32] *Suida. et Politian lib. 15. Miscellan.

[33] Cf. below, pp. 238–239, 246, and *The Worth of a Penny*, ed. 1669, pp. 10 ff.

[34] *Iuvenal. Satyr [vi. 304–305].

By the Levitical Law, who had a glutton or a drunkard to their son, they were to bring him before the elders of the city and see him stoned to death. And in Spain at this day they have a law that the word of him that hath been convicted of drunkenness shall not be taken in any testimony. Within these fifty or threescore years it was a rare thing with us in England to see a drunken man, our nation carrying the name of the most sober and temperate of any other in the world. But since we had to do in the quarrel of the Netherlands, about the time of Sir John Norris his first being there, the custom of drinking and pledging healths was brought over into England; wherein let the Dutch be their own judges if we equal them not. Yea, I think rather excel them.

Tricongius and the old Romans had laws and statutes concerning the art of drinking,[35] which, it seems, are revived and by our drunkards observed to an hair, it being enacted "that he who after his drink faltered not in his speech, vomited not, neither reeled, if he drank off his cups cleanly, took not his wine in his draught, spit not, left nothing in the pot, nor spilt any upon the ground," he had the prize and was accounted the bravest man. If they were contented herewith, it were well, but they daily invent new and damnable kinds of carousing (as that in north Holland and Friesland, though among the baser sort, of "Upsy Monikedam," which is, after you have drunk out the drink to your friend or companion, you must break the glass full upon his face, and, if you miss, you must drink again), whence proceed quarreling, reviling, and many times execrable murders,[36] as Alexander was slain in his drunkenness,[37] and Domitius, Nero's father, slew Liberius outright because he would not pledge him a whole carouse. And hence arise most quarrels among our gallant drunkards, unto whom if you read a lecture of sobriety and how in former ages their forefathers drank water,

[35] *Plin[ius] lib. 4. Historiae sub finem.*
[36] *Prov. 23.
[37] Peacham's error for "Clitus was slain by Alexander," etc.

they swear water is the frog's drink and ordained only for the driving of mills and carrying of boats.

Neither desire I you should be so abstemious as not to re-member a friend with a hearty draught, since wine was created to make the heart merry, for "what is the life of man if it want wine?" [38] Moderately taken, it preserveth health, comforteth and disperseth the natural heat over all the whole body, allays choleric humors, expelling the same with the sweat, etc., tem-pereth melancholy, and, as one saith, hath in itself ἑλκυστικόν τι πρὸς τὴν φιλίαν,[39] a drawing virtue to procure friendship.

At your meat to be liberal and freely merry is very healthy and comely, and many times the stranger or guest will take more content in the cheerliness of your countenance than in your meat. Augustus the Emperor had always his mirth greater than his feasts. And Suetonius saith of Titus, Vespasian's son, he had ever his table furnished with mirth and good company. And the old Lord Treasurer of England, Lord William Burghley, how employed soever in state affairs, at his table he would lay all business by and be heartily merry.

Charles the Great used at his meats to have some history read, whereof he would afterwards discourse. And Francis the First, King of France, would commonly dispute of history, cosmogra-phy, poetry; his Majesty, our sovereign, altogether in points and profound questions of divinity.[40] When I was in Utrecht and lived at the table of that honorable gentleman, Sir John Ogle, lord governor, whither resorted many great scholars and cap-tains, English, Scottish, French, and Dutch, it had been enough to have made a scholar or soldier to have observed the several disputations and discourses among many strangers, one while of sundry forms of battles, sometime of fortification, of fire-works, history, antiquities, heraldry, pronunciation of languages, etc., that his table seemed many times a little academy.

---

[38] *Ecclesiast[icus]. 31. vers. 27.   [39] *Athenaeus.
[40] Sleidan[us]. lib. 19.

The Complete Gentleman

In your discourse be free and affable, giving entertainment in a sweet and liberal manner, and with a cheerful courtesy seasoning your talk, at the table among grave and serious discourses, with conceits of wit and pleasant invention, as ingenious epigrams, emblems, anagrams, merry tales, witty questions and answers, mistakings, as a melancholy gentleman, sitting one day at table where I was, started up upon the sudden and, meaning to say "I must go buy a dagger," by transposition of the letters, said "Sir, I must go die a beggar."

A plain country man, being called at an assize to be a witness about a piece of land that was in controversy, the judge calling, said unto him, "Sirrah, how call you that water that runs on the south side of this close?" "My lord," quoth the fellow, "our water comes without calling." [41]

A poor soldier with his musket and rest in Breda came one day in and set him down at the nether end of the Prince of Orange his table as he was at dinner, whither none might be privileged under the degree of a gentleman at the least to come. The gentleman-usher of the prince demanded of him if he were a gentleman. "Yes," quoth the soldier, "my father was a goldsmith of Antwerp." "But what can you do in your father's trade?" Quoth he, "I can set stones in mortar, for he was a bricklayer and helped masons in their works."

For epigrams, Pasquin [42] will afford you the best and quickest I know. You shall have them all bound in two volumes. I remember he tells us once upon a Sunday morning Pasquin had a foul shirt put on and, being asked the cause, Pasquin made answer, "Because my laundress is become a countess." [43]

You shall have a taste of some of my anagrams, such as they are.

---

[41] *This happened in Norfolk.
[42] *Pasquin, a marble image in Rome, on which they use to fix libels.
[43] *Because an earl in Rome had married a chambermaid. [See below, pp. 196–197.]

Henry Peacham

Upon the Prince

CAROLUS
O clarus [44]
Charles, Prince of Wales
All France cries, "O help us."

Of the Queen of Bohemia and Princess Palatine of the Rhine, my gracious lady,

ELISABETHA STEUARTA
Has artes beata velit.[45]

Being requested by a noble and religious lady who was sister to the old Lord De La Warr, to try what her name would afford, it gave me this:

JANE WEST
En tua, Jesu.[46]

And upon the name of a brave and beautiful lady, wife to Sir Robert Mordaunt, son and heir to Sir Le Strange Mordaunt, knight and baronet in the County of Norfolk:

AMIE MORDAUNT
Tu more Dianam.
Tum ore Dianam.
Minerva, domat.
Me induat amor.
Nuda, O te miram.
Vi tandem amor.[47]

Upon the name of a fair gentlewoman in Italian:

[44] "O distinguished one."
[45] "May the happy one like these arts." This anagram had been used in 1612 for an emblem in Minerva Britanna, p. 14.
[46] "Jesus, behold thine own."
[47] "Thou outdoest Diana in behavior. Thou outdoest Diana in presence. Minerva conquers. May love envelop me. O unadorned one, I wonder at thee." "To the end, love with strength (virtue)."

156

The Complete Gentleman

ANNA DUDLAEIA
E' la nuda Diana.[48]

Upon a sweet and a modest young gentlewoman, Mistress

MARIA MEUTAS
Tu a me amaris.[49]

To comfort myself living in a town where I found not a scholar to converse withal, nor the kindest respect, as I thought, I gave this my posy, the same backward and forward,

SUBI DURA A RUDIBUS.[50]

Of Master Doctor Hall, Dean of Worcester, this, added to the body of a glory, wherein was written "Jehovah" in Hebrew, resembling the Deity,

JOSEPH HALL
All his hope.

Of a virtuous and fair gentlewoman at the request of my friend who bare her good will:

FRANCIS BARNEY
Barres in fancy.

And this,

THEODOSIA DIXON
A DEO DIXIT HONOS: or
O Dea, dixit honos.[51]

Of my good friend, Master Doctor Dowland, in regard he had slipped many opportunities in advancing his fortunes, and

---

[48] "She is the unadorned Diana." This anagram had appeared in *Minerva Britanna,* p. 175.
[49] "Thou art loved by me."
[50] "Endure harsh things from rude people."
[51] "Honor has spoken from God," or "Honor has spoken, O goddess."

a rare lutenist as any of our nation, besides one of our greatest masters of music for composing. I gave him an emblem with this:

JOHANNES DOULANDUS
Annos ludendo hausi.[52]

There were at one time in Rome very witty and unhappy libels cast forth upon the whole Consistory of Cardinals in the nature of emblems. I remember Cardinal Farnese had for his part a stork devouring a frog, with *Mordeo non mordentes;* [53] Bellarmine, a tiger fast chained to a post, in a scroll proceeding from the beast's mouth in Italian: *Da mi mia liberta, vederete chi io sono;* that is, give me my liberty, you shall see what I am, meaning, perhaps, he would be no longer, etc. And those were very knavish that were thrown up and down the court of France, the escutcheon or arms of the party on the one side of a pasteboard and some ingenious device on the other; as one had the arms of the house of de Medici of Florence on the one side, on the other an inkhorn with the mouth turned downward, with this tart pasquil: *Elle faut d'encre;* [54] and so of the whole court.

Emblems and impresas, if ingeniously conceited, are of dainty device and much esteem. The invention of the Italian herein is very singular. Neither do our English wits come much behind them, but rather equal them every way. The best that I have seen have been the devices of tiltings, whereof many are reserved in the private gallery at Whitehall, of Sir Philip Sidney's, the Earl of Cumberland, Sir Henry Leigh, the Earl of Essex, with many others, most of which I once collected with intent to publish them, but the charge dissuaded me.

But above all in your talk and discourse have a care ever to

[52] "I have used up years in playing." This anagram had appeared in *Minerva Britanna,* p. 74.
[53] "I do not devour those who bite."   [54] "Ink is needed."

speak the truth, remembering there is nothing that can more prejudice your esteem than to be lavish-tongued in speaking that which is false, and disgracefully of others in their absence. The Persians and Indians had a law that whosoever had been thrice convicted of speaking untruth should, upon pain of death, never speak word all his life after.[55] Cato would suffer no man to be praised or dispraised, but used always such discourse as was profitable to the hearers, for, as one saith, *Dicteria minuunt majestatem.* Jests and scoffs do lessen majesty and greatness, and should be far from great personages and men of wisdom.

CHAPTER XVIII

Of Travel

I will conclude with travel,[1] which many disallow in gentlemen, yea, and some great travelers themselves; but methinks they are as one who hath filled his own belly and denieth the dish to his fellow. In my opinion nothing rectifieth and confirmeth more the judgment of a gentleman in foreign affairs, teacheth him knowledge of himself, and settleth his affection more sure to his own country than travel doth. For if it be the common law of nature that the learned should have rule over and instruct the ignorant, the experienced the unexperienced,[2] what concerneth more nobility, taking place above other, than to be learned and wise, and where may wisdom be had but from

---

[55] *Plato saith it is only allowed physicians to lie for the comfort of the sick.

[1] The first edition of 1622 ended with this chapter. For further remarks on travel, see the essay below, pp. 217 ff.

[2] *Dionys. Halicarnass.*

many men and in many places? Hereupon we find the most eminent and wise men of the world to have been the greatest travelers (to omit the patriarchs and apostles themselves in Holy Writ), as Plato, Pythagoras, Aristotle, Theophrastus, Osiris, King of Egypt, who traveled a great part of the world and caused to be engraven upon his sepulcher,[3] "Hereunder I lie, King Osiris, eldest son of Saturn, who have left no part of the world unsearched whitherto I have not come, teaching again whatsoever I have found, for the use and commodity of mankind." And Xenophon, to intimate unto us the benefit and excellent use of travel, saith that Cambyses by his travel learned many excellent things which he taught Cyrus, his son, and, having traveled as far as Meroë, as a perpetual monument of his long voyage he built a city in the form of a Persian shield. And it was the usual boast of Alexander, said Archelaus,[4] a cosmographer, that he had found out more with his eyes than other kings were able to comprehend in thought. And to no small commendation of himself Menelaus in Homer reporteth that he had been in Egypt, Cyprus, Phoenicia, and seen Thebes, having an hundred gates, and at every gate two hundred horsemen for the guard. But, say some, few of our gentlemen are bettered by their travel, but rather return home worse than they went in manners and many times in religion. Therefore it were better they tarried still at home, according to Claudian:

> *Foelix qui patriis aevum transegit in agris;*
> *Ipsa domus puerum quem videt, ipsa senem,*
> *Qui baculo nitens, in qua reptavit arena,*
> *Unius numerat saecula longa casae.*

He's blest who in's own country ends his days,
Whose homestead sees his old age and his birth, etc.[5]

[3] *Diodor. Sic[ulus] lib. 1.*

[4] *Diog. Laert[ius] lib. 2. in vita Archel[ai].*

[5] Claudian, *Carminum minorum corp.* xx (lii). P's translation is meager and free: "Happy is he who has passed his life in his paternal fields, whose

But this happiness is but *puerorum beatitudo*,[6] as one saith, and the greatest unhappiness to the truly generous and industrious mind.

If, therefore, you intend to travel, you must first propound unto yourself the end, which either is *ad voluptatem vel ad utilitatem*, pleasure or profit. For the first, everyone naturally affecteth, and the fool himself is tickled, with the sight of strange towns, towers, and habits of people. Therefore you must hold you to the other, which is profit, which again hath two branches, your own private or the public; your private, as the recovery of your health by some outlandish means, as the water of the spa, some physician famous for his cure in such and such kinds, change of air, or gaining, as a merchant, by traffic, or some profession wherein you excel others. The public is the general good of your country, for which we are all born, it challenging a third part of us.

But before you travel into a strange country, I wish you, as I have heretofore said, to be well acquainted with your own. For I know it by experience that many of our young gallants have gone over with an intent to pass by nothing unseen or what might be known in their places, when they have been most ignorant here in their own native country, and strangers to their just reproof could discourse and say more of England than they.

In your passage I must give you in either hand a light: preservation and observation—preservation of your mind from errors and ill manners; of your body from distemperature either by overeating, drinking, violent or venereal exercise.

For there is not any nation in the world more subject unto surfeits than our English are, whether it proceedeth from the

---

house sees him as a boy and as an old man, who, supported by his staff, counts the great age of the same cottage and the ground whereon he crawled as a baby."

[6] "The happiness of boys."

constitution of our bodies, ill agreeing with the hotter climates, or the exchange of our wholesome diet and plenty for little and ill-dressed, or the greediness of their fruits and hot wines, wherewith only we are sometime constrained to fill our bellies, I am not certain. No less peril there is *ab istis callidis et calidis solis filiabus*,[7] which almost in every place will offer themselves or be put upon you by others.

Keep the fountain of your mind from being empoisoned, especially by those serpents, error and atheism, which you shall find lurking under the fairest flowers. And though you hear the discourses of all and listen to the charms of some, discover your religion or mind to none, but, resembling the needle of the compass, howsoever for a while moved or shaken, look northerly, be constant to one. To be carried away with every fancy and opinion is to walk with Cain in the land of giddiness,[8] the greatest punishment that God laid upon him.

Before you enter into observation, first seek the language, that you may be fit for conference, and where the language is best spoken there settle and furnish yourself with the discreetest and most able master. For as here in England, so in other places, the language is spoken with more elegancy and purity in some places more than others. For the French, Orleans and thereabout is esteemed the best; Florence for the Italian; Leipzig for the High Dutch; and Valladolid for the Spanish.

To help you in conjugating your verbs you may use the help awhile of a grammar of that language, but in general you must expect your perfection from conference. For hereby the true accent and the native grace of pronunciation, which no book can teach, is only attained.

Now, as well for neighborhood sake as that the French tongue is chiefly affected among our nobility, it being a copious and a sweet language wherein so many famous works by as great

---

[7] *Lipsius.* ["From those cunning and passionate daughters of the sun"; cf. below, pp. 218, 247.]

[8] *Nod.* Genesis 4.

wits as any ever Europe bred have been published, I wish you first of all to see France, being seated under a temperate and most wholesome climate, and shall not endanger your health so much as being sent upon the sudden from a cold country into the scorching heat of another more remote.

I will not stand to make any topographical description of the country, I being herein both prevented long since [9] by a faithful pen.[10] Besides, I remember I am to write only one chapter, not a volume.

You shall find the French, I mean of the noblest and better sort, generally free and courteous, unto whom, even among their princes, state and majestic retiredness are burdensome, so that sometime you shall see them familiar with the meanest. La Noüe, speaking of the French nobility, saith *Elle est très vallereuse et courtoise, et ny à estat en la Chrestiente ou elle soit in si grand nombre:* They are exceeding valiant and courteous and there is no estate in Christendom where they are in so great number.

They delight for the most part in horsemanship, fencing, hunting, dancing, and little esteem of learning and gifts of the mind, contrary to the custom of the ancient Romans, as Cato the Censor, Caesar, Paulus Aemilius, and many others no less famous for knowledge than action; whereof themselves and their friends oftentimes complain. Commines layeth the fault upon the remissness of parents in their education. *Ils nourissent leur enfans seulement à faire les sots, en habilements et en parolles: de nulle lettre ils nont cognoissance:* They breed their children to play the wanton fools both in apparel and words, but for learning they know nothing.

The French are full of discourse, quick-witted, sudden in action, and generally light and inconstant, which Caesar [11] found long since, writing of them, *Quod sunt in consiliis capiendis*

---

[9] Anticipated long ago.
[10] *M. Dallington* [i.e., Sir Robert Dallington's *View of France* (1604)].
[11] *Caesar com. 3.*

mobiles et novis plerumque rebus student, and elsewhere he calls *Gallorum subita et repentina consilia.*[12] Moreover, as among the Spanish and Dutch, one fashion of apparel still observed amongst them argueth a constancy of mind and humor, so their change and variety, their vainness and levity, for every two years their fashion altereth.

Their exercises are for the most part tennis play, pall-mall, shooting in the crossbow or piece, and dancing.

Concerning their diet, it is nothing so good or plentiful as ours, they contenting themselves many times with mean viands. Only in the solemn feasts and banquets of entertainment they are bountiful enough, yea, far exceed us. As for the poor peasant, he is fain oftentimes to make up his meal with a mushroom or his *grenouilles* (in English, frogs), the which are in Paris and many other places commonly sold in the market.

Concerning their building, it is very magnificent, and I know not whether in all Europe any buildings may for majesty and state be compared with those of France, though they have been miserably spoiled by the last civil wars, they being the best architects of the world, upon the view of some of which, as breathing on a fair hill, I will detain you a while. And first we will begin with the Louvre in Paris. The Louvre is the royal seat of the kings of France, famous throughout all Europe, situate near to the town walls on the west side, by which runneth the river of Seine, which in old time served rather for a fortress than a king's house. And herein was a tower wherein were kept the king's revenues and treasure, which after by King Francis the First was pulled down and in this place was begun the building of the front, which is of masonry so enriched with pillars, friezes, architraves, and all sort of architecture with such symmetry and beauty that throughout all Europe

[12] "That they are capricious in forming designs and subject usually to change (*Com.* iv. 5) . . . spasmodic and sudden in their resolutions" (*Com.* iii. 8).

you shall hardly find the like. It was begun by Francis the First, finished by Henry, his son, under the appointment of the Lord of Clagny, and afterwards increased by Francis the Second, Charles the Ninth—last of all made the wonder of all other works by that beautiful gallery, the work of Henry the Fourth.

The Tuileries sometime belonged to the suburbs of St. Honoré in Paris by the side of the Louvre, and was indeed a place wherein they made tiles, and by reason there were many fair gardens about it, the Queen Mother, drawing the plot herself, seeing it a pleasant and fit place, began first to build here. It is a royal work, all of freestone. The portal or entrance is very stately, of marble pillars and jasper.

Fontainebleau is situate in the forest of Bierre,[13] in a plain encompassed with great woods, and was in old time a retiring place for the kings of France. Francis the First, who loved to build, took great pleasure in this seat and builded here the house as we see it at this present. The base court hereof is esteemed the fairest of all France. In the second court there is the purest and fairest fountain esteemed in the world; wherefore it was called *belle eauë*, and so *Fontaine belle eauë*. King Francis loved this place so well that he spent most of his time here, beautifying it while he lived with all sorts of commodities, goodly galleries, stoves,[14] etc., and caused the rarest masters of Europe in painting to be sent for for the beautifying it with all manner of histories. Also here he placed the rarest antiquities he could get. In brief, whatsoever he could wrap or wring he thought too little for this place. It is about fourteen leagues from Paris.

Blois is an ancient castle situate from the river of Loire upon an hill. Here the old kings of France were wont to reside. Especially Louis the Twelfth took delight in this place, who was called *Pater Patriae*.[15] It hath belonging unto it two goodly

[13] 1622 Biere; 1634, 1661 Becro.   [14] From 1622; 1634 Stroves.
[15] "The Father of His Country."

forests, one on this side the river, the other on the other. Going
forth of the gardens of the house, you pass into the forest under
four rows of elms at the least twelve hundred spaces. This is
rather remarkable for the antiquity than for the beauty. The
town standeth beneath, about the which are these fair places
within two or three leagues: Bury, Beauregard, Ville-sansin,
Chindony, and some others.

Amboise is one of the principal buildings of France. It
standeth upon the Loire upon a high seat. At the foot hereof
is the town, and near that a goodly forest. This castle is seen
a great way off, both by the hill and the valley yielding so
goodly a prospect as I never beheld a better. For from the ter-
races that environ the castle you may easily discern Tours and
the Abbey of Marmoustier seven leagues off. The castle standeth
upon a rock, at the foot whereof there is a cloister.

This house [16] is in Picardy, upon the way from Paris to Soissons, distant from Paris sixteen leagues, five from Soissons. It
standeth close upon the forest of Retz. It is of very great receipt,[17] as may appear by the enclosure of the park. Here King
Francis, whose only delight was in building, for many years
together set masons awork, the rather because it adjoined unto
the greatest forest of all France, himself loving hunting exceed-
ingly. Here are the goodliest walks in Europe, for the trees
themselves are placed in curious knots, as we use to set our
herbs in gardens.

Charleval is in Normandy upon the way from Paris to Rouen,
near to the village of Fleury. It was built by Charles the Ninth
at the instance of the Lord of Durescu. It standeth in a valley
enclosed with mountains above,[18] which is the forest of Lyons.
Among these mountains are many goodly prospects, one within
another. It is three leagues by a pleasant valley easily discerned

[16] *Villiers Costerets.* [17] Income; hence, wealth.
[18] From 1622; 1634 about.

to the River Seine. Had it been finished, it had been the chief building of France.

This castle [19] or royal house is called Bois de Vincennes. It is situate within one league of Paris and two of St. Denis, the place of burial of the French kings, so that these three stand in a manner in a triangle. It is a very sumptuous work and of admirable art. It was begun by Charles, Count of Valois, brother to Philip the Fair, and finished a good while after by Charles the Fifth. This house hath many fair courts in it, withal about it a park containing in circuit sixteen or seventeen thousand paces, which amount to two leagues and a half, stretching on the south even unto the river of Seine and by north unto the river of Marne, which, joining at the village of Confluence (so called of their meeting) near Charenton, fall down unto Paris. This in ancient times was the usual court and abode of the French kings, but now little frequented and falling in a manner to ruin.

But I omit farther to speak as well of the royal houses, as those of the nobles, being indeed the beauty of France, whereof there are many other, as St. Maur, Chenonceau, Chambourg, Boulogne, Creil, Coussie, Folembray, Montargis, St. Germain, and La Muette, which are all the King's houses and worthy your view and regard if you happen to find them in your way. In brief, hold France for one of the most rich, fertilest, and bravest kingdoms of the world.

And since Spain and France are but one continent, let us pass the Pyrenean hills and take some observations there.

Spain lieth southerly from France, in northern latitude from thirty-seven to forty-four degrees or thereabout, in the same height and parallel with the Azores Islands. It is far hotter than France, a very dry country, yet abounding in sweet springs, rivers, and all sorts of fruits. Pasture there is little or none in

[19] *The Castle of *Vincennes.*

respect of the great heat, but infinitely furnished with vineyards, olive trees; having corn sufficient save only in the skirts of the country, which are mountainous, hilly, and barren, yet abounding in goats and other cattle.

For victuals, you shall find it very scarce. Not that the country affordeth not a sufficiency, but that the people, being by constitution hot and dry, are not able to digest heavy and more solid meat like unto ours, but rather choose fruits, salads, and sweetmeats, as marmalade, by them called *membrillada* (for *membrillo* is a quince), and conserves of all sorts for coolness and lightness of digestion. The people are by nature generally proud and haughty, but withal very civil, faithful to their friend, and above all to their prince, for seldom or never have any of that nation been known to have been traitors. Their soldiers are infatigable,[20] resolute, and obedient unto their commanders, but withal lasciviously given and too cruel in victory.

The gentry affect not the country but desire to live in walled towns altogether, where they dedicate themselves either to some employment of state or business of war, save such who are of the better sort, dedicate to the church, of whom there is at the least a third part.

Their habit in apparel is all one for color and fashion, which hardly makes a distinction of parts. Only they are discerned by their servants, in whom they observe an excellent equipage, their *regalado*[21] horses, caroches, and horselitters.

The women are black and little, but very well favored and for discourse admirable. These have a more eminent distinction of habit and are all discerned by their apparel of what quality they are. They affect strangers much and are liberal in their converse with them.

The heart of the country is very scarce of fish. That which they have are either tons[22] or pilchards, brought salted from Biscay on the one side and from Valencia on the other. Yea,

---

[20] Indefatigable.　　　[21] "Dainty."　　　[22] Tunnies.

the church for want of fish is fain to give a license to eat the entrails of beasts upon fasting days.

All their meat, fruit, and bread are sold by the pound, and not except before an officer which they call *alcalde,* so that no stranger can be deceived either in weight or price.

They tread their corn out with oxen in the field as soon as it is reaped, their mules and horses eating the straw with barley, for oats they are not so well acquainted with. It is a country for travel very cumbersome in respect of lodging and diet, except when you come into the walled towns, where you shall according to their manner be accommodated well enough.

They travel all on mules, keeping their horses for beauty and show, putting them to no use save only to be led up and down.

Their coins are the best of Europe, since all their neighbors make a gain of them, as a piece of eight reals (or sixpence of our money) goeth in France for four shillings and sixpence. A doubloon in gold, that which is a pistolet with them, being thirteen shillings, is in France and other places twenty-nine reals, which is fourteen shillings sixpence of our money. Most of the coin that passeth for ordinary and trivial things, as wine, bread, melons, peaches, is of brass, which they call *quartas* and *quartillias.*[23] Of their *maravedis* twenty make threepence. Their buildings are fair and stately, and the King, though he hath many goodly houses and palaces, as in Seville, Granada, Toledo, Cordova, Valladolid, etc., yet the Escorial, seven leagues from Madrid, is the place where the King most resides, and this exceeds all the buildings of Christendom for beauty and curiosity in contriving; to which is adjoined one of the goodliest monasteries of the world, wherein are to be seen the rarest waterworks that men can devise.

Spain being divided into many kingdoms or provinces, you are allowed to carry about you only but an hundred reals. What

[23] I.e., cuartas, cuartillas: fourths.

you have above it is forfeited, and for that purpose at every bridge or passage where the countries part you are to be searched.

And I hope you have heard so much of the Inquisition and the danger thereof that I shall not here need to give you any caveat.

Navarre affordeth, by reason of the mountains, a very hard passage, whereof Pamplona is the chief city. Herein are the best muttons [24] and made the strongest wines. This country is so abundant in rosemary that they make it their ordinary fuel in heating their ovens and for their other uses.

Aragon aboundeth in wine and corn, which Portugal so wanteth that all the corn in that kingdom is not able to suffice Lisbon only, but they are fain to have it of the Britons, Hollanders, and from the Azores Islands.

Last of all, it is worth noting how that in their universities, as Salamanca, Alcala, Coimbra, etc., and other of their colleges, they care little for the Latin, but dispute and keep their exercises in Spanish or the Portuguese tongue, yet have they great scholars in all professions.

Thus have I only given you a taste how and what especially to observe in your travel. I willingly omit to speak of Italy, Germany, and other countries by reason they have been so exactly described by Master Sandys [25] and others, unto whose ample discourses, excepting your personal experience, I refer you, it being here mine only intent but to give you some few directions in general. And so I conclude, wishing you all happiness to yourself and prosperous success to your studies.

.   .   .   .   [26]

[24] *Yet the finest wool is of Segovia.

[25] George Sandys, whose popular book, *The Relation of a Journey Begun An. Dom. 1610. Four Books* (1615), which dealt with the Turkish Empire, Egypt, the Holy Land, and parts of Italy and neighboring islands.

[26] For reasons given in the introduction, Chapter XIX, "Of Military Observations," is here omitted.

CHAPTER XX

Concerning Fishing

I HAVE taken so much delight in the art of angling that I may well term it the honest and patient man's recreation, or a pastime for all men to recreate themselves at vacant hours.

For angling, there are of divers kinds, but the most useful are of two, either at the top of the water with a fly or at the bottom with other baits.

But for the description of the anglers' implements I leave it to their own discretion whether to use either hazel or cane, but if with a fly the hazel is better; for the cane is to carry for privacy either in a bag or, framed like a staff, to walk withal, whose joints doth many times fail and deceive when a man doth strike at [1] his bait.

For the lines, they must be framed according to the fish where you angle: for the small fish three good hairs taken from the tail of a good stonehorse that is lusty and in flesh (for your poor jade's hair is not good), but if you come in place where great fish are you must fish with lines of six or eight hairs.

For the floats, they are of divers kinds, as some made of cork with a quill, but in my opinion the float made of two swan's quills, made one in the other so it take no water, or the bustard's quills, are the neatest.

And for your hooks, they are to be fitted in size as the fish are either great or small.

Thus far, having showed the necessary instruments appertaining to this harmless and modest recreation, I will set down the

[1] Pull at.

baits to angle with and their seasons. For baits, they are of three kinds, which are live baits, dead baits, and artificial baits. For your live baits, they are worms of all kinds, especially the red worm, the maggot (or gentle), the bob, the dor, brown flies, frogs, grasshoppers, hornet, wasps, bees, snails, small roaches, bleaks, gudgeons, or loaches, minnows, etc.[2] Your dead baits are pastes of all kinds, young broods of wasps dried or undried, the clotted blood of sheep, cheese, brambleberries, corn, seeds, cherries, and suchlike. Your baits which seem to live, yet are dead, are flies of all sorts and shapes made of silk and feathers about the hooks, fitting the season severally for the times of the year, which, being moved in the water, the fish will greedily strive to devour.

For the seasons in which these baits are to be used, the red worm will serve for small fish all the year, the maggot or gentle in July, the bob and dor in May, the brown flies in June, frogs in March, grasshoppers in September, hornets in July, wasps and bees in July, snails in August; for the roach, bleak, gudgeon, and minnow—they serve for the pike and trout at any season. All pastes are good in May, June, and July, dried wasps in May, sheep's blood and cheese in April. For brambleberries, corn, and seeds, at the fall of the leaf. For flies, those for the trout, the dun fly is good in March, the stone fly in April, the red and yellow flies in May, the black and moorish[3] fly in June, the wasp and shell fly in July, the cloudy fly in August.

For the making of these flies, the best way is to take the natural fly and make one so like it that you may have sport. For you must observe what flies haunt the waters for seasons of the year, and to make their like with cottons, wool, silk, or feathers to resemble the like.

---

[2] P.'s categories are not mutually exclusive, but the red worm and the bob are the earthworm and the grub; the bleak, gudgeon, and loach are all small fish, minnows.

[3] Marsh.

You must not keep your live baits all together, but every kind by itself, and to feed them with such things they delighted in when they had their liberty. And to begin with the red worm, you shall put them in a bag of woolen cloth (if it be red the better) and put ground moss or fennel cut small, in which they will scour themselves. But if you mix earth that is fat and black or neat's dung, they will live the longer. For your maggots or gentles, they are fed with sheep's suet or livers of any beasts cut into small bits, but to scour them use sand, loam, or bran. And keep them warm—they will live the longer. For frogs and grasshoppers, wet moss is best to keep them in, and when you angle with the frog, cut off their legs at the knees and the grasshoppers' wings near the body. For other worms, as the bob, caddis worm, canker, or suchlike, you may keep them with the same things you take them with. Paste is a made-bait, and there are divers kinds of them, but to make paste to last long, you may use bean flour and those parts of the cony's legs which are called the almonds,[4] or a young whelp or cat is as good, and put the like quantity of virgin's wax [5] and sheep's suet, and beat them together in a mortar till they become one body; then with a little clarified honey temper them before the fire and make them into balls. These will keep long. With this you must bait your hook.[6] Some use the purest white bread they can get and make it into paste to fish at the hook. The coarser pastes are used to bait the ground, to entice the fish to gather together to that place which you angle in, by flinging in small balls or pellets of coarser paste. Thus much for your baits.

Now I have named the baits, it is necessary to show what fish are delighted therewith, as the gudgeon, roach, and dace, which are fish of eager bite and soonest deceived, and feed at the red worm, gentle, or paste.

[4] The ears of the rabbit or "some part of a rabbit's leg" (NED).
[5] Virgin wax: "fresh, new, or unused bees-wax" (NED).
[6] 1634 hook with.

To angle for the carp your rod and line must be strong. He is dainty to bite (his times [7] of feeding are early in the morning, or in the evening); therefore is to be enticed by baiting the ground with coarse paste. The red worm he seldom refuseth in March, the caddis in June, the grasshopper in July, August, and September.

The chevin and trout are taken at the top of the water with flies, snails, and grasshoppers; at the bottom, with the great red worm.

The eel and flounder are two greedy fish and bite at the red worm. The best season to angle for bream is from the latter end of February till September. The baits which he delights in are worms of all sorts, butterflies, green flies, paste of all the crumbs of white bread, and the brood of wasps.

The tench is a fish that ever loveth the bottom of rivers, where the ooze or mud is thickest. The best angling for him is in the height of summer, for at other seasons he bites more sparingly. The baits which delight him are pastes, very sweet, the browner the better, being mixed with sheep's blood—also at the great red worm. The perch biteth at the red worm about the midst of the water.

Thus have I briefly set down the art of angling and will conclude with all seasons which are naught to angle in, as the violent heat of the day, high winds, great rain, snow and hail, thunder, lightning, or any wind that bloweth from the East, land floods, and thick waters, the falling of leaves into the water, and suchlike impediments, which are enemies to anglers.

[7] 1634 time.

FINIS

THE TRUTH OF OUR TIMES

Revealed out of One Man's Experience
by Way of Essay

(1638)

By Henry Peacham

To my honored and much respected friend, Mr. Henry Barnwell of Turrington in Marshland near to King's Lynn in the County of Norfolk

Sir,

When I had finished this little piece, and bethought myself to whom I should present the dedication, I often, as Pliny adviseth authors to do, considered the title, which was *experience*. Now lest the porch or forefront might not be suitable to the whole fabric, I begin with the experience I formerly have had of your friendly respect of me ever since our first acquaintance at Lynn, which you have continued by many years, even to our late and last meeting in London.

The consideration whereof hath moved me to be publicly thankful (for I ever hated ingratitude) and desirous at so far a distance not to be forgotten so long as you shall have this little book, the pledge of my affection, lying by you. Little it is, indeed, but of little books let me say, as Virgil said of little bees,

Ingentes animos in parvo corpore versant.[1]

Whatsoever it is, accept, I pray you, who can both judge and understand and I am sure will take in good part whatsoever shall proceed from the pen of him who truly and affectionately will be ever ready to do you any friendly service.

HENRY PEACHAM.

[1] "They display enormous courage in small bodies."

To the Reader

It FARETH with me now, honest reader, as with a traveler in winter, who, having foolishly ventured over some dangerous river or passage quite frozen with ice, stands on the other side pointing with his finger and showing his following friends where it cracked. In the same manner I have ventured before, tried the coldness of these frozen and hard times, together with the slippery ways of this deceitful and trustless world. Standing, I hope, now at the last safe on this other side, I show those that are to follow me where the danger is. I have seen and known much, as well in England as somewhere else abroad, and have had much acquaintance (and which hath been my happiness, if it be an happiness) with the most famous men of our time in all excellent professions. Whence I am not altogether ignorant in the noble sciences, as well the theoric as practic, but, to say the truth, I have ever found multiplicity of knowledge in many things to have been rather an hindrance than ever any way tending to advancement. Having hereby found much employment to no purpose, but as we see a carrier's horse when he is heavily laden hath bells hung about his neck to give him some content on the way and to allay the pain of his burden, so have I taken pains and deserved well at the hands of many of good rank, yet got I never anything hereby save the horse-bells of praise, thanks, and fruitless promises, which, like the carriers, they can put on and take off at their pleasure. *Vix vivitur gratiis,* saith Plautus.[1] The peacock, as Mantuan hath it,

[1] "One can scarcely live on thanks."

was admired for his plumes, which every beholder would be ready to snatch off, but in the meantime there was none of them all would give him so much as a grain to fill his belly. In a word, the main and most material of my observations, and which the nearest concerned myself, reader, I present thee withal; the less will fall in of themselves and are obvious. But, fearing thou shouldst give me such a jeer as Diogenes did unto those of Mindum, I make my gate but little lest the whole city should run out. Thus leaving what I have known by mine own experience to be certain unto thy friendly censure, I rest thine

H. P.[2]

[2] Here follows: "*Imprimatur* Tho. Weekes. *R. P. Episc. Londi. Cappel. Domest.*"

Of God's Providence

I WILL begin my first observation, which from a child I have seriously considered, with the contemplation of God's providence, which is never wanting to the protection of them and their posterity who in singleness of heart have sought and sincerely served Him all their lives, averring with David [1] that "I never saw the righteous forsaken nor his seed begging their bread."

When, on the contrary, oppressors, atheists, cruel men, idle and lewd livers have with the curse of Reuben [2] been as water spilt upon the ground, they have either sunk into the earth or ran without consistence, every one his several way so far that their place of birth or being in a second or third generation hath been quite lost and utterly forgotten. "I have seen the ungodly flourish," etc. [3]

I never knew any sacrilegious vulture digest that which he snatched from the altar, or any demolisher of churches or such as had converted them to profane uses, as turning them into stables, sheepcotes (after the depopulation of the whole town), thrive in their estates. And many of them have I known to have come to infamous and desperate ends, yea, being their own executioners.

I have again observed the especial providence and goodness of God extended toward the meanest and poorest whom the world hath contemned, as a poor man in the country, who by

---

[1] *Psa[lm] 37:25.   [2] *Gen[esis] 49:4.   [3] *Ps[alm] 37:35.

his only hand-labor earning a groat or sixpence by the day, to
have brought up a charge of six or seven children, who, poor
things, get seldom their bellies full of bread, and their drink
is many times, as I have seen it, but a roasted crab crushed into
a dish of fair water, and for the greatest part of the year go
barefooted and barelegged. Yet, commonly, like Daniel with
his pulse are they as fresh-colored, healthy, cheerful, as free
from diseases as the best men's children in the country, who
usually are pampered and crammed with the greatest dainties
that may be gotten, many times till their bellies are ready to
burst. And though the parishes where they are born commonly
account of them no better than beggars' brats not worth the
looking after, and caring not how soon they were rid of them
to avoid charge, yet by the blessing of God attaining, as many
of them have done, to the most eminent places of dignity, as
well in church as commonwealth, they have obliged their
native places to them by erecting schools, hospitals, almshouses,
and doing other charitable works, which of itself the whole
parish had never been able to have performed.

I might fill a whole volume if I should reckon up all such
great and eminent personages the cottage hath afforded as
principal pillars to the support of our commonwealth, or tell
you what magnificent works have been done by bishops, lord
mayors, and citizens of London whose parents have been
extreme poor and obscure, and, which is more, not a son but
sons of one poor man have participated and shared in honorable advancement.[4]

Chicheley,[5] a very poor man of Higham Ferrers in Northamp-
tonshire, about the time of Henry V, had two sons, the one
Archbishop of Canterbury, the founder of All Souls' in Oxford,

[4] For other remarks on the rise from poverty to eminence, see *The Worth
of a Penny*, ed. 1669, pp. 8–9.
[5] Thomas Chicheley, whose son Henry was Archbishop of Canterbury
from 1414 to 1443. A Robert Chicheley was Lord Mayor of London in
1411, and a Richard Chicheley held the same office in 1421.

and the other Lord Mayor of London, both at one time. Patten of Wainfleet in Lincolnshire, a man of mean estate, had also two sons.[6] The one was William de Wainfleet, Bishop of Winchester and founder of that magnificent college, Magdalen's in Oxford, besides a school at Wainfleet, where he was born; and the other was Dean of Chichester; which brothers, one in the habit of a bishop, the other of a dean, support the pillow under their father's head upon his monument in Wainfleet Allhallows Church, who lieth cut out in alabaster in a side coat, a great pouch and a dudgeon dagger at his girdle. I could instance many others even of our own times, whose mean beginnings no whit can derogate from their esteem and worthiness, but I had rather look backward and farther off.

I have also with great comfort observed the merciful goodness of God in providing for fatherless and motherless children, who, being left in trust with some hard-hearted executor, or sometime to the miserable mercy of some poor parish to be maintained, God miraculously hath taken them into his protection by kindling love and piety in the hearts of those who are his to receive and take them in, they keeping the true fast which God commandeth in Isaiah.[7] And how in time with their growth He guides them with His grace to live honestly and uprightly, which were else impossible for these young and tender souls to do, especially in populous cities and public places, whither they are constrained at fourteen or fifteen years of age to come up with a silly country-carrier and some small sum of money (the benevolence of friends) to bear their charges, to seek services and means of living, where they know nobody, neither are they known of any, being left as poor chickens, having lost their mother hen and defender, unable to protect themselves, to the merciless mercy of a most cruel

---

[6] William Patten, who was Bishop of Winchester from 1447 to 1457, and John Patten, Dean of Chichester, 1425–1434.

[7] *Esay [i.e., Isaiah] 58:7.

and pitiless age; wherein, besides, they are in danger through want and necessity to be seduced to lewd and ill courses and, as the Wise Man saith, "To seek death in the error of their lives." [8] Neither hath poverty anything more unhappy in it than perverting good natures and drawing them into vicious courses, as a poet justly complaineth: *O mala paupertas, vitii sclerisque ministra.*[9]

Hence let all parents, while they are living, be seriously careful to the uttermost of their powers to provide something to maintain their poor children in their livelihood after their deaths; if they cannot, to give them that education and knowledge in some art or other, seasoned with the fear of God, that they may be able to encounter the manifold miseries of this wretched world and withstand all lewd temptations and allurements unto vice.

And being able in an honest calling to subsist of themselves, bless God for his care and goodness toward them, and say with the Psalmist, "When my father and mother forsook me, thou, O Lord, tookest me up," [10] which, freely I confess, I may say myself, being left young to the wide world to seek my fortune, and acknowledge the providence of Almighty God to have attended me both at home and abroad in other countries, for which I had rather be silently thankful than to proclaim the particularities which to some may seem to be fabulous and incredible. And for anything I know, I and mine must say yet, though in a far different condition, with that noble and great earl of Ireland,[11] "God's providence is our inheritance."

---

[8] ° Wisd[om of Solomon] 1:12.

[9] °Mantuan. ["Wicked poverty, the encourager of vice and crime." Cf. below, pp. 204, 209 and *The Worth of a Penny*, ed. 1669, p. 15.]

[10] Psalm 27:10.　　　　　　　　　[11] °Earl of Cork.

Of Schools and Masters

THERE is no profession more necessary to the erecting the frame of a famous commonwealth than that of schoolmasters, yet none in more disesteem among the common vulgar, yea, and illiterate great ones. I know not the reason of this, except that the greater part of the multitude being ignorant, they are desirous that their children should be so likewise. But I rather believe that which I have found true: reward to be out of reach and livings nowadays like lotteries—some principal prizes, as gilt basins and ewers; some of a middle rank, as fruit dishes and candlesticks; some of the least value, as spoons and saucers. Yet one of these least many times costs him more than it is worth in expense of many years in the university, his labor in search and making friends, his money, hardly gotten, largely expended, and, as in a lottery, all this getteth nothing.

Some few prime schools in England serve as a foil for the rest. I mean Westminster, Winchester, Eton, Paul's, with some few others, which at this day, as all others in general, have lost of their former greatness and esteem, not because there are not learned and able masters (there being now as sufficient as ever) and sound grammarians among the scholars, but because men have found shorter cuts in the way of preferment for their children.

Neither do our nobility and gentry so much affect the study of good letters as in former times, loving better the active than the contemplative part of knowledge, which in times of the monasteries was more esteemed and doted on than now; when kings and princes were so devoted to the services of God that they consecrated their sons, nephews, and other kinsmen to the church, some of whom have become cardinals, as Beaufort

185

and Pole, whose mother was a Plantagenet. I also omit many bishops and clergymen who for the singular estimation of their sincerity, truth, and learning have been made by the prince his treasurers, chancellors, masters of the rolls, and preferred to other the like honorable places of trust and credit. And why may we not expect re-advancement of learning *Carolinis hisce temporibus*,[1] wherein so many works of piety have been undertaken and the worthiest advanced?

Louis the Eleventh, King of France, would say that his son should learn no more Latin than *Qui nescit dissimulare, nescit regnare.*[2] Of which opinion are many of our times, which is the reason that after travel they come home as wise as they went, and hold their tongues where wise and learned men are in discourse, and are left like wrecks in the open sea of the world, without man, mast, or rudder to direct them in a right and orderly course. Now where knowledge is undervalued, what reward can a master expect, teaching being one of the most laborious callings in the world and the school well termed *pistrinum paedagogicum?*[3] Hence the most masters making teaching a shift but for a time, till a better fortune falleth. And to say truth, *In grammatica senescere miserrimum.*[4] A master of a free school is more absolute.[5] To teach in private houses is subject to many inconveniences. The master becometh more servile than their servants, who observe him to an inch, and, as commonly they are pickthanks, lay all the blame of their young master's unlucky behavior upon his master. If he falls in climbing a daw's nest, his master is in fault; if he be asked a question at the table by a stranger and is dumb, his mother swells and tells his master he loseth his time and doth no good, though he taketh all the pains with him that possibly he can.

But imagine there is a good correspondency held on all sides.

---

[1] "In these times of [King] Charles."
[2] "He who does not know how to dissemble knows not how to rule."
[3] "Pedagogical drudgery."
[4] "It is most wretched to grow old in grammar."   [5] Independent.

He pleaseth the parents as well in painstaking as using the children mildly and gently. They again love their master. Let him expect no future preferment, but only for the present his bare stipend. But some may tell him his master hath many benefices in his gift, but, believe me, not any that ever he shall be better. But why not, since he will bestow them *gratis?* Yes (in the adjective but not in the adverb), to them that will give most. Sometimes, if he happens to marry a chambermaid of the house, he may fare the better: neither much, *computatis computandis,*[6] for his wife, for charge, may stand him in as much as a small living may be worth; or if he be a neighbor's child, and his father or some friend for him will lay down a matter of seven- or eightscore pounds to a second or third man. For simoniacal patrons are like pickpockets in a throng. They will not have the purse and money found about them; they presently turn it off to another of their consorts not far off, who, to avoid the danger of the law, hath taken in lease his advowsons. So hereby both the king, bishop of the diocese, or the universities are cheated of their right in the next presentation. But perhaps his scholars, when they come to be men and of themselves, will not be forgetful of him. Let me tell him he must get him a pair of leaden shoes if he means to attend upon so long and tedious hopes, and withal remember that old monkish verse wherein the reason is much better than the rime:

> *Servitium pueri, mulierum*
> *Et* Black-*monachorum,*
> *Est, et erit semper* small
> Thanks *in fine laborum.*[7]

Indeed, in the universities many young noblemen and ingenuous learned gentlemen have been very grateful afterward to their tutors and teachers, and have proved the only raisers of their fortunes. Neither is here any long expectation, they

[6] "Necessary reckonings having been made."
[7] "Service to boys, women, and Black Monks is and always will win small thanks at the end of your labors."

being of years of judgment to discern a benefit, which commonly they requite ere it be outworn and forgotten. So that I conclude it is most fitting that good schoolmasters should be as well in public cities and towns as private gentlemen's houses. But, more fitting, they should be better dealt withal than commonly they are in most places. Besides, it were greatly to be wished that those who took that profession upon them and found themselves able to endure it, should follow none other calling so long as they lived, and, as in other countries, to be maintained by the public with large and sufficient stipends, so themselves would not be unprovided in their age and their scholars not be turned over to seek every year new masters, than which nothing can hurt or more hinder proficiency in learning. For my part, I have done with that profession, having evermore found the world unthankful, how industrious soever I have been.

Of Making and Publishing Books

SOLOMON saith, "There is no end of making books," and books many times are made to no end, since, according to that, *Nihil dictum quod non prius*.[1] For writers nowadays, like cooks, dress but the same meat after another manner, which in substance is but one and the same. All the libraries of the world have been ransacked and tossed over and over, and whatsoever hath borne the stamp of antiquity, now vindicated from dust and moths and brought to see the light of the Hebrew, Arabic, Greek, and Latin, having broken through the midnight and mists of many barbarous ages, have now regained their proper luster and purity.

[1] "Nothing has been said that has not been said before."

The Truth of Our Times

Neither are the bare making of books nowadays sufficient, but new authors are made and brought to speak and determine controversies, not only in divinity, but in other sciences, and, like painted wooden cannons against the walls of a weak town, do terrify for a while, but the stratagem is quickly discovered; and many ancient authors that are made to speak more than they would if they were living, if Manutius hath spoken the truth. But this by the way. I would know whether out of a superlative singularity or, like the griffins in Bactria, they envy the world should partake and be sharers of that gold which they have digged for. Many famous and great scholars love not to be seen in print, except a necessity by command of superiors be laid upon them, being, as they suppose, able to do as much with their tongues. There being already such a mass of books in the world, which hath swallowed more than it can digest, it were a folly to burden it with more, especially there being not the third reader to the fortieth book, and the better part of these vain, useless, yea, sometimes impious. Of what sort are those of Casa, Bishop of Beneventum, Aretino, Machiavelli, and many other, so that among the learned and wise it is a great question whether printing hath done more hurt or good in the world! Certain it is we have knowledge now almost at the height, according to the prophet Daniel,[2] of these last times. *Scientia multiplicabitur*,[3] but practice of piety, charity, and devotion at the lowest, as St. Paul foretold of the same times.

But say thou, being a general scholar, a traveler, an excellent artist in one kind or other, and desirest, not out of vainglory *digito monstrarier hic est*,[4] but of a good mind of profiting and doing good to others, to make the world partaker of thy knowledge if thou beest a scholar, or thy observations, being a traveler, or thy experience or invention, being an artist. Having

[2] *Daniel 12.   [3] "Learning will be enlarged."
[4] "To be pointed out with the finger."

189

spent many years, much money, and a great part of thy life hoping by thy labors and honest deserving to get a respect in the world, or by thy dedication the favor and support of some great personage for thy preferment, or a good round sum of a stationer for thy copy—and it must be a choice and rare one too, which he for his own gain will look to—it will hardly by a tenth part countervail thy labor and charge. For the respect of the world is nothing. Nay, thou shalt find it altogether ingrate and thy reader readier to requite thee with a jeer or a scorn than a good word to give thee thy due—and perhaps out of envy, because thou knowest more and art learneder than he. And though thou hast a general applause, thou shalt be but a nine days' wonder.

But then you may say the dedication will be worth a great matter, either in present reward of money or preferment by your patron's letter or other means. And for this purpose you prefix a learned and as panegyrical epistle as you can, and bestow great cost of the binding of your book, gilding and stringing of it in the best and finest manner. Let me tell thee, whosoever thou art, if nowadays, such are these times, thou gettest but as much as will pay for the binding and strings, thou art well enough. The rest thou wilt have in promises of great matters. Perhaps you shall be willed to come another time, but one occasion or other will so fall out that, come never so often, you lose but your labor. Your great patron is not stirring, he is abroad at dinner, he is busy with such a lord. To be short, you and your labor are forgotten, some of his pages in the meantime having made himself off with [5] your book.

See now, learned authors and you modern poets, what end your elabored lines tend unto, and what gain you by your neat and eloquent epistles, wherewith many times you gild senseless statues that will teach you, as they did Diogenes, patience when they are sought and sued unto.

[5] Original: of your.

190

Aretine, I remember, giveth a reason why poets have not that esteem and fall short of the munificence of kings and princes which formerly they did partake of. Poets, saith he, nowadays are not rewarded for their verses because their patrons in their conscience find themselves not guilty [6] of any desert or merit why they should be extolled by them. Again, an ingenuous and a free spirit cannot *dorer les oreilles d'asne*,[7] as the Frenchman says, do honor to the undeserving. There are many that befool themselves this way. Therefore let the book you dedicate sort with his judgment and understanding to whom it is presented, as near as may be, you having formerly known him. I had rather present any work of mine to a private patron with whom I might confer of the subject, hear his judgment, and speak mine freely. Besides, books are evermore best taken of such, and you be esteemed less ambitious. There be some so highly upborne by the bladders of their honor and greatness that they receive your gift but as an homage or a tribute due to their transcendency.

Leaving those farther off, let us look a little back to the authors and poets of late time and consider how they have thrived by their works and dedications. The famous Spenser did never get any preferment in his life, save toward his latter end he became a clerk of the council in Ireland and, dying in England, he died but poor. When he lay sick, the noble and pattern of true honor, Robert, Earl of Essex, sent him twenty pound either to relieve or bury him. Joshua Sylvester, admired for his translation of Bartas, died at Middelburg,[8] a factor for our English merchants, having had very little or no reward at all either for his pains or dedication. And honest Master Michael Drayton had about some five pound lying by him at his death, which was *satis viatici ad caelum*,[9] as William Warham, Bishop of Canterbury, answered his steward when, lying

[6] Worthy.   [7] "Gild the ass's ears."   [8] In Holland.
[9] "Enough for a journey to heaven."

upon his deathbed, he had asked him how much money he had in the house. He told his Grace thirty pounds. I have, I confess, published things of mine own heretofore, but I never gained one halfpenny by any dedication that ever I made save *splendida promissa* and, as Plutarch saith, *byssina verba*.[10] Neither cared I much, for what I did was to please myself only. So that I would wish no friend of mine in these days to make further use of English poesy than in epitaphs, emblems, or encomiastics for friends, yet if his vein be for Latin, not to restrain himself herein, for hereby he shall do honor to our nation and become a man, though not of Mars, yet of Martes, getting himself hereby the name and reputation of a scholar. As all other excellency, so Latin poesy is valued at an higher rate abroad than with us in England—albeit our wits are nothing inferior to theirs—and more bountifully in all places rewarded.

> *Sint Maecenates, non deerunt, Flacce, Marones.*

> Among us let Maecenases but be,
> And, Flaccus, Virgils thou enow shalt see.

I confess I have spent too many hours in this folly and fruitless exercise, having ever been naturally addicted to those arts and sciences which consist of proportion and number, as painting, music, and poetry, and the mathematical sciences. But now, having shaken hands with those vanities, being exercised in another calling, I bid them (though unwillingly and as friends do at parting with some reluctancy) adieu, and am with Horace his old censor forced to say,

> *Veianius armis*
> *Herculis ad postem fixis latet abditus agro.*[11]

[10] "Splendid promises . . . silken words."
[11] *Epist.* i.1.5: "Veianius hangs up his arms at Hercules' door and then lies hidden in the country."

Of Liberty

THERE is nothing so sweet and agreeable to the nature of man, next unto his health, as his liberty, which, according to Tully's definition hereof, is an *arbitrium vivendi ut velis,* the choice of living as a man list himself. Wherefore Paracelsus, that glory of Germany for his depth of knowledge in the nature of minerals, to show his true happiness herein, when he traveled by the way and came to his inn at night, the first thing he did he would lay his sword upon the table, professing he would not give the same to be Emperor of Germany. It was a long broadsword, and had engraved upon the blade this:

Alterius non sit qui suus esse potest.[1]

as being the emblem of his liberty. In the pommel, which was hollow and to be opened with a screw, were all his chief quintessences and spirits of metals and herbs wherewith he cured the most desperate diseases, gaining hereby infinite treasure and sums of money.

And the old Burgundians possessing that part of Germany which belongeth at this time to the Landgrave of Hessen, to express their hatred of bondage and their love of liberty, gave in their warlike ensign a cat, because no creature in the world is more impatient of bondage than it; for put her into a cage or grate, she never will be quiet, but rather beat herself to death there than want her liberty. Hence that prince is called *Princeps Catorum,*[2] and in the German *der*[3] *Landgrav von Hessen, Hesse* as well in the High as Low Dutch signifying a cat. For, as we call here *puss,* so they there *Hesse,* yet in Gelderland they call her *pous,* as we do.

---

[1] "Let no man be another's hireling if he can be his own master."
[2] "Prince of Tomcats."   [3] Original: *die.*

Servitude was as a curse pronounced to them who had offended God and transgressed his law, as Noah cursed Canaan,[4] saying, "A servant of servants shall he be unto his brethren," and we find indeed bondage to be but an effect of vice, as in unthrifty, idle persons and offenders of the law, with all intemperate persons, who by their ill-living fall into many long and loathsome diseases, are as it were in bonds bound to their beds and imprisoned within their chambers and set in the stocks by the gout.

There is also the want of half a man's liberty in marriage, for he is not absolutely himself, though many believe when they are going to church upon their wedding day they are going into the land of liberty. But Solomon telleth them, "The fool laugheth when he is going to the stocks." For my part, I am not married. If I were, I should find my wings clipped and the collar too strait for my neck.

The Low Countries, having tasted the sweetness of their liberty when they had shaken off the yoke of Spain, gave for their emblem a lion, who, having slipped his collar, looked behind him to the same, with this: *Liber leo revinciri nescit.*[5] An absolute [6] man cannot be he who wanteth his liberty.

Who enjoy their liberty commonly are longer lived than others who want it. They are more able in wit and judgment; they are more useful to the commonwealth when the rest are but *umbratiles,* but shadows of men. They have done the best works either of wit or expense; they are the fastest and truest friends; lastly, they have been the fairest precedents of piety and goodness.

But, you tell me, every man cannot enjoy that condition, but some, yea, the most, must serve and obey. It is true. I only speak of the ingenuous and those as may, if it please them, be

[4] °Gen. 9:25.
[5] "A free lion cannot know how to be bound down again."
[6] Independent.

fabri fati sui, shape out their own fortune, yet rather choose a servile condition before liberty and freedom. As if a master of arts should turn gentleman-usher to an ordinary lady, or a lieutenant in the wars leave his honorable profession to become a lord's porter, or like a foolish vicar in Lincolnshire who would suffer his wife to raise him in cold winter mornings to make her a fire. Some again are by nature so base and obsequious that, being overcome with the presence of those who were greater or braver than themselves, they soothe him up and foolishly applaud and admire whatsoever he says, and, if he speaks in his own opinion anything wisely or like a statist [7] and looketh about him for applause, they reply, "Your Honor or Worship is in the right; the best counselor the King hath could not have spoken to better purpose. God maintain your life. If some would be ruled by you it would be better for all England"—with the like gross and palpable flattery. And if haply he utter anything savoring of a jest, they feign a sardonian smile by way of allowance of his facetious conceit. And indeed many there are so stately and affecting greatness after so foolish a manner that they become ridiculous in suffering men ofttimes as good as themselves to stand bare before them three or four hours together; and therefore many times they hold them in talk for the purpose, in expecting the title of "Honor" or "Worship" at every word that is spoken, as if they were the constables of the next wappentake.[8] Sometime they will be bold to command you as their menial servant, which also you must take as a favor. In brief, I will ever commend that genteel freedom of the French nation, who affect servility least of all other, especially that of standing bare, yea, even in waiting at the table, were it before the greatest lord in France (they usually bringing up their dishes with their hats on their heads), as also in freedom of speech, whereof none save slaves are debarred. For

[7] Statesman.
[8] A judicial court of a wappentake, a subdivision of an English shire.

mine own part I affect freedom so much and I have found such happiness therein that I had rather dine even at a threepenny ordinary, where I may be free and merry, than to be a dumb tenant for two hours at a lord's table, preferring health and liberty, *bonae corporis*,[9] before those of fortune and all the wealth the greatest usurer hath in the world, and will ever say,

O bona libertas, pretio pretiosior omni.[10]

Of Opinion

OPINION is a monster of more heads than Hercules his Hydra. And if one happily be cut off, another ariseth forthwith in the room. One day when[1] walking in Breda in Brabant not far from the market place, I passed by a gentleman or merchant's house, over whose great gates was written in letters of gold upon a blue ground, *Totus mundus regitur opinione.*[2] I stood still and, pondering upon it, I found it[3] witty and weighty, to concern the whole world and everyone in particular, and myself especially at that time, since I thought it to be the best that I had seen, which perhaps another would have disliked.

And I have often wondered why the ancient pagans, in their deifying so many, passed by opinion, bearing far greater sway than dogs, onions, and leeks in Egypt, *Cui numen crescebat in hortis.*[4] Yet it is no great wonder. Since deifying was wont to be done with a general consent, Opinion was never to expect it, every man where she reigns being of a several mind. It was but opinion that caused Count Martinengo of Italy, of a noble

---

[9] "Goods of the body."
[10] "O good liberty, more precious than all wealth."
[1] Original: when I.   [2] "The whole world is ruled by opinion."
[3] Original: found witty.
[4] "Whose god was growing in gardens." Original: *nomen.*

house and of an exceeding great estate, to marry a common laundress. Whereupon, within two or three days following, Pasquin in Rome had a foul shirt upon his back and underneath this in Italian: *Perche Pasquin,* etc. "Pasquin, how haps it thou hast a foul shirt on upon a Sunday morning?" *Riposto.* "Because my laundress is made a countess." [5]

It is but opinion that makes all the marriages in the world. For there is no beauty, favor, or complexion but is loved and liked of by one or other, nature so providing that none might be lost for having.

It is but opinion that great ladies many times marry their grooms, refusing great men and of great means.

It is but opinion that one goes to Rome, another to New England, and a third to Amsterdam. It is also but opinion that a proud coxcomb in the fashion, wearing taffeta and an ill-favored lock on his shoulder, thinks all that wear cloth and are out of fashion to be clowns, base and unworthy of his acquaintance.

So that opinion is the compass the fool only saileth by in the vast ocean of ignorance. For hereby vices are taken for virtues, and so the contrary. And all the errors that men commit in their whole lives is for want of the line and level of an even and true judgment. And it is the very rock whereat many, yea, the most, make shipwreck of their credits, estates, and lives.

That emblem was a pretty one which was an old woman who, having gathered up into her apron many dead men's skulls which she found scattered upon the ground, with an intent to lay them up in a charnel house, but her apron slipping upon a hill where she stood, some ran one way and some another; which the old woman seeing, "Nay," quoth she, "go your ways, for thus ye differed in your opinion when ye had life, everyone taking his several way as he fancied." There is no writer, none

[5] This squib, apparently a favorite with P., had appeared much earlier (p. 155) and later in *The Worth of a Penny,* ed. 1669, p. 12.

of public or private employment in the commonwealth, but passeth in danger by the den of this one-eyed Polyphemus. And while I write, by how many opinions am I censured, one saying one thing and another another! But I am not so unhappy as to fear or care for them. I hold on a direct course and will never strike sail to rovers.

Of Following the Fashion

ECCLESIASTICUS saith that "by gait, laughter, and apparel a man is known what he is." [1] Truly nothing more discovereth the gravity or levity of the mind than apparel. I never knew a solid or wise man to affect this popular vanity, which caused Henry the Fourth of France to say usually of his counselors and learneder sort of his courtiers that they had so much within them that they never cared to beg regard from feathers and gold lace.[2] And himself would commonly go as plain as an ordinary gentleman or citizen, only in black, sometime in a suit no better than buckram. The Emperor Charles the Fifth seldom or never wore any gold or silver about him save his Order of the Fleece.[3] And the plainness of our English kings in former times hath been very remarkable. King Henry the Eighth was the first that ever wore a band about his neck, and that very plain, without lace, and about an inch or two in depth. We may see how the case is altered. He is not a gentleman, nor in the fashion, whose band of Italian cutwork now standeth him not at the least in three or four pounds. Yea, a seamster in Holborn told me that there are of threescore pound price a piece, and shoeties that go under the name of roses, from thirty shillings to three, four, and five pounds the pair. Yea, a gallant of the time not long since paid thirty pound for a pair. I would have had him by himself to have eaten that dish of buttered

---

[1] Cf. above, p. 144.   [2] *Ibid.*   [3] Cf. above, p. 150.

eggs prepared with musk and ambergris, which cost thirty and
five pounds, and when his belly had been full, to have laid
him to sleep upon my Lady N.'s bed, whose furniture cost her
ladyship five hundred and threescore pounds.

I never knew any wholly affected to follow fashions to have
been any way useful or profitable to the commonwealth, except
that way Aristotle affirmeth the prodigal man to be, by scatter-
ing his money about to the benefit of many—tailors, seamsters,
silkmen, etc. Neither ever knew I any man esteemed the better
or the wiser for his bravery but among simple people. Now this
thing we call the fashion is so [4] much hunted and pursued after,
like a thief with an hue and cry, that our tailors dog it into
France even to the very door. It reigns commonly like an
epidemical disease, first infecting the court, then the city, after
the country, from the countess to the *chambrière*,[5] who rather
than she will want her curled locks, will turn them up with a
hot pair of tongs instead of the irons. The fashion, like an
higher orb, hath the revolution commonly every hundred year,
when the same comes into request again; which I saw once
in Antwerp handsomely described by an he- and she-fool turning a wheel about, with hats, hose, and doublets in the fashion
fastened round about it, which, when they were below, began
to mount up again, as we see them. For example, in the time
of King Henry the Seventh the slashed doublets now used were
in request. Only the coats of the King's guard keep the same
form they did since they were first given them by the said
King, who was the first King of England that had a guard
about his person, and that by the advice of Sir William Stanley,
who was shortly after beheaded for treason, albeit he set the
crown, found thrown in a hawthorn bush, upon the King's head
in the field. After that the Flemish fashion in the time of King
Henry the Eighth came in request—of straight doublets, huge
breeches let out with puffs and codpieces. In Queen Mary's
time the Spanish was much in use. In Queen Elizabeth's time

---

[4] Original: fashion, so.   [5] Chambermaid.

were the great-bellied doublets, wide saucy sleeves that would be in every dish before their master, and buttons as big as tablemen [6] or the lesser sort of Sandwich turnips, with huge ruffs that stood like cartwheels about their necks, and round breeches not much unlike St. Omer's onions, whereto the long stocking without garters was joined; which then was the Earl of Leicester's fashion, and theirs who had the handsomest leg. The women wore straight-bodied gowns with narrow sleeves drawn out with lawn or fine cambric in puff, with high-bolstered wings, little ruffs edged with gold or black silk. And maids wore cauls of gold, now quite out of use. Chains of gold were then of lords, knights, and gentlemen commonly worn, but a chain of gold now (to so high a rate is gold raised) is as much as some of them are worth.

The like variety hath been in hats, which have been but of late years. Henry the Fourth is commonly portrayed with a hood on his head such as the liveries of the city wear on their shoulders. Henry the Sixth, the Seventh, and Eighth wore only caps. King Philip in England wore commonly a somewhat high velvet cap with a white feather. After came in hats of all fashions, some with crowns so high that, beholding them far off, you would have thought you had discovered the Tenerife. Those close to the head like barber's basins, with narrow brims, we were at that time beholden to Cadiz in Spain for. After them came up those with square crowns and brims almost as broad as a brewer's mashvat or a reasonable upper stone of a mustard quern, which among my other epigrams gave me occasion of this:

> Soranzo's broad-brimmed hat I oft compare
> To the vast compass of the heavenly sphere:
> His head, the earth's globe fixed under it,
> Whose center is his wondrous little wit.[7]

---

[6] Pieces used in any game played on a board.
[7] This epigram appeared as no. 11 in *Thalia's Banquet* (1620).

No less variety hath been in hatbands, the cypress being now quite out of use save among some few of the graver sort.

Wherefore the Spaniard and Dutch are much to be commended, who for some hundreds of years never altered their fashion, but have kept always one and the same.[8]

The Switzers, ever since the fatal and final overthrow which they gave to the Duke of Burgundy at Nancy in Lorraine, have worn their parti-colored doublets, breeches, and codpieces, drawn out with huge puffs of taffeta or linen, and their stockings, like the knave of our cards, parti-colored of red and yellow or other colors. I remember at the taking in of the town of Rees in Cleveland between Wesel and Embrick upon the river of Rhine (I being there at the same time), when a part of the Swiss quarter, being before the town, was by accident burned. I demanded of a Swiss captain the reason of their so much affecting colors above other nations. He told me the occasion was honorable, which was this. At what time the Duke of Burgundy received his overthrow and the Swiss recovering their liberty, he entered the field in all the state and pomp he could possible [9] devise. He brought with him all his plate and jewels; all his tents were of silk of several colors, which, the battle being ended, being torn all to pieces by the Swiss soldiers, of a part of one color they made them doublets, of the rest of other colors breeches, stockings, and caps, returning home in that habit. So ever since, in remembrance of that famous victory by them achieved and their liberty recovered, even to this day they go still in their parti-colors. Let me not forget to tell you the occasion of this mortal war. It was only, as Guicciardini tells us, but for the toll of a load of calfskins coming over a bridge, which toll the Duke claimed as his right and the Swiss theirs. But this by the way.

I have much wondered why our English above other nations should so much dote upon new fashions, but more I wonder

[8] Cf. *The Worth of a Penny*, ed. 1669, p. 27.   [9] I.e., possibly.

at our want of wit that we cannot invent them ourselves, but, when one is grown stale, run presently over into France to seek a new, making that noble and flourishing kingdom the magazine of our fooleries. And for this purpose many of our tailors lie ledger [10] there and ladies post over their gentlemen-ushers to accouter them and themselves as you see. Hence came your slashed doublets (as if the wearers were cut out to be carbonadoed upon the coals) and your half shirts; piccadillies, now out of request; your long breeches, narrow toward the knees like a pair of smith's bellows; the spangled garters pendant to the shoe; your perfumed perukes or periwigs to show us that lost hair may be had again for money; with a thousand such fooleries unknown to our manly forefathers.

It was a saying of that noble Roman Cato, *Cui corporis summa cura, ei virtutis maxima incuriae.*[11] And most true it is, since on the contrary we daily find by experience our greatest scholars and statists [12] to offend on the contrary part, being careless and sometime slovenly in their apparel that many times—their thoughts being taken up with studious and profound meditations—they forget to button or to truss themselves. They love their old clothes better than new; they care not for curious setting their ruff, wearing cuffs, etc.

Erasmus in *Epistolis,* I remember, reporteth of Sir Thomas More that *a puero in vestitu semper fuit negligentissimus.*[13] And I believe it to be most true that God hath said by the mouth of his prophet, that "He will visit or send his plague among such as are clothed with strange apparel." [14]

[10] Reside as agents.   [11] Cf. above, p. 149, note 24.   [12] Statesmen.
[13] "From his boyhood he was always most neglectful of his dress."
[14] Zephaniah 1:8.

Of Friendship and Acquaintance

I HAVE ever found the most solid and durable friendship to have been among equals—equals in age, manners, estates, and professions. That with inferiors is subject to many inconveniences, as lavish and needless expending, lending, importunity of entreaty, and sometimes discredit. On the contrary, that with superiors, which I cannot properly call friendship, but raiseth or depresseth a man in valuation high or low, as they please themselves. And this friendship is but a kind of subjection or slavery. As he is your friend, a great man inviteth you to dinner to his table; the sweetness of that favor and kindness is made distasteful by the awe of his greatness—in his presence not to be covered, to sit down and to be placed where and under whom he pleaseth, to be tongue-tied all the while, though you be able to speak more to the purpose than himself and all his company. While you whisper in a waiter's ear for anything that you want, you must endure to be carved unto many times of the first, worst, or rawest of the meat. Sometime you have a piece preferred unto you from his own trencher, but then imagine his belly is full or he cannot for some other reason eat it himself, so that for true and free content you were better seek your dinner with some honest companion in Pie Corner.[1] Besides, they love you should have a kind of dependency of them, that they might make use of you at their pleasure, if you be well qualified, rewarding you with promises and overtures of great matters of future hope. In the meantime you must live only by countenance and shift for yourself. In a word, to trust to this superlative friendship is but as an earthen pot to join

---

[1] A street between Newgate and Smithfield noted chiefly for its cooks' shops.

yourself to one of brass, who under a color of assisting you in the stream will crack your sides one way or other. And it is one thing to be necessitous and stand in need of great ones' friendship, and another out of your election to apply yourself to such whereof I only speak.

So that the first point of discretion in the choice of a friend is to know whether he be real or superficial, whether he aimeth at his own ends or tendereth and is willing to advance your good. Indeed, poverty and necessity, according to St. Jerome, be touchstones for the trial of real friendship. *Ob hoc unicum,* saith he, *amanda est paupertas, ut a quibus ameris intelligas.*[2] Yet according to Seneca not the truest and the best: *Amor virtutis est morum similitudo,* the love of virtue and likeness of manners begetteth amongst men the most solid durable friendship.

Sometimes there is a sympathy in nature whereby one man affecteth the friendship and acquaintance of another whom before he never saw in his life, yea, and it may be whom he never saw at all, as a duchess of Burgundy fell in love with a nobleman whom she only heard two strangers commend for his person and rare qualities, walking on the other side of the river near to her court.

The common and ordinary friendship of the world is measured by the benefit that one man reaps by another, according to Ovid.

> *Turpe quidem dictu sed si modo vera fatemur*
> *Vulgus amicitias utilitate probat:*
> *Sed vix invenias multis in millibus unum*
> *Virtutis pretio qui putat esse sui.*[3]

---

[2] "Poverty ought to be loved for the sole reason that you then know by whom you are loved."

[3] Ovid *Ex ponto* ii.3.8–9, 11–12: "It is shameful to say, but if we confess the truth, the herd always value friendships for profit; but hardly will you find one in many thousands who considers virtue its own reward."

The Truth of Our Times

And this friendship for the most part lives and expires with men's lives and their fortunes, and indeed merits not the name of friendship. I confess myself to have found more friendship at a stranger's hand whom I never in my life saw before, yea, and in foreign parts beyond the seas, than among the most of my nearest kindred and old acquaintance here in England, who have professed much toward me in empty promises.

The ordinary friendship of our times is but mere acquaintance, whose utmost bound and extent is, in the country, entertainment for you and your horse a night or two. In the city, an old acquaintance meets you, and with admiration "Good Lord," saith he, "are you alive yet!" when he sees you and speaks to you; [4] then at the next tavern gives you a pint or a quart of wine; at the court you are shown the king or queen at dinner. So that if among one hundred of your acquaintance, yea, five hundred, you meet with two or three faithful friends, think yourself happy. Such is the world in our cunning age.

You may also be much deceived by overweening, taking those for friends which indeed are not. Such friendship you ordinarily meet with over a cup of wine in a tavern, where they will call you brother and promise you all kindness by giving you their hands, and the next morning when the grosser parts of the wine are turned to melancholic dregs, as is usual with Dutchmen, they look on you like lions and never were the men.[5]

The vows of such vanish into air, to the often loss of your labor in visiting, soliciting, and attending them at their houses or chambers. Sometimes you shall be so injuriously dealt withal, as, by believing their promises, you shall in hope take tedious journeys to London, the court, and other places, and when you have done all, you shall only find your horse tired, your purse emptied, and yourself in your expectation merely [6]

[4] Original: sees him and speaks to him.
[5] I.e., the men you knew the night before.   [6] Wholly.

abused. So I wish thee, whosoever thou art, to have as little to do with these transcendent great ones on the one side as the useless inferiors and *vaultneants* [7] on the other.

I have often considered with myself whether a man were the better or the worse for multitude of acquaintance. I concluded generally the worse, considering the most are of no use unto us, casting into the account the expense of money, loss of time, and neglect of business.

The best acquaintance is with such as you may better yourself by any way, especially in knowledge of discourse and conference (which was the ancient course of learning; according to Euripides, ὁμιλία ἔτεκε τέχνας, converse was the mother of arts) either with general scholars, travelers, such as are skilled in the tongues and in mechanical arts. For by conversing with such you shall husband your time to the best and take the shortest cut to knowledge. Besides, the keeping of such company getteth you the reputation of being understanding and learned as they are, though yet a puisne and a novice in their studies and professions.

The best way to preserve a gotten friend is thankfully to acknowledge the benefit you have received from him; to endeavor all you can to requite his courtesy some way or other; to use him tenderly and not oft, and then but in cases of necessity when, as a good sword, you shall see what metal he is made of; to give him no occasion by your ill carriage or unthriftness to think ill of you; to go on in an honest way and calling, that he may think his courtesies well bestowed and be the readier to assist and further you. For commonly friends accumulate one good turn upon another, especially where they have found the former to have been seasonably and profitably bestowed.

[7] "Good-for-nothings, rascals."

Of Parents and Children

ALL parents are naturally indulgent to their children, especially while they are young. Yet the height of their affection or coldness of love toward them appeareth not until they are of riper years, at what time they do them equal wrong, either in giving them the rein of liberty and spending or being overharsh, unnatural, and hard-hearted over them. I have known excellent spirits and many noble wits lost and undone either way.

Some mothers, when their children are young, are so fond [1] over them as by no means they will endure them out of their sight, much less send them abroad to school or to be nurtured by others abroad, by whom they profit more than at home. Hence it comes to pass that so many great and rich men's sons and heirs, when they come toward men's estate, are so simple and easy to be wrought upon by crafty knaves and cheaters. Hence we see them often brought upon the stage under the names of Sir Simple, John Daw, Abraham Ninny, and the like, their study being nothing else but the newest fashion, what tavern to go to dinner to, or stare at every post to see where the newest play is that afternoon.

I knew a great lady that had only one son of some fourteen or fifteen of age, whom indeed she would have brought up at school, but he must go when himself listed and have two men to carry him thither and to bring him home again to dinner and supper. He was once in my charge, and I remember not a bit of meat would down with him without sauce, which must be extraordinary too, as the juice of lemons with sugar and rose water. Sometime if it were a dainty fowl, as partridge, gray plover, or the like, he must have wine mixed with bread

[1] Foolish.

crumbs and the juice of an orange. Pepper he could not abide, for it bit him by the tongue. His breakfast was either a caudle or a manchet spread with almond butter. Being one day with his mother at dinner, she seemed to be overjoyed in that her son fell to eating of beef, which, she protested, he never did before in his life. And now she verily believed he would prove a soldier. Indeed he proved very valiant after, for he kicked his mother and told her he was better descended than ever she was, so that it seems strong meats have strange effects. In earnest this young gentleman was the only one whom I ever knew to prove towardly and good after such a motherly education. Indeed, as I said, he was sometimes my scholar and at this day is as understanding, civil, discreet, and as thrifty a gentleman as is in the west part of England.

Some, again, in the universities maintain their sons at such an height that there, instead of studying the seven liberal sciences, they study seven couple of hounds. Yet I must needs say they there grow perfect in the Spanish, French, and the Dutch, that is, sack, claret, and Rhenish, while poor scholars make their exercises. And some of these now and then (unknown to their friends) clap up a match with some seamster, chambermaid, or tradesman's daughter. That news is carried to their fathers, how their sons have profited so well in the university that they have gotten more in an hour than they know what to do withal all their lives after.

Hence, being men, they become unserviceable both for the church and state, and, being no scholars, they hate learning in others. Whereupon, when in learned company they can say little, they break jests upon others, or, which is the more generous and commendable, if it be a tavern and upon a spending occasion, they will *numerando symbolum officium sarcire,* as Erasmus saith, make amends by paying a good part of the reckoning and, being no scholars, show their loves to scholars.

On the other side there are some fathers so unnatural and

harsh toward their children that they are not only careless in giving them any education at all, but no means of maintenance to support their livelihood, turning them off young to shift in the wide world, seek their fortunes among strangers, and become servants to others, or, if they stay at home, use them in that manner by blows and beating or ill and uncomfortable words, withdrawing timely help for their preferments, that all their lives after they loathe their father's house and the very sight of the place where they were bred and born.

I knew a very rich and able man in Norfolk that while he lived would allow his children no means at all to live upon (they being at man's estate and very civil and honest gentlemen) save the windfalls of trees in his woods, and to make their best by selling them; but, no winds stirring, they were fain to help themselves by digging the roots loose within the earth, then covering them again with turfs that the least wind in a manner would lay them along. And these shifts do merciless fathers put their children unto, who, though by nature towardly, ingenious, and no way viciously given, are oftentimes through poverty and want wrested from the bent and that natural and inbred honesty of mind to do things base and unbeseeming. Whereupon Mantuan wisely complaineth of poverty, saying, *O mala paupertas vitii scelerisque ministra.*[2] I have known some, whom their fathers having sent to the universities or the Inns of Court, have left their houses and course of studies for want of maintenance, making money of books, bedding, and such as they had, to shift elsewhere. Hence they have not been able to keep company with the better sort. They are undervalued all their lives after, whatsoever their good parts are. They are constrained to walk on foot, take up their lodging in base alehouses, be hail-fellow with every tinker by every fireside. Many times driven by necessity, they borrow of their kindred or father's tenants, lie at their houses. Sometimes for

[2] "O evil poverty, the abettor of vice and crime." Cf. above, p. 184.

debt or despair they are fain to leave the land and seek means in foreign countries, either by turning soldiers or seminaries.[3] Sometimes not going so far, they take purses about home, ending their miserable days at the gallows, where they cry out against their parents'—fathers' especially—hardness and carelessness of them in neither giving them maintenance or settling them in some course wherein they might have lived and proved honest men and good members in the commonwealth.

Neither must parents have all the share in their children's undoing, since I know, though many are hard enough, they all would have their children to do well and the most are careful enough to bring them up in all virtuous education. Yet many times their children are refractory and averse to all goodness, out of an ill temperature of the mind by nature, and prove so notoriously evil that nothing can reduce them to civility and honesty. Such a one was Troilo Savelli of late years in Rome. Descended of noble and honest parents, being their only child and hope of their house, who, by that time he was sixteen years of age, joining himself to the *banditti* or outlawed thieves and robbers, became the arrantest villain one of them that ever Italy bred. And before those years his mother laid him up in prison, being glad to keep him alive there, but he, breaking out and falling to murdering, robbing, and acting all manner of mischief, was afterward beheaded. If I mistake not, there is a story of his life translated out of Italian into English by Sir Tobie Matthew.[4] I have often seen and read it over in Dutch. But this by the way.

Sometimes among children the parents have two hopeful and the third void of all grace; sometimes all good saving the eldest.

I remember, when I was a schoolboy in London, Tarlton acted a third son's part, such a one as I now speak of. His

---

[3] Seminarians, students in a seminary.
[4] A work by G. Blondo, translated as *A Relation of the Death of T. Savelli* (1620); STC 3134.

father, being a very rich man and lying upon his deathbed, called his three sons about him, who with tears and on their knees craved his blessing, and to the eldest son, said he, "You are mine heir, and my land must descend upon you, and I pray God bless you with it." The eldest son replied, "Father, I trust in God you shall yet live to enjoy it yourself." To the second son said he, "You are a scholar, and what profession soever you take upon you, out of my land I allow you threescore pounds a year toward your maintenance and three hundred pounds to buy you books." As his brother he, weeping, answered, "I trust, father, you shall live to enjoy your money yourself. I desire it not," etc. To the third, which was Tarlton (who came like a rogue, in a foul shirt without a band, and in a blue coat with one sleeve, his stockings out at the heels and his head full of straw and feathers), "As for you, sirrah," quoth he, "you know how often I have fetched you out of Newgate and Bridewell. You have been an ungracious villain. I have nothing to bequeath to you but the gallows and a rope." Tarlton, weeping and sobbing upon his knees as his brothers, said, "O father, I do not desire it. I trust in God you shall live to enjoy it yourself." There are many such sons of honest and careful parents in England at this day.

I have also known many children to have proved and become honest and religious through the loathing of the parents' vices and lewdness of behavior, as, if they have been addicted to drunkenness, the child would never abide it, or, if to swearing, their son was free from that vice. Yea, many times children have proved their parents' best advisers and reclaimers from their vices.

I never knew any child thrive in the world that was rebellious against father or mother by cursing them, abusing them, scorning them, as many do that come to preferment and high place from a poor parentage and a mean beginning, but the judgment of God hath fallen heavy upon them at one time or other.

211

Solomon saith,[5] "The ravens shall pick out the eyes of such in the valley," meaning they shall be hanged and left for ravens and other fowls to feed upon.

I have also known very religious and honest parents, withal of very great ability, who have had but only one son in the world, heir not only to their own inheritance, but also to brothers' and other of kin, to whom they have given allowance according to his own desire, as his horse to ride on whither it pleased him, money to spend among gentlemen, to stay at home or go whither and when he listed. Yet all this and all the care they could take could not keep him at home, but, like a vagabond, to wander up and down the country with common rogues and gypsies till at the last he came to the gallows. I have known two of this humor, being the sons of very rich and able men, my loving friends.

From sons I come to daughters, of whom I have known many proper young gentlewomen, daughters to rich and miserable clowns, who, to save their money for portions and servants' wages, keep them at home unmarried, making drudges of them to do all manner of work about the house, till, growing stale maids, they bestow themselves on their fathers' horsekeepers, servingmen, many times on tailors that come to work at their houses, and so are oftentimes undone forever.

That among these extremes we may come to a mediocrity, let both the parent and the child listen to and remember the short but pithy advice of St. Paul in their reciprocal duty: "Children, obey your parents; parents, provoke not your children." [6] I never knew a race to thrive and prosper but where there was a firm and mutual love of one toward the other: in the child a true filial and fearful to offend; in the father that same στοργή, or natural affection, descending and applying itself without bitterness to the disposition of weak and childish age.

Likewise between brother and sister. And this is preserved

[5] Prov. 30:17.   [6] Col. 3:20–21.

and cherished by a moderate and wise indulgence of the parents, as, if ought be amiss, by familiar admonition, teaching, gently rebuking, discoursing with them as with strangers of years and understanding; and, growing to men and women's estate, to supply their wants, keeping them neat, and, with the best of their rank, fashionable in apparel, which addeth spirit unto them, maketh them to think well of themselves, and teacheth them to make good choice of their company and acquaintance; lastly, it maketh them in all places to be respected and their friends commended. It is also fitting that a father, when his son grows near man, not only to supply his corporal necessities, but also to allow him money in his purse to keep company with his equals and sometimes to lay out upon a good bargain which unexpectedly he may meet withal. Hereby he will learn to love and keep his money, lay it out to the best advantage to keep and maintain his credit. He shall be known and get reputation in the world. He will become more obsequious to his parents and friends when those penniless and, long of [7] their parents, poor ones are a disgrace to their parents, the object of pity to their friends, and a scorn to every golden ass and their enemies, and, which is most lamentable, are sometimes driven to be beholding [8] to these. There was a miserable slave not long since that had kept three- or fourscore load of hay two or three years, hoping it would be still dearer when it was at five pounds and ten shillings the load, but presently it falling to forty shillings, went into his barn, takes a stool to stand on, and, throwing a rope over a beam, kicks down the stool and so hangs. His son, being threshing on the other side of the wall, hearing the stool fall, runs in and, seeing his father hanging, takes his knife and cuts him down, rubs him and recovers him. His son a week after, coming for his week's wages for threshing (for his father allowed him nothing but what he dearly earned), he abated him twopence, which the son told

[7] On account of.   [8] Beholden, indebted.

him was wanting. His father answered, the rope which he cut cost him so much and he should pay for it. The son, departing heavily, told his father, if he would forgive him that twopence, he should not want a new rope at any time, withal wished for his own sake he might not find him at the like business again.

It is also worthy the observation that when God would destroy and root out a wicked family or generation from the face of the earth, he suffers enmity and discord to reign and divide a kindred in their affections one toward another. The father hates the child, the child the father; the sister cannot abide her brother, the brother speaks ill of the sister, purloining one from the other. They seldom or never see or visit in kindly manner one another. In sickness one will not relieve or comfort one another, nay, many times grudge a night's lodging. In a word, no more regard of blood or alliance amongst them than among swine. This I have often observed and, when of such a family, in a few years not one of the name hath been left.

Of Clowns and Rude Behavior

SCALIGER reporteth [1] that our English country husbandmen and Gascons to be of all other the most clownish and uncivil, wherein he is much deceived. For the boors of High and Low Germany are ten times worse, as well in their education, manners, and civility, in respect of whom ours in general are most genteel, humane, and courteous. Some we have, I confess, merely *terrae filii*,[2] mushrooms in a night shot up and nourished by the dung of the earth, that have neither religion, wit, or moderation—

[1] *Angli rustici et Vascones sunt omnium inhumanissimi.* [The Vascones were not the people of Gascony, France, but the old Basques of what is now modern Navarre.]

[2] "Sons of the soil."

professed enemies to understanding, learning, civility, and all manner of gentility, by nature commonly so base and miserable that they could find in their hearts they had come into the world like calves, with skins of hair, that they might never have gone to a draper's for cloth, or, like Pan, to have got feet of horn, [that] they could have kept their money from the shoemaker. Like that emblematical sow, their noses are ever rooting in the earth, with *Ulterius* over her back.[3] They commonly love the church so well that they had rather spend ten pounds in suit than allow him one tithe pig out of nine. *Erra Pater*[4] and this year's almanac, if he can read, are the two only books he spends his time in. And if a shower of rain extraordinarily happens in haytime or harvest, he grumbles against God, beats his maids, and looks currishly upon any that speaks to him.

Of all men in the world he cannot endure lawyers, but evermore he is barking against them, as dogs do at tinkers, not because they stop holes in their dame's kettles, but because they make their budgets of their skins. If a gentleman or nobleman happens to ride in hawking time over his grounds, he bans and curses him and his followers to the pit of hell; for between your clown and gentleman there is ever an antipathy. If I should tell you how the late Prince of Orange, Grave[5] Maurice, hath been answered amongst his boors as he passed through the country, you would say our country of England was a school of civility in regard of those countries.

Charles the Fifth, that religious and puissant emperor, when by fortune of war he was pursued and chased by the Duke of Saxony and the Landgrave of Hesse and, in a very dark and rainy night having lost his way among the heaths and woods, having only two or three in his company, fortuned to come

[3] This emblem appeared in Geoffrey Whitney's *Choice of Emblems* (1586), p. 53.
[4] *The Prognostication forever of Master Erra Pater* (1536?); STC 10515–10526. Cf. *Notes and Queries*, 10th ser., VIII, 518.
[5] Landgrave, Count.

to a boor's house that stood under a wood's side and, knocking, desired entertainment but to sit up by the fire till it were day. The boor, looking out at his window, as boars thrust their heads of the frank,[6] said he and his wife were in bed, and he was some skellum or rogue that would be out so late. If he would, to use his own words, *Met siin verkens slaepen*, rest him with his pigs in an outhouse, he might. In he should not come. The Emperor then desired of him to know what time of night it was. The boor told him *all by twee heuren*, near two of clock in the morning. The Emperor asked him how he knew. The clown replied, *Ick hebt nu ghepist*, he had but newly made water.[7] These entertainments are common amongst them, yea, were he the greatest prince of the empire. I once lived in a town where scarce a gentleman or any of civil carriage lived, and, having found but ill requital for good deserts, I caused this to be written over the porch of their free school door: *Subi dura a rudibus*.[8] It is a palindrome, the letters making the same again backwards. To know an absolute clown, observe these his conditions. He had rather be spreading of dung than go to the leanest sermon in the shire. He murmurs at all payments and levies, especially the money to be collected for the maintenance of his Majesty's navy royal. If he fortune to be churchwarden of his parish, at every brief gathering in the church he reserves a groat or sixpence to himself. If he do affect to follow the fashion in his clothes, it is long of [9] his wife, some gentleman's daughter who was matched unto him for his wealth, and, being fine, he takes his place above her and all women at the table. Salute him on his way, he will give you never a word. His hands are commonly unwashed, and his doublet unbuttoned but never trussed. His ordinary discourse is of last year's hay,

---

[6] Pigsty.

[7] P. has an epigram upon this incident in his *Thalia's Banquet* (1620), no. 116.

[8] "Endure rude things from boors." Cf. above, p. 157.

[9] Because of.

which he hopes will give six pounds the load in Smithfield, and of the rate of swine in Rumford market. All his jests consist in rude actions with the hand or foot. His speech is Lincolnshire about Wrangle and Frieston; [10] if he be westward, about Taunton and ten miles beyond. And though the most of them wear russet and have their high shoes well nailed, yet they are often too hard for velvet and satin, in law tricks and quiddities, and commonly hold their own the longest. Great men that hold them hard and keep them under have them as they list. Yield unto one of them or stand to his mercy, you shall find no tyrant more imperious and cruel. Most true is that old verse:

Rustica gens est optima
Flens et pessima ridens.[11]

Of Travel

THE true taste of our lives' sweetness is in travel upon the way, at home, or abroad in other countries. For not only it affordeth change of air, which is very availful [1] to health, but variety of objects and remarkable occasions to entertain our thoughts, besides choice of acquaintance with able and excellent men in all faculties and of all nations, and perhaps some such as you would ever after think your labor and expense of money well bestowed if you had but only passed the sea for their acquaintance. Such an one I met withal traveling in a very rainy evening through a muddy part of Westphalia where I had lost my way, and it grew near night and, in Latin demanding of him the way toward Oldenburg and how I had lost my way, using the

[10] Small villages of Lincolnshire.
[11] "Rustic people weep at good fortune and laugh at bad."
[1] Advantageous.

word *deviavi hic,* he answered *humanum est errare.*[2] To be short, he would not suffer me to pass any further, but carried me home to his own house, which was almost half a mile off, where I never found better entertainment or had more friendlier respect in all my life.

The first thing in any good town wherever I came, so soon as I had made choice of mine inn and lodging, was of my acquaintance, for in all places you shall meet with very civil and courteous people, evermore of the better sort, in Italy especially, who will show you all respect and kindness, but without charge. You must never put them to any expense or charge, no, not so much as to come to dinner to their houses, though you be solemnly invited. And, on the contrary, look that nobody be chargeable to you. You shall have many times, as also here in England, as soon as you are alighted at your inn or harbory, fellows that will insinuate themselves into your company and acquaintance, beginning either by commending your horse or demanding how far you have come that day, or of what country you are, and the like, and after perhaps will offer their service to show you the town, to bring you acquainted with some famous man there living, or carry you *ad calidas et callidas solis filias,*[3] as Lipsius calleth them, to the handsomest wenches about the town. *Sed aures obtura ad has Sirenum cantiunculas;* [4] rather be alone perusing some good book in your chamber, or walk by yourself.

You shall in travel never lose ought by silence. Many have paid dearly for their lavish tongues in strange countries, especially being far from home and where they must not be allowed to be their own interpreters, especially in matter of religion and

---

[2] "I have gone astray here, . . . To err is human." Original: *hic,* answered.

[3] Cf. p. 162 above, and note.

[4] "But stop your ears against the enticing songs of the Sirens."

state, when you shall find it safer and better to talk of the Great
Turk than the Pope.

Let your observations be of such things whereby you may
profit yourself or your country—yourself by procuring and win-
ning the acquaintance of the famous men in science or art for
the bettering of your understanding and skill in whatsoever
you pretend unto. If you study physic, you shall have in Paris
and other places of France the most learned and able physicians of the world. If you would be a civilian, Bononia [Bo-
logna] and other cities of Italy will afford you the rarest men
in that way. If you delight in painting and the use of your
pencil, the Netherlands everywhere will afford you rare masters;
if in other mechanical arts, the higher Germany, which Bodin
calleth *hominum officinam* [5] for the variety of artists there. And
therein Speyer, Strasbourg,[6] Nuremberg, and many other famous cities will furnish you with skillful men abundantly.

I have observed as I have gone along those countries many
excellent points of good husbandry in fields and gardens which
we here in England have not been acquainted withal, as in
manuring their land so at one time that it shall bear a great
crop seven or ten years together; their artificial plows that shall
turn up in a day as much as two of ours; their neat and handsome stacking of their corn abroad to stand dry all the winter;
their many devices for draining of grounds, casting of moats
and town ditches; many excellent forms of grafting, adulterat-
ing plants and flowers, with infinite such devices.

Apparel abroad is much dearer than here in England, especially cloth. Stuffs are cheap and ordinary in the Netherlands;
so are velvets and silks about Naples and other parts of Italy,
and commonly worn of tradesmen's wives and daughters.

Boots and shoes are very dear everywhere, especially in
France, for leather is there very scarce, so that if I had but

[5] "The workshop of men."   [6] Original: Spires, Shasbourge.

the monopoly of carrying old shoes, newly mended, and mastiff whelps into France, I should think to live as well and as happily as Master Mayor of Quinborrow.[7] For diet I bought what I liked and learned one thing not usual with us in England save in cooks' shops; that is, to know the price of meat before you eat it. If our young gallants would observe this rule in costly taverns, who only call for a bill at the end of dinner, they would have money many times when they want it. But they esteem it a disgrace better befitting carriers and aqua vitae men than gentlemen of rank. Hence it cometh to pass they pay eight shillings for a capon, as my L. of N.[8] gentleman did once at Greenwich; another, a mark or fourteen shillings for a pair of soles, I having often bought as good at Bennington [9] in Holland for threepence. And as I would not have you to be familiar with everyone, so it is good so to retire yourself as you scorned to eat or drink in any other company. For, note, you cannot take up your chamber and call for your meat thither, but commonly an ordinary is kept where all the guests sit down together, of what country or condition it makes no matter. If they be merry, you must be so too, or at least feign yourself to be. If they drink to you, you must pledge them, for their draughts are but sippings, not carousing whole pints and quarts as among our tosspots in England. So shall you be beloved and made welcome amongst them. Otherwise, they will suspect you to be a spy from the enemy or to scorn their company, whereby you come into danger of being quarreled withal, suddenly stabbed among the Dutch with a knife, in Italy to be poisoned, etc.

Travel, like physic, upon several complexions works diversely. With a staid and mature judgment it doth best; such return

[7] Queenborough in Kent. This legendary figure is introduced into Middleton's *The Mayor of Queenborough* (1661).

[8] Lord of N.'s gentleman?

[9] Did P. intend to write *Benekom*, a village near Arnhem? I find no such English name as *Bennington* in Holland.

much bettered by it. Those who are sent young and childish, whom foolish fathers and mothers would have thought to be rare and ripe-witted, become the worse by it for wanting judgment to understand the true use of travel, to know with whom to converse, and what to observe, but only to follow and to wear a lovelock on the left shoulder, return home as wise as the ass who, undertaking to travel into far countries and to acquaint himself with strange beasts abroad, at last returning home, he asked the fox how he liked him since he undertook his journey. The fox replied and told him plainly he saw no difference in him but that his mane and his tail were grown longer. If they chance to go into the Netherlands, and perhaps get to be gentlemen of a company but of three weeks' standing, then at their return among their companions they must be styled by the name of captain, they must stand upon that airy title and mere nothing, reputation, undertake every quarrel and challenge or become seconds to those that will. It is a great want of discretion, besides very dangerous, to tell or show your money openly in strange places where you are unknown, or to travel upon the way extraordinary rich in your clothes. Hereby many have been betrayed and lost their lives, as a gentleman and an acquaintance of mine, Master W. T., was pistoled by his guide in the forest of Ardennes because, riding in a suit laid thick with gold lace, he was supposed to have had store of crowns.

Erasmus, I remember, in his *Epistles* tells us how narrowly he escaped his throat-cutting one night in an inn where he drew store of money out of his velvet pouch, which commonly he wore at his girdle; that he was fain to rise in his shirt with another that lay in the same chamber, to barricade the door with a form and some stools to keep his host out, who was an arrant thief.

Be as thrifty as possible you can, as well in your apparel as diet, for you shall many times be hard beset for money. And if you can otherwise avoid it, go seldom upon credit, which is not gentlemanlike abroad, but much more base in England, where for the most part hosts and hostesses are far more un-conscionable than they are there. For spend five pounds at a sitting, you shall not be misreckoned a penny, and they expect as just dealing from you. Here you shall be shamefully wronged except you very narrowly look to your layings-out, besides meet with ill pennyworths,[10] paying as good many times as forty in the hundred for the use of your credit.

I could wish every young gentleman, before he travels into foreign parts, *non esse domi peregrini,*[11] because here are many rarities in England, and our coast towns are worthy the view and the knowing, if it were but only to satisfy strangers who are many times inquisitive of the state of England, yea, and many times know it better than most of our homeborn gentlemen. Herein Sir Robert Carr of Sleaford in Lincolnshire, a noble gentleman and my worthy friend, was much to be commended.

A Religious Honest Man

I never knew any man of sound judgment and fit for employ-ment either in church or commonwealth but he endeavored to be religious. For *Virtutum vel optimarum actionum basis re-ligio,*[1] and there are many who, though they make not outward show thereof by those actions and gestures which may also be common to hypocrites, yet the bias of the life of an honest man would ever lean, for doing and discourse, to a serious service of God. Hence such men keep their church together with their families constantly, there carrying himself with the greatest reverence and humility.

You shall know a religious honest man by humility, charity,

---

[10] Very poor value for your money.

[11] "Not to be strangers at home." See also above, pp. 63, note 31; 161.

[1] "Religion is the foundation of the virtues as well as of the best actions." Original reads *Virtutem.*

love of hospitality. Hence he is discreet in his discourse, affable, pleasant, and peaceable among his neighbors, loving, and beloved.

He backbiteth and traduceth none, meddleth not with matters and affairs of state, well knowing, like those builders of the Tower of Babel, that a rash affection of things too high bringeth discord and confusion. And if any controversy shall arise among his neighbors, he commonly hath compounded the strife ere the la[w]yer can finger his fee.

His tithes he payeth cheerfully and with the most, well knowing that God by Malachi hath promised a blessing by the opening of the windows of heaven upon such as pay their tithes truly and with alacrity.[2]

He is versed and very ready in the Holy Scriptures and their orthodox exposition, never wresting or misapplying them, as sectaries do to serve their purposes and suit with their fantastical or willful opinions.

As Mahomet and his followers affirmed that place of St. John,[3] where our Saviour saith, "I will send you a comforter," to be meant of himself, or in that place something to be written of Mahomet which the Christians have scraped or blotted out.

So not long since a false prophet affirmed that himself was one of those two witnesses St. John speaketh of in the eleventh of the Revelation.

The like examples may be produced from David George, Knipperdollink, Hacket,[4] and others, which we pass.

---

[2] Malachi 3:10.　　　　　　　　[3] *John 14.

[4] David George, an account of whose "life and damnable heresy" was published at Basel in 1592 (STC 14794), was a Dutch painter who made himself chief of the Davists or Davidians and proclaimed himself the Messiah; Bernhardt Knipperdollink was one of the leaders of the Anabaptists of Münster who was brutally tortured to death; and William Hacket, the English fanatic, who claimed he had been sent to prepare the way for the Messiah, was later found guilty of conspiracy against the Queen and was executed in 1591.

Again, the moderate religious man forbears with open mouth to rail against the Pope, but speaks of him in a modest reverence as of a great bishop and a temporal prince.

He is also to his power a benefactor to poor scholars, and though not learned himself, he is a prompter [5] of learning. So was Wykeham, Bishop of Winchester, who, being no great scholar himself, said, to make amends he would make scholars, and soon after he founded Winchester School and New College in Oxford.

He loveth unity and praiseth it as well in church or commonwealth as his own parish and family. Hence is he opposite *ex diametro* [6] to separatists and schismatics, who, since they fall in my way, let me tell you what out of my own experience I have known and found by them, having remained a good time at Leyden in Holland and other places where they have their congregations and conventicles. There are about thirty-two several sects, among some whereof are called *huiskoopers,* other *huisverkoopers,* i.[e.], housebuyers and housesellers, and such enmity there is among them that the pride of their heads or ringleaders will never permit [7] an unity one with another.

Now why the sectaries should single out themselves after this manner I confess I know not; perhaps not without the divine providence, and for that very same reason Joseph Acosta giveth of beasts and birds of prey, whom God as pernicious and hurtful to mankind hath set at odds and at enmity one with the other. For if they should accompany together in herds and flocks, they would overrun and devour a whole country, as among beasts, lions, bears, wolves, foxes, badgers, polecats, etc.; and among birds, eagles, hawks, kites, ravens, vultures, buzzards, etc., when nature for the behoof of man hath set others which are most profitable unto him at unity among themselves and to live peacefully one with the other, as kine, horses, deer, sheep,

[5] Promoter.   [6] "Diametrically opposed."
[7] Original: never an.

goats, conies, etc.; of birds, pigeons, geese, ducks, partridges, the most of the daintiest of sea birds, with sundry others.

I have heard some of their sermons and been present at their private ordinary discourse, and somewhat alway seasoned the same that savored either pride or malice or both, especially against our church and the happy and well-settled estate of the same.

We must make a difference between our stricter people in England, whom your profaner sort call Precisians, and those who are superintendents over a few buttonmakers and weavers at Amsterdam. For of ours we have many conformable to his Majesty's laws and the ceremonies of the church, carrying themselves very honestly and conscionably; among which I reckon not the professed Puritan, of whom I know many who gladly take that name and profession upon them, being tradesmen in cities and market towns, only to get custom to their shops. And working themselves into the opinion of the world to be honest, religious, and upright-dealing men, they procure to themselves many salutations—like the Pharisees—in the market place, and hence they become the prime men at feasts and meetings, and are trusted with the estates and education of men's children at the death of the parents, out of the opinion of their zeal and honesty, whereby they become marvelous rich and by consequent so proud that, as St. Augustine saith of the Donatists, *ne nostri cuiquam dicant Ave*, they will not bid a conformist good morrow or good even, and, sitting in their fur- or velvet-faced gowns, with their neat-set double ruffs, they tax, with Augustus, all the world. But some of these men have not many years since reformed themselves.

There is yet another sort amongst us worse than these, who like double-faced Janus one way look to their own parish church and the other eastward toward St. Peter's in Rome. These indeed are *filii huius seculi*,[8] and here only have their reward,

[8] "Sons of this age."

making religion only as a cloak or waistcoat to be worn both sides alike. Some profess themselves Roman Catholics that their families might keep Lent, all the Saints' eves, Ember, and all other fasting days, whereby their masters save in their victuals their whole year's wages. Another while they are Protestants and will monthly visit the church to avoid the penalty of the law or to insinuate themselves into some gainful employment or other in the commonwealth. These be those lukewarm Laodiceans [9] whom God cannot digest and whom I have known both Protestant and Papist alike to have discarded. There, I remember, is a country, whether Utopia or no, where those who side equally with contrary factions wear parti-colored coats and stockings. Besides, they are great rackers of their tenants, backward and resty [10] in all levies and payments for the common good, seldom charitable to the poor, and the worst payers of their tithes and duties to the church and minister that may be.

Of Discretion

THE old Lord Burghley, sometime treasurer of England, coming to Cambridge with Queen Elizabeth, when he was led into the public schools and had much commended their convenience, beauty, and greatness they had sometime received from their founder, Humphrey, the good Duke of Gloucester, "Yea, marry," said he, "but I find one school wanting in our universities, and that is the school of discretion." In what sense he meant it I know not, but most true it is that though discretion be none of the liberal sciences it is an art that gives all other their value and estimation, and without which, as a ship without an helm, an horse without a bridle, or a blind man without a guide, men

[9] * Rev. 3:16. [10] Stubborn, sluggish.

do they know not what, go they know not whither, and instead of steering a right course run upon the rocks of their irrecoverable ruin.

Discretion is so called of *discerno*, which properly is to sever or part one thing from another, as to divide or sift the flour from the bran, silver from the lead, a quintessence from elementary parts. So that metaphorically it is applied to our judgments in severing or dividing virtue from vice, that which is honest from that which is profitable, the necessary from the superfluous, a friend from a foe, etc., and indeed it is the highest pitch of understanding and judgment, which the most men seem to have but fall short of, yea, in their weightiest actions; in which our actions of it claimeth so great an interest that without discretion the whole course of our lives is nothing else but folly or rashness, as I found well expressed in this distich which I found engraven upon the heft of a learned lady's knife in Brabant:

> *Omnia si repetas humanae tempora vitae,*
> *Vel male, vel temere, vel nihil egit homo.*[1]

Whence cometh it to pass that so many men undo themselves and their posterity forever by selling and making away such fair estates left them by their friends, but lack of discretion, their judgments being so corrupted that they think they shall never want—their children will otherwise be provided for. While they wear the best clothes they shall be respected, beloved of ladies, saluted by citizens, congeed [2] by courtiers, and the like. Now the salt of discretion should first have seasoned his brains in this or the like way. While walking in his garden in the country or under a solitary woodside, he should have thought with himself,

[1] "If you will recall all the stages of human life, you will find that man acts either evilly or rashly or not at all."
[2] Bowed to.

God hath blessed me with a fair estate, and, as Henry the Fourth said to his son, the prince, "Getting is a chance, but keeping is a wit." And what a difference of happiness is there in enjoying and coming freely to an estate left by friends than in attaining to the same by continual labor of my body, hazarding my health in sitting up late, rising early, to endure heat, hunger, cold, and the like extremities; then to be only master of the same a very few years, yea, sometime days. That most truly Martial as a principal happiness accounted,

Res relicta, non parta labore.

An estate left, and not by labor gained.

Now if I part with this, let me believe and assuredly say with the philosopher, *A privatione in habitum nulla est regressio.*[3] I may another day come by and view, saying with a sigh of me and mine, *Fuimus Troes;* [4] this was ours once. How have I wronged you, my poor children! Who will feed and entertain you? But you are like to wander up and down and seek untimely death in the errors of your lives. And for myself, who will relieve me when all is gone? I would be loath to depend upon any, being of a generous and free spirit, and *debere quibus nolis miserrimum.*[5] And these times are grown so cunning and flinty hard that necessitous men can hardly borrow five shillings of their best friends and acquaintance. And how many great heirs have I known to have begged and died in alehouses and barns, surfeiting of that abundance which hath been left them?

These and the like notions mature discretion should have suggested and been mistress of the key before the house had been parted withal.

Out of the heat of thy youth, unknown to thy parents or friends, thou matchest thyself to some snout-fair young thing not worth a groat, whereby thou art forever after to be dis-

---

[3] "From deprivation there is no returning to fortune."

[4] "We were once Trojans."

[5] "It is a most miserable thing to owe to those to whom you would not.

esteemed and undervalued. Discretion, hadst thou been acquainted with her, would have told thee, *nil temere*, do nothing rashly, and how marriage, with one's calling and profession, is the greatest action he shall undertake in his whole life and, like a stratagem in war, in which he can err but once. And how beautiful soever she be, the Dutch women can tell you, "Good looks buy nothing in the market." Moreover, instead of honorable (many times) or worshipful kindred and alliance, you shall have on her side a needy kindred always relying upon you by begging or borrowing. Lastly, after the springtime of her beauty and your amorous desire is over, you begin to loathe her more than ever you loved her. Hence proceeds your perpetual discontent, homebred quarrels, scoffs and jeering from the neighbors, a weary life to servants, and, to conclude, a parting or divorcement between yourselves, which discretion, had you been a scholar in her school, would have easily taught you to have prevented. Let these two examples, instead of many other, show the inestimable value of discretion in all our actions.[6] I will now come to speak of discretion we ought to have in speech and discourse.

An ill tongue in the Holy Scripture is compared to a two-edged sword, bitter words to arrows, slanderous and malicious to the poison of asps. And it is the instrument many times of life and death, as well to the soul as the body. Wherefore the old Egyptians dedicated their persean tree, whose leaves are like tongues and the fruit or apples like hearts, to Isis, meaning hereby the tongue and heart agreeing together should be consecrated to God only and his honor, and not in profaning or blaspheming his sanctified name—usual even in these days among children in the streets—or slandering and lyingly traducing others behind their backs. Wherefore we show our discre-

---

[6] For more on rash marriages, see *The Worth of a Penny*, ed. 1669, p. 10.

tion in nothing more than in our speech and discourse, and hence came the word *Loquere ut te videam.*[7] For a natural fool, so long as he is silent, for ought we know, may be the wisest man in the company, and a great wit by too much babbling and suffering his tongue to run at random oftentimes proves a more fool than he, speaking their pleasure of princes, statesmen, and bishops, raising them higher or lower, as Dutchmen do their coin, to their own advantage. Hence they crave pardon, being questioned, of their ears that heard them and stand in awe even of strangers and waiters upon them. Homer attributes it as a prime virtue in Ulysses that his words were few but to the purpose. I confess the table, as with good dishes, so should be furnished with good discourse, for mirth at feasts and banquets hath ever been commended. And I deny not but where men of several dispositions meet, something τὸ παρέργον [8] may slip beyond the bounds of discretion and these impertinencies. And *quicquid inter pocula liberius dictum fueret in mappa proiciatur cum micis,*[9] as Erasmus holdeth, sitting without more ado, having learned as much of Horace.

> *Ne fidos inter amicos*
> *Sit qui dicta foras eliminet.*[10]

And Plutarch in *Symposiasis* saith it was a custom among the Lacedaemonians that when they invited any kinsman or friend unto their houses, they with a finger would point to the door or porch and say ταύτη οὐκ ἐξέρχεται λόγος, "No words must come from hence," which was the law of Lycurgus. Hence proceedeth it that in many places, as well in England as the Low Countries, they have over their tables a rose painted, and what is spoken

---

[7] "Speak that I may see you," a speech attributed to Socrates.

[8] Incidental.

[9] "Let whatever may have been said with some abandon among the cups be thrown away with the crumbs in the table napkin."

[10] "Among true friends let there be none who will blab."

under the rose must not be revealed. The reason is this: The rose being sacred to Venus, whose amorous and stolen sports, that they might never be revealed, her son Cupid would needs dedicate to Harpocrates, the god of silence. Hence these not inelegant verses.

Est rosa flos Veneris, cuius quo surta laterent;
Harpocrati matris dona dicavit Amor.
Inde rosam mensis, hospes suspendet amicis,
Convivae ut sub ea dicta tacenda sciant.[11]

And for the same reason Gerusa and Oblivo [12] were dedicated to Bacchus, meaning what had been done or spoken freely among merry cups should either have been quite forgotten or very slightly punished.

Of Common Ignorance

THE world hath taken so much upon trust from credulous and superstitious antiquity that nowadays it will hardly believe common experience. Whereof I will produce some neither unpleasant nor unprofitable examples.

There are many that believe and affirm that the manna which is sold in the shops of our apothecaries [1] to be of the same which

[11] "The rose is the flower of beauty because its stratagems lie concealed. Love presented roses as votive offerings of his mother to Harpocrates. Then let the host suspend for his friends a rose above his table, so that they may know that things said under it at his feasts may be kept secret."

[12] These words offer some difficulty. *Gerusa* could mean *goad* (suggesting slight punishment) in Low Latin, and *oblivo* may be an error for *oblivio*, forgetfulness.

[1] A medicine, chiefly mannitol, from the European flowering ash, used as a gentle laxative, demulcent, and expectorant.

fell from heaven and wherewith the Israelites were fed forty years in the wilderness—which cannot be by these reasons.

1. That manna in the wilderness was miraculous; this of ours natural, falling from the heaven in fair, clear, and hot days at certain seasons of the year in Calabria and upon Mount Libanus.

2. That manna in the wilderness was kept but only one day, excepting the eve of the Sabbath, when it remained uncorrupt for two days together. Ours in shops will abide a year and more sweet and good.

3. That was a meat, ours a medicine to loosen the body, withal most excellent to purge choler, and ours so unfit to use for food that if we eat much and continually of it, our bowels will melt within us and we die forthwith.

Now from that affinity and likeness it hath from the other in some things it borroweth the same name; that is, the whiteness, the taste of an honeylike sweetness, and the place whence it cometh, that is, the air.

It is called in Hebrew *Man,* derived either from *Mana,* to prepare, because it was prepared by God himself, or else because, when the Israelites saw it first fall, one said to the other, "Man, huh? What is this?" Exodus 16:16.

Manna Thuris or the Manna of frankincense, as Pliny showeth, is like neither of these, but only the smaller and finer corns of frankincense falling and tossing to and fro.

If there be any, as there be many, that cannot away with an ordinary purgation, their stomachs taking offense thereat, let them take but two ounces and a half of manna, and it will purge choler most easily and gently and without any offense at all.

The like error hath antiquity been possessed with concerning the bear, who is said to bring forth, instead of a proportioned whelp, a lump of flesh without form, which by often licking she bringeth to its right shape—which Ovid verily believed when he saith,

232

The Truth of Our Times

Nec catulus partu quem reddit ursa recenti,
Sed male viva caro est. Lambendo mater in artus
Fingit et in formam quantam capit ipsa, reducit.[2]

It is most false, for I have seen a bear whelp newly littered in all respects like unto the dam—in head, back, sides, feet, etc., like unto other young creatures. It is true the bear licks it; so doth the cow her calf, the mare her foal, and other creatures in like manner. But that by licking she gives it form and shape is most untrue.

Scaliger affirmeth as much, saying, "In our Alps" (meaning those about Piedmont) "the hunters caught a she-bear big with young, who being cut up, they found a whelp within her of perfect form and shape," etc.

The diamond, saith Pliny, never agreeth with the loadstone (*l. 37. c. 4.*), but are so far at enmity, each with either, that the diamond will not suffer the loadstone to draw any iron unto it, and happily if it do, it will pluck and withdraw the same away unto itself; which is most untrue, as Garzias ab Horto and many other great physicians and learned men have proved. And as true it is that the diamond can be broken by no means but by the blood of a goat only. I know not whether there be several kinds of diamonds, but I am sure I have seen in the city of Antwerp the powder of a diamond, and the aforenamed Garzias affirmeth with an iron hammer it may be easily done, and himself hath seen it beaten into a fine powder.

It is moreover as commonly believed as reported that the swan before her death singeth sweetly her own funeral song, which not only poets and painters ever since the time of Aeschylus but even the chief among philosophers themselves have

---

[2] "A cub which a mother-bear has just given birth to is not a cub but a half-alive lump of flesh; but the mother licks it into shape and so gives it her own form."—*Metam.* xv. 379–381.

believed and published, as Plato, Aristotle, Chrysippus, Philostratus, Cicero, and Seneca. Yet this hath proved a mere fable, so confessed by Pliny, Athenaeus, and others, and confirmed by daily experience. See Bodin in *Method. hist. c.* 4.

The vulgar ignorance and simplicity is in these days notably wrought upon by cunning sectaries, pretending under a severe kind of carriage and show of religion the cure of their souls and, by medicinal impostures, for the cure of their bodies. Of the former I have spoken; of the later I will now say something.

For the first, true it is they suffer themselves to be bitten of serpents, especially vipers, but cleared and rid of their poison, for they take their vipers in winter when they lie half dead and benumbed with cold, and with a fine or small pair of tongs take away certain little bladders about their teeth wherein their poison lieth; which being gone, their biting is never deadly after. Others keep their vipers lean and half hunger-starved, and then throw amongst them some hard dried flesh, which when they fall upon, their teeth stick so fast in the same that at once they pour out all their poison and become harmless ever after. And of these they suffer themselves to be bitten to the great admiration of the standers-by. But if you happen to get a viper fresh out of the field and offer that to him to show his skill, he will rather be hanged than venture upon it. Hereby their notorious cheating is discovered.

The other will have nothing to do with serpents, but only swalloweth down poison—or seemeth to do—to utter his trade or antidote to the people at as dear a rate as he can. These, when they take poison, take beforehand in summertime lettuce well steeped and soaked in oil, but in winter the tripes or fattest entrails of beasts; for by these meats they retund [3] and abate the strength of the poison, the coldness of the lettuce and fatness of the oil and entrails only availing hereunto. Neither is this all, but returning to their lodging, they drink good store

[3] Render ineffective.

234

of thick milk and cast it up again. And if all cannot be brought upward, the milk digested conveys it the other way.

But they having been many times deceived by arsenic, which having tarried so long with some it ate out their guts, they have found out a new trick, which is, when they are upon their stage they send a boy forthwith to the apothecary's for arsenic or mercury, which [4] being brought, he shows it to the multitude about him, with the apothecary's testimony that it [5] is right and good. All the people see it. What then? He presently conveys into the cover of a box lid turned upward, upon which sticks sugar made into the form and color of arsenic, which sugar he takes out and puts into water or wine, drinks it off, falls down, and keeps his breath, that you would certainly say he was quite dead. But he remembers his treacle, takes it, and is raised to life. Then he commends his antidote and treacle to the skies. The people fetch it from him as fast as he can utter it, but if any afterward happen to use his treacle when they are poisoned indeed, it never does good, but they die without all question. I have spoken the more at large of these kind of people that our magistrates in cities and towns may have a care of seeing themselves and the people abused by such runagates and artificial pickpockets. But we are not much troubled with them here in England.

Of Quietness and Health

WE DO find by daily experience that the age of man very much declineth, and that men now for the most part are not half so strong and vigorous as they were in the memory of our fathers, as we may easily perceive by those arrows of a yard or an ell

---

[4] Original: mercury, being.   [5] Original: that is.

long which hang by the walls in many places of the north and west part of England, which the owner's grandfather or great-grandfather left behind him for a monument of his loyal affection to one of the roses under whose conduct he served an archer. The shooting butts in country towns have lost much of their length since the beginning of Queen Elizabeth's reign. Who can wield that lance which Charles Brandon, Duke of Suffolk, tilted withal, yet to be seen in the Tower? Neither can so heavy arms be borne as were not many years [ago]. Our pikes and muskets are made far less because our lesser bodies find them rather for burden than use. Now if we look into the cause and true reason hereof, we shall find first the world declining and, like a mother in her age, to bring forth but weak and short-lived children. Neither is this all, but we are living in the last age of the world, wherein all iniquity and vice doth abound. Men shorten their lives by overeating and drinking, ease and want of exercise, luxury and incontinence, temperance and continency being the main and only supporters of our health, as incomparable Fernelius affirmeth. There are two things more (as these to our health) which conduce to our happiness in this world, which are liberty and tranquillity or quiet of mind. These, I confess, fall not to every man's share, most men living being involved in so many affairs, variety of cares and business which attend us in this our earthly pilgrimage, that this quiet of mind is as rare as Homer's Nepenthe, many men, not out of necessity, but of self-willfulness, vexing and disquieting themselves without cause or reason. As how many rich and men of great estates be there in this kingdom of whose care of getting and purchasing there is no end, they never in all their lives (like the ass that carried venison, pheasants, capons, bottles of wine, and other dainties upon his back) tasting the sweetness of what they had about them, but fed upon the thorns and thistles of vexation, grief, and needless carefulness to enrich some unthrifty son or kinsman, or scrape up thousands for some dainty thing troubled with the green sickness, who within a year or two is stolen and married by a tailor or hosteler.

Others again are by nature choleric, fretful, quarrelsome, and evermore enemies to their own rest, delighting to be meddlers and brokers in other men's business, as eels in troubled waters and mud. Some out of curiosity or the search of some deep and uncouth invention, as firing ships under water, making traps for the monstrous bear of Nova Zembla, etc., or secret in nature, as setting the loadstone and jet at enmity about iron and straws. Others draw misery and vexation as with cords unto them, through weakness of judgment, when they marry disadvantageously to themselves either for estate or their own dispositions. I mean when themselves, being gentle and addicted to peace, match with arrant scolds; honest of life meet with whores and the like.

So, since we cannot make ourselves master of this so sweet a benefit, tranquillity of mind, let us, which is in our own power, look unto our health, whereof the most men are careless and negligent. To the conservation whereof let us first consider the quality of the air in that place where we live, which is not only an element, but an aliment. For by it, if it be pure and good, our spirits are clarified and quickened, our blood rarefied, and our hearts recomforted. For the whole body fareth the better for the goodness of a pure and sweet air, so that we find by experience that men are more sprightly, lively, and merry in an upland perfumed and fanned with the flower-scented air of the country, and of better complexions than in close lanes and noisome alleys about the city, where the air in such places is not good but raw and cold. You may better it, especially in infectious and dangerous times, by burning of several sorts of sweet wood, as cypress, juniper, bay, rosemary, pine, the turpentine-and rosin tree. If it be too hot, open your windows and place your bed toward the north, strewing the floor with rushes, water lilies, nenuphar, lettuce, endive, sorrel, and ever and anon sprinkle cold water with a little vinegar of roses. If any in Rome were troubled with ulcers of the lungs or fell into consumptions, Galen would presently send them to Mount Tabian, a most sweet air near unto Naples, where through the dryness of the place and drinking the milk of goats and kine, which fed upon many medicinable herbs (and proper to those diseases growing in that place), they recovered in a short time, having perhaps learned out of Hippocrates that in long and languishing diseases there is nothing better than air and place of our dwelling.

The next thing for our health, we must have especial care of our eating and drinking. Our meat wherewith our bodies are nourished proceedeth either from living creatures or vegetables, that is, plants, and of these there must be a choice had. That of plants nourisheth far less than the flesh of living creatures, excepting that grain whereof we make our bread, as wheat, rye, barley, oats, etc., wheat being the chief. Fruits nourish very little. Of fruits, cherries and grapes are the best. Melon, cucumbers, and citrals are good for choleric stomachs. They breed gross blood, are very cold and hard of digestion. Platina tells us in his life of Pope Paul the Second how the said Pope two hours before night was taken suddenly with an apoplexy—being a little before very well and complaining of no disease or pain—which came through eating of a whole muskmelon *An.* 1471.

And how many in these our times kill themselves with overmuch drinking, the cause of many long and deadly diseases, as apoplexies, dropsies, palsies, the gout, and many others. And I know not whether any of the colder northern nations herein excel us, drunkenness nowadays being grown into that request that it is almost esteemed a virtue, at least a gentlemanlike quality, to carouse, sit up whole days and nights at it,

The Truth of Our Times

Donec vertigine tectum
Ambulet et geminis exurgat mensa a lucernis,[1]

keeping neither method nor measure in their eating and drinking, which the ancient Grecians and other nations were so precise in,[2] England formerly having been accounted the most sober and temperate nation in the world. Neither were we ever noted for this vice till, as Mr. Camden saith, we had to do with the Netherlands in their wars, ales[3] being from all antiquity our English drink. *Britanni,* saith Pliny, *habent potus genus quod alicam vocant,*[4] which doubtless was our ale. Beer and bass viols came into England in one year in the time of King Henry the Seventh. But that I may conclude concerning those things whereon ours[5] doth principally depend, which are air, eating, drinking, sleep and waking, moving and exercise, rest, evacuation of excrements, venereal recreation, and passions of the mind: that we may live to serve God, to do our king and country service, to be a comfort to our friends and helpful to our children and others that depend upon us, let us follow sobriety and temperance, and have, as Tully saith, a diligent care of our health, which we shall be sure to do if we will observe and keep that one short, but true, rule of Hippocrates: "All things moderately and in measure."[6]

[1] Cf. above, p. 152 and note 34.   [2] Original: in it.
[3] Original: wars. Also being.
[4] "The Britons have a kind of draught which they call *alica.*"
[5] I.e., our health.   [6] *Πάντα μετρίος.*

FINIS

THE ART OF LIVING IN LONDON

(1642)

By Henry Peacham

The Art of Living in London [1]

It is a greater piece of skill to live in a populous place, where multitudes of people reside, than in a solitary and private place among a few. Yet some natures are so carried and led away with variety of acquaintance and company that it is a death unto them to live by and to themselves, which indeed is the happiest life of all and hath ever been most contenting and pleasing to the best and wisest men.

Now our most populous places are cities, and among us London or κατ' ἐξοχήν,[2] the city whither all sorts reside, noble and simple, rich and poor, young and old, from all places and countries, either for pleasure (and let me add besides, to save the charge of housekeeping in the country) or for profit, as lawyers to the terms, countrymen and women to Smithfield and the markets; or for necessity, as poor young men and maids to seek services and places; servingmen, masters; and some others, all manner of employment.

Now the city being like a vast sea, full of gusts, fearful-dangerous shelves and rocks, ready at every storm to sink and cast away the weak and unexperienced bark with her fresh-

[1] This essay was published in four leaves quarto with the following title: *The Art of Living in London; or, A caution how gentlemen, countrymen, and strangers, drawn by occasion of business, should dispose of themselves in the thriftiest way, not only in the city, but in all other populous places. As also, A direction to the poorer sort that come thither to seek their fortunes. By H. P. Printed for John Gyles, and are to be sold by Samuel Rand at his shop at Barnard's Inn in Holborn. 1642.*

[2] "Par excellence."

water soldiers, as wanting her compass and her skillful pilot, myself, like another Columbus or Drake, acquainted with her rough entertainment and storms, have drawn you this chart or map for your guide as well out of mine own as my many friends' experience.

Who therefore soever shall have occasion to come to the city for the occasions before mentioned, the first thing he is to do is to arm himself with patience and to think that he is entered into a wood where there is as many briers as people, everyone as ready to catch hold of your fleece as yourself. For we see that sheep, when they pass through a thorny or a bushy place, they leave locks of [3] wool behind them; so imagine a populous city could not live nor subsist (like the stomach) except it have help and nourishment from the other parts and members. Therefore the first rule I give you, next to the due observation of God and the Sabbath and at other times, is the choice of your company and acquaintance. For according to that, every man finds his own valuation high or low. That is, we are esteemed to be such as we keep company withal, as well in estate as condition. If you cannot find such fitting for you, apply yourself to your friends, if you have any, or the friends of your friend. If you have not them neither (I speak to the meaner and more inferior), be sure that you take your lodging at least in some honest house of credit, whether it be inn, alehouse, or other private house, which latter [4] I could rather wish because in the other the multiplicity of resort and company of all sorts will draw you to much needless and vain expense, as in pots of beer or ale, tobacco, perhaps cards, dice, the shovelboard table, etc.

But first of all have an eye to and a care of your main business or the end of your coming to town; as it were, at what mark you would shoot your arrow; which, being thoroughly considered, for your purse sake pursue it with all expedition. For

[3] Original: or.   [4] Original: which I.

the city is like a quicksand: the longer you stand upon it the deeper you sink, if here money or means to get it be wanting.

But imagine you have money of your own and come hither only for your pleasure, as being tired and weary of your country. If you husband it not thriftily you may quickly take a nap upon penniless-bench—so many are the occasions here offered that are ready every hour to pick your purse: as perpetual visits of vain and useless acquaintance; necessitous persons ever upon borrowing hand with you; clothes in the fashion; this or that new play; play at ordinaries, tavern feasts, and meetings; horse and coach hire, besides those brittle commodities they carry; boat hire to Kingston, Windsor, and other places; with the like. For an antidote to these several poisons let me prescribe to my city-country gentleman these receipts or remedies.

First, being come to the city, avoid idleness, which commonly draws after a train of many vices. I call idleness keeping your chamber, consuming the day lying in bed, or, risen, in walking up and down from street to street, to this or that gentleman's chamber, having no business at all, and cannot meet with useful company. Let the Bible and other books of piety such as treat of philosophy, natural or moral, history, the mathematics, as arithmetic, geometry, music, sometimes heraldry, and the like, be your chief company. For you shall find books no flatterers, nor expensive in your converse with them. Besides, you shall meet with those who can instruct you in all those arts which Tully calls *venales,* which are taught for money, as the mathematics themselves, dancing, fencing, riding, painting, and the like.

Next, have a care of saving and improving your money to the best, as who would bespeak a supper or a dinner at all adventure at a tavern, and not know the price of every dish, as the Italians and other nations do, while they laugh at our English for their vain profuseness and simplicity, who, when the dinner is ended, must stand to the courtesy of a nimble-tongued drawer or of a many-ringed whistling mistress, whether they or you should be masters of your money. Besides, one dish, well dressed, gives a good stomach more and better content than a variety of twenty.

And above all things beware of beastly drunkenness, which, as Horace truly saith, doth *affigere humo divinae particulam aurae.*[5] And well he may *affigere humo*, or "nail to the ground," for some are found sometimes so drunk, who, being fallen upon the ground or, which is worse, in the kennel, are not able to stir or move again. Drinking begets challenges and quarrels and occasioneth the death of many, as is known by almost daily experience. Hence are Newgate, the Counters, and other prisons filled with our young heirs and swaggering gallants, to the sorrow of their friends and joy of their jailers. Again, men, when they are in drink, are apt to say or do anything, as become sureties for decayed companions or lending them ready money out of their purses, which, when they have slept upon it, they curse and are ready to hang themselves—besides the terror of conscience and extreme melancholy which sticks by them a long time after. Drunken men are apt to lose their hats, cloaks, or rapiers, not to know what they have spent, how much money they have, and full oft have their pockets picked by whores and knaves. There is less danger in outdoor recreations then, as shooting, bowls, riding, tennis, etc.

Next, let every man beware of play and gaming, as cards, especially dice, at ordinaries and other places, for in the city there are many who, when they live only by cheating, are so cunning that they will so strip a young heir or novice but lately come to town, and woodcocklike so pull his wings that he shall in a short time never be able to fly over ten acres of his own land.

These and the like errors are the cause why so many fair estates, being near or not very far from the city, have been so

---

[5] "Fasten upon the ground a part of a divine being."

often bought and sold. And the truth is, very few have held out
in a name to the third generation.

Let a moneyed man or gentleman especially beware in the
city, *ab istis calidis solis filiabus,*[6] as Lipsius saith,[7] these over-
hot and crafty daughters of the sun, your silken and gold-laced
harlots everywhere, especially in the suburbs, to be found.
These have been and are daily the ruin of thousands. And if
they happen to allure and entice him, which is only to cheat
him and pick his pocket to boot, with the bargain she makes,
but let him resolutely say, as Diogenes did to Lais of Corinth,
Non tanti emam poenitentiam, I will not buy repentance at such
a rate.

Let him also in the city have a special care whom he entertains
into his service. Let him or them [8] have friends of his acquaintance who may undertake [9] for them, but not at all adventure
every straggler. What says old Tusser in his book of good husbandry?

> Take runagate Robin to pity his need,
> And look to be filched as sure as thy creed.

And if you bring one with you out of the country, except you
have a great eye over him he will quickly be corrupted in the
city with much acquaintance. Then shall you help yourself to
bed, see your horse starved in the stable and never rubbed,
your linen lost at the laundresses; in a word, yourself everywhere
neglected. Think it therefore no disgrace in a city inn to see
your horse every day yourself, and to see him well meated,
rubbed, and watered. He shall make you amends in your journey: *Occhio di patrono ingrassa lo cavallo,* the master's eye
makes the horse fat. Besides, remember what Solomon saith:
"The righteous man regardeth the life of his beast, but the ungodly have cruel hearts." I saw, I remember, a carrier flay his

---

[6] Cf. above, pp. 162, 218. [7] Original: Lipsius, these.
[8] Original: they. [9] Assume responsibility.

horse alive, being able to go on the way no farther, his too heavy burden having broken his back, insomuch that he tumbled raw in his own skin.

Next let the gentleman living in the city have a care to keep himself out of debt. Let him owe as little as he can to his tailor for following the fashion, than which there can be no greater misery. For then, if he walks abroad he is ready to be snapped up at every lane's end by sergeants, marshal's men, or bailies [10] or, keeping his chamber, let him stir never so little, be betrayed by some false knave or other. In the meantime his creditors, if they be of the inferior sort, nay, their scolding and clamorous wives and every saucy apprentice, will be ready to disgrace him. And if arrested, he shall be hauled to prison many times like a dog if he returns but the least ill word. If he be a landed man, let him take heed of usurers and their factors, of whom he shall find as much mercy in cities as an oxcheek from a butcher's cur. But I will turn my discourse now to such as accidentally make their abode here, either through business, to see friends, or sent for by authority.

Next after the setting up of their horses and seeing them well used, which should be your chiefest care at your first alighting in the city, with all diligence follow your business. Let not vain and by-occasions take you off from it, as going to taverns, seeing plays, and now and then to worse places—so lose your time, spend your money, and sometimes leave your business uneffected. To avoid these, take a private chamber wherein you may pass your spare time in doing something or other, and what you call for, pay for, without going upon the score, especially in city alehouses, where in many places you shall be torn out of your skin, if it were possible, even for a debt of twopence. And though you have spent twenty or forty pounds in one of their houses, your host, especially your hostess, will hardly bid you drink in a twelvemonth; but if they be at dinner

[10] Bailiffs.

or supper, never to eat a bit with them, for that were an undoing to them in their opinion.

Again, walking abroad, take heed with what company you sort yourself withal. If you are a countryman and but newly come to town, you will be smelt out by some cheaters or other, who will salute, call you by your name—which perhaps one of their company meeting you in another street hath learned by way of mistaking you for another man, which is an old trick—carry you to a tavern, saying they are akin to someone dwelling near you, etc. But all tricks of late years have been so plainly discovered and are so generally known almost to every child that their practice is out of date and now no great fear of them. Yet an *item* can do you no hurt.

You shall not do amiss if you send for your diet to your own chamber a hot joint of meat, of mutton, veal, or the like; what you leave covered with a fair napkin will serve you to break-fast the next morning, or when you please. Keep out of throngs and public places where multitudes of people are—for saving your purse. The fingers of a number go beyond your sense of feeling. A tradesman's wife of the Exchange one day, when her husband was following some business in the city, desired him he would give her leave to go see a play, which she had not done in seven years. He bade her take his apprentice along with her and go, but especially to have a care of her purse, which she warranted him she would. Sitting in a box among some gallants and gallant wenches and returning when the play was done, she [11] returned to her husband and told him she had lost her purse. "Wife," quoth he, "did I not give you warning of it? How much money was there in it?" Quoth she, "Truly, four pieces, six shillings, and a silver toothpicker." Quoth her husband, "Where did you put it?" "Under my petticoat, between that and my smock." "What," quoth he, "did you feel nobody's hand there?" "Yes," quoth she, "I felt one's hand there, but I

[11] Original: done, returned.

did not think he had come for that." So much for the guard of the purse.

Now for such as are of the poorest condition and come to the city, compelled by necessity to try their fortunes, to seek services or other means to live. Let them presently provide themselves if they can—for here is employment for all hands that will work—or return home again before they find or feel the extremity of want. Here are more occasions to draw them into ill courses than there, as being constrained to steal and to shorten their days; to seek death in the error of their lives, as Solomon saith; young maids, who never knew ill in their lives, to be enticed by impudent bawds to turn common whores; and the like. But if they can provide themselves and take honest courses, by the blessing of God they may come to as great preferment as aldermen and aldermen's wives. For poverty of itself is no vice, but by accident. Whom hath the city more advanced than poor men's children? the city itself being the most charitable place of the whole, and having done more good deeds than half the land beside. In a word, for a conclusion, let me give all comers, not only to London, but all other populous places, this only rule never to be forgotten, which is: To serve God, avoid idleness, to keep your money, and to beware of ill company.

FINIS